Psychoses of Power

Psychoses of Power

African Personal Dictatorships

Samuel Decalo

Westview Press BOULDER AND LONDON

African Modernization and Development Series

All rights reserved. No part of this publication may be reproduced or transmitted in any form or by any means, electronic or mechanical, including photocopy, recording, or any information storage and retrieval system, without permission in writing from the publisher.

Copyright © 1989 by Westview Press, Inc.

A portion of the author's material has been incorporated into this book from his article, "African Personal Dictatorships," *Journal of Modern African Studies*, vol. 23, no. 2, pp. 209-237, 1985, with the kind permission of the publisher.

Published in 1989 in the United States of America by Westview Press, Inc., 5500 Central Avenue, Boulder, Colorado 80301, and in the United Kingdom by Westview Press, Inc., 13 Brunswick Centre, London WC1N 1AF, England

Library of Congress Cataloging-in-Publication Data
Decalo, Samuel.
  Psychoses of power : African personal dictatorships / by Samuel Decalo.
    p. cm.—(African modernization and development series)
  ISBN 0-8133-7617-3
  1. Bokassa I, Emperor of the Central African Empire, 1921–
2. Macias Nguema, Francisco. 3. Amin, Idi, 1925–   . 4. Dictators—
Africa, Sub-Saharan—Biography. 5. Central African Republic—
Politics and government—1966–1979. 6. Equatorial Guinea—Politics
and government—1968–   . 7. Uganda—Politics and
government—1971–1979. I. Title. II. Series.
DT352.8.D44 1989
967'.4105'0924—dc19
[B]   88-17593
                                                                    CIP

Printed and bound in the United States of America

∞ The paper used in this publication meets the requirements of the American National Standard for Permanence of Paper for Printed Library Materials Z39.48-1984.

10   9   8   7   6   5   4   3   2   1

To Roma, as always

Contents

Preface, ix

1 The Face of Dictatorship in Africa — 1

   Socioeconomic Origins: From Rags to Riches, 5
   Patterns of Repression and Political Decay, 12
   On Physiology and Psychology, 21
   The Legacy of Dictatorship, 25
   Notes, 27

2 Francisco Macias Nguema: Tyrant of Equatorial Guinea — 31

   Socioeconomic Background, 33
   Basic Features of the Economy, 38
   Prelude to Independence, 42
   The Events of 1969 and the Onset of Dictatorship, 47
   Profile of a Dictator, 49
   Equatorial Guinea Under El Unico Miraclo, 54
   Patterns of Control and Repression, 60
   The Fall of a Dictator, 64
   The Second Republic and the Obiang Dictatorship, 66
   Notes, 70

3 Idi Amin: The Brutal Reign of the Iron Marshal — 77

   Ugandan Social Dynamics, 78
   The Economic Context, 84
   Prelude to Dictatorship: The Civilian Era, 85
   Consolidation and Collapse: 1966–1971, 90
   Military Politics and Coup d'Etat, 92
   Idi Dada Amin, 95
   Personal Dictatorship and Societal Terror, 99
   Administrative and Economic Decay, 104

The "Solution" to the "Asian Problem," 109
The Collapse of a Dictator, 111
Rebirth and Decay, 113
The Second Overthrow of Obote and the Rise of the South, 116
Notes, 119

4 Jean-Bedel Bokassa: "Emperor" of the Central African Republic 129

The Ethnic Mosaic, 131
The Colonial Heritage, 133
Economic Limitations, 137
Forestry and Mineral Resources, 138
Decolonization and the Dacko Presidency, 140
The 1966 Coup d'Etat, 144
Military Dictatorship and Personalist Rule, 145
Jean-Bedel Bokassa, 146
Thirteen Years of Personal Dictatorship, 151
The Final Years: Political Decay and Personal Empire, 155
The Central African Empire, 160
The Fall of a Dictator, 162
The Legacy of Dictatorship, 164
The Military Tries to Rule, 167
Notes, 172

5 The Authoritarian Syndrome in Africa 179

The Roots of Tyranny, 179
The Future of Dictatorship in Africa, 184
Personal Rule in Africa, 185
The Personalist Coup, 188
The Aberrant Personality in Africa, 191
Notes, 196

Selected Bibliography, 199
Index, 213

Preface

Three brutal and highly idiosyncratic personal dictatorships sprang up in Africa in the 1960s and 1970s. Yet only Idi Amin's bloody interregnum in Uganda has received adequate analysis in the professional literature. The other two tyrants—Jean-Bedel Bokassa of the Central African Republic and Francisco Macias Nguema of Equatorial Guinea—have attracted surprisingly little academic attention, their polities remaining among the least studied of the African countries.

The purpose of this book is to survey the recent social, economic, and political histories of these three countries, the specific conditions that facilitated the rise of the dictatorial triumvirate, and the key characteristics of personal dictatorship in Africa. The first chapter compares and contrasts the three dictatorships on a multiplicity of systemic and personal planes. Despite the quite distinct societal fabrics from which dictatorships emerged in these countries, and the unique personalities of the three tyrants, certain similarities are clearly visible and bear underscoring. The subsequent three chapters are essential in-depth case studies. They trace in greater detail the salient socioeconomic features and the political evolution of the three countries concerned, both before and after the rise of dictatorship, and the specific modality of governance of dictatorial rule in each instance. Self-contained, the case-studies provide useful introductions to the political evolution of two of the lesser known countries in Africa. The concluding chapter briefly examines the tyrannical dimensions of the three dictatorships that set them apart from other instances of authoritarian rule in Africa. It then assesses the prospects of further instances of such aberrant regimes emerging on the continent.

Although by 1979 all three tyrants currently under analysis had been toppled from office (in two instances—Amin and Bokassa—through external force of arms), future instances of brutal personal dictatorship cannot axiomatically be ruled out. The highly personalist nature of political power in Africa, the slow drift toward increased societal repression and authoritarian rule on the continent, the never-ending pattern of military coups (through which both Amin and Bokassa seized power) set against a legitimacy void, and the highly personalist motivations that suffuse some of these power-grabs hardly preclude the possibility of the emergence of the kinds of personality and power aberrations that Amin, Bokassa, and Nguema so cogently represent. Ultimately, therefore, the current study may have wider implications in that it attempts to throw some light on the inner mechanics of the dictatorial syndrome in Africa.

Samuel Decalo

1 The Face of Dictatorship in Africa

As long ago as the 1960s, Aristide Zolberg suggested that the most visible features of independent Africa might well be instability and not stability, cleavage and conflict rather than unity and consensus.[1] The formula ensuring the establishment of a viable and integrative political order has eluded many African states. Their failure to create viable political institutions and to forge ahead in the direction of national integration and socioeconomic development has been documented in the voluminous literature that has sprung up since Zolberg's original analysis. Early expectations of a relatively smooth transition from colonialism to meaningful independence have been dashed in an Africa ravaged by natural disasters, international conflict, civil war, and military coups. Although striking exceptions do exist, neither the richer nor the more developed nations are necessarily assured of stability and unity, given the continental context of scarcity and conflict.

Apart from so much political instability there is the increasing phenomenon of authoritarian rule. Often glossed over due to its relatively innocuous nature in Africa or because of more virulent examples elsewhere, authoritarian patterns of government have become a permanent feature of political life in many African states. Whether romanticized as Africa's contribution to democratic centralism, or defended as axiomatically necessary in societies in rapid socioeconomic flux beset by a multiplicity of stressful cleavages, or ideologically anchored in Marxist class dogma, authoritarian rule has become ingrained as the norm in much of the continent.

At any point in time, a large number of African states are ruled by civil or military hierarchies of varying degrees of oppressiveness, with or without sustaining patrimonial credentials and supports. Only in a minority of instances are these systems legitimated by elections, and most often the elections are intermittent, tightly circumscribed exercises in which the masses participate for a variety of nonpolitical reasons that, in any case, do not obviate the reality of authoritarianism.[2] Where meaningful political choice is present and electoral fraud absent, elections are orchestrated by traditional power-wielders and are dominated by parochial and corporate concerns. They catapult to power elites whose prime concern seems to be the centralization and retention of power at all costs. Their policies once in office—circumscribed by external factors beyond their control and by the necessity of rewarding cohorts and allies—often set the stage for societal tumult that may bring in coups, strife, or increasing repression. As was grimly noted in the London weekly *West Africa* in January 1985, "Nowhere, apart from Mauritius in 1982, has a ruling party been voted out of office in an election."[3]

Politics, even in the heyday of Africa's independence, has always been an elite activity, with social repression used as a method of retaining power in the context of declining legitimacy and societal scarcity. Only the inherent pluralism and inertia of traditional African society, and the relative weakness of central structures and bureaucracies, have prevented the imposition in most states of more repressive authoritarian rule. This societal resilience to tighter centralization of power has been both lauded and lamented, depending upon the leadership's goals.

Not all those in high positions have authoritarian inclinations, and certainly not all are concerned with personal or political aggrandizement or with a nonequitable distribution of the spoils of office based on ethnic or regional considerations. Yet most African leaders, from the urbane Félix Houphouët-Boigny, Habib Bourgiba, and Omar Bongo to the ideological Sassou Nguesso and Mathieu Kerekou, including the "populist" Jerry Rawlings and Thomas Sankara, have found that "clamping down the political lid" has been a basic precondition for effective government and for their own political survival. Authoritarian trends are also linked to the frustration of leaders incapable of bringing about fundamental socioeconomic change due to the resilience of societal values to directives from above and the administrative weaknesses of the African state itself. However that may be, political authoritarianism from paternalism to personal tyranny has, to date, attracted scholarly attention mostly when accompanied by large-scale societal terror (Uganda), crass venality (Zaire), or racial domination (South Africa), or in ex post facto explanations of systemic violence and military coups. Its incidence is high, however, and its systemic implications are important. The long-term effect of political authoritarianism extends beyond reinforcement of the absence of legitimacy, the absence of political accountability, the escalating corruption in already largely unaccountable social systems, and political decay.

More important by far, a political culture of authoritarianism may be a legacy of such regimes, even if they do attain other socioeconomic goals, such as cementing society's inherent fissions.[4] The authoritarian proclivities of many contemporary African leaders may reinforce the tradition of authoritarian rule inherited from colonialism, which in itself was superimposed on an indigenous concept of the functional indivisibility of power and authority in traditional African society. One need not be a cultural determinist to perceive the potential dangers of authoritarianism becoming for insecure political elites the preferred (easiest) and possibly most culturally sanctioned modality of governing complex multicleavaged societies. Although some experimentation has occurred on the part of elites seeking greater sources of legitimacy, few of the options available to political leaders—and suggested by the experience of areas outside the continent—have been truly explored. Africa may be following *mutatis mutandis* the route of Latin America, where "authoritarianism, whether personalist, oligarchic, socialist or radical, has persisted . . . since colonisation."[5]

Within this context of varying degrees of authoritarian rule in Africa, the emergence of a number of personal dictatorships stands out. It is not easy to differentiate sharply between authoritarian and dictatorial rule. As Amos Perlmutter notes, "conventional definitions of autocracy, tyranny, and authoritarianism are quite similar."[6] In Africa specifically, the image of omnipotence projected by the rhetoric of militant leaders frequently conflicts with the reality of weak hierarchies of social control (coupled with administrative inefficiency) that militates against the establishment of meaningful social, economic, and political control. Analytical distinctions between autocratic regimes often break down when empirical realities are taken into account, quite apart from the fact that the criteria for making assessments are not universally accepted. The authoritarian regimes of Kamuzu Banda (Malawi), Sékou Touré (Guinea), Omar Bongo (Gabon), and Thomas Sankara (Burkina Faso), for example, have been assessed in diametrically different fashions by scholars, in part due to the different ideological hues of their regimes.

As part of a continuum of oligarchically controlled political power and of the quest for total societal subservience, dictatorships often differ only in degree from the run-of-the-mill authoritarian systems. The fact that aspects of freedom and choice are given different weight in various cultures complicates not only efforts of assessment and comparison but also those of determination and classification. Moreover, authoritarian rule is differently perceived by subgroups in society, with the criteria of ethnicity, region, traditional standing, and even the religion of the oligarch assuming dominant roles. Conversely, the legitimacy of relatively open political systems may well be denied or undermined by the popular application of such parochial "subnational" criteria, rather than assessed by universalistic considerations.

At one extremity of the continuum of authoritarianism is found the *tyrannical* variant of dictatorship. A highly idiosyncratic, brutal, and personalist system of social repression set up by a civilian or military leader,[7] tyranny is the epitome of personal rule unfettered by moral constraints or political structures and unsupported by society. Although governmental structures may at times be retained, pro forma, all policy dictates derive directly from the personal dictator, no secondary loci of power are allowed to exist, and all of society is viewed as the personal fief and private domain of the dictator. Of the several dictatorships to emerge in Africa, three personal tyrannies stand out starkly by virtue of their sheer brutality and the highly arbitrary nature of their dictatorial rule. These three dictatorships—that of Idi Amin in Uganda, Macias Nguema in Equatorial Guinea, and Jean-Bedel Bokassa in the Central African Republic—are the focus of this study.

Ruling through auxiliary hierarchies of social repression (in the form of family kinsmen, secret police, armed forces, or mercenaries) with the tacit or intimidated consent of the bureaucracy, such systems employ levels of terror—a mechanism of social control—that may be high (Uganda, Equatorial Guinea) or moderate (Central African Republic), the ultimate distinctive characteristic being their "imperial" modality of rule.[8] Totally unfettered by checks on their power (in contradistinction to an autocracy or oligarchy, where some informal give-and-take exists, even if pragmatically arrived at), personal tyrants possess maximum power to the extent feasible within a given society. Socioeconomic patronage and plunder, status and prestige, and ultimately naked fear are the glue that binds cohorts to the potentate. Personal tyrants rule in an absolute imperial manner, often for the sole purpose of self-gratification or glorification, molding society in their own image and exploiting it to their own advantage. They create a vast societal void within which they often enact their personal fantasies and whims, a vacuum that is particularly destabilizing for successor regimes that must painstakingly rebuild from brutalized societies the new cornerstones of state authority and popular legitimacy.

Not all policies emanating from such dictators need be socially destructive, but all, in one way or another, are linked to the dictators' self-perceptions or simplistic visions of an ideal (though often objectively perverse) social order. The precise personality idiosyncracies of each leader manifest themselves in diverse particularistic concerns once the leader is in power; but in all instances the modality of rule is the same. Because such rulers are primarily preoccupied with themselves (the socioeconomic and political forces at their disposal are merely means for the attainment of personal goals), their legacy is completely negative and destructive.

Socioeconomic Origins: From Rags to Riches

The three African tyrants were born within a few years of one another: Jean-Bedel Bokassa in 1921, Francisco Macias Nguema in 1924, and Idi Amin in 1925. They each came to power at the age of forty-five, ruled their countries for periods of between eight and thirteen years, and were overthrown by 1979.[9] Of the three, only Nguema paid with his life for the atrocities committed under his administration—although he too could have eluded capture and slipped into exile. The other two ex-dictators retired in isolated splendor—Amin in Saudi Arabia and Bokassa in a chateau in France until his surprise return to Bangui in October 1986—their protestations of poverty negated by the existence of numerous Swiss bank accounts.

Amin, Bokassa, and Nguema all possessed low traditional status. The first two are members of small ethnic groups known as the Kakwa and the Mbaïka, respectively, whereas the third belonged to the numerically dominant but socioeconomically backward Fang (Esengui clan) in Equatorial Guinea. There is little doubt that their ethnic and socioeconomic backgrounds directly conditioned their behavior while in power.

The Kakwa are one of the smallest ethnic groups in Uganda, isolated to the northwest in the remote West Nile District. Totally outside the mainstream of Ugandan life, neglected by colonial and postcolonial governments alike, they played no political role whatsoever until the rise to power of Amin. Indeed, lagging on all socioeconomic indicators behind most ethnic groups in Uganda, the Kakwa were best known for their high rates of homicide and bellicosity. Within this very marginal ethnic group, Amin was born of humble origins. His father was an itinerant farmer/laborer who had worked for considerable periods in the Sudan, and his mother was a sorceress/mendicant. The completely unlettered Amin was able to escape his humble origins only by enlisting in the colonial army as a cook, later becoming an orderly.

The Mbaïka are part of the relatively more Westernized riverine inhabitants of the Central African Republic who, despite their modest numbers, have traditionally dominated the administration, economy, and armed services of that country. Bokassa himself came from a petty chiefly lineage in some disrepute. His father died at the hands of the French—allegedly in "error" over some minor colonial infraction—and his mother committed suicide shortly afterward. Raised by his grandfather, and bearing the societal stigma of the violent death of his parents,

Bokassa opted for a military career. The "glory" of soldierhood offered the dual prospects of escaping from the Oubangui-Shari backwaters of the French empire and leaving behind the family stigma for which he had been taunted during childhood.

The small Essengui clan forms part of the Fang group, the largest ethnicity of the mainland Río Muni enclave (and, hence, in Equatorial Guinea), although they constitute a minority on the island of Fernando Póo, the nerve center of the country. Within the artificially compressed union of Fernando Póo and Río Muni, the Fang have always been "disenfranchised," with the Bubi and Fernandinos of the main island holding social and economic power and leading on most socioeconomic indicators. Very little is known of Nguema's origins beyond the fact that he was born in Gabon (the Fang "heartland") of very humble stock and that his father was a commoner, albeit a feared traditional sorcerer.

As children, all three had troubled home lives that deeply affected their developing personalities. Nguema was taken away at an early age from his home in Gabon to Río Muni, where he was raised by an uncle. He rarely saw his father, never his mother, and always felt ill at ease within his adopted family. Regarded as introverted and not especially intelligent, Nguema carried with him a sense of inferiority vis-à-vis foreigners, especially those with a modern education, even after he had risen to political preeminence and wielded absolute power over the life and death of all his subjects. His introverted nature led him to mull over past slights, real or imagined, that he remembered years later. Both his disdain for intellectuals, science, and technology and his purges of the entire educated class of the country are at least in part traceable to this unease in a world in which he had always felt threatened. His ban of all modern drugs (which contributed to the decimation of an entire island by cholera) and his shift of the Guinean economy toward barter and autarky were further symptoms of his "back to nature" drive, a return to the idealized, uncomplicated precolonial life in which he felt most comfortable.

Bokassa's childhood was also marred by the traumatic loss both of parents and of social status. He was raised by a very strict paternal grandfather and was constantly taunted by village children regarding his dual family tragedy. Both then and later as a soldier in the French colonial armies, Bokassa felt an internal compulsion to prove his personal worth through acts of courage and daring, which he more than adequately demonstrated during the war in Indochina.

Amin likewise had a grueling childhood. His parents separated immediately after his birth, and he was taken south by his destitute, part-Lugbara mother to the outskirts of various military camps and ultimately to Jinja. There he peddled *mandazi* biscuits and developed his anti-Asian hatreds, while his mother practiced petty witchcraft and consorted with camp personnel. Anxious to escape the marginality of his rootless life, he too saw salvation in a structured and secure army career, even if, at the outset, he was merely a cook and an orderly.

Bokassa was able to acquire a secondary education before enlisting in the armed forces, having been sponsored by missionaries who worked among the riverine ethnic groups. By contrast, Amin received no schooling at all; he was functionally illiterate even upon his promotion to the post of chief of staff. Grossly deficient in both English and Luganda (the *lingua franca* of Uganda) but possessing a smattering of six different languages (a detail that impressed his superior officers), Amin was rarely seen reading or writing anything. He could neither master the intricacies of normal banking procedures nor handle a checkbook, as was revealed in the aftermath of the 1965 Congo/Kinshasa ivory fiasco. Even the massive overspending and huge budgetary deficits of the armed forces during the civilian era when Amin was chief of staff were, in part, a function of his inability to set priorities or to exercise self-restraint. Later, as president, his solution to Uganda's financial morass, which had been triggered by his profligate spendings, was to order the governor of the Central Bank to print more currency. In any task requiring mental effort, his attention span was extremely brief. All these deficiencies became acutely visible once Amin seized power in Kampala, as he could neither preside over cabinet meetings (their function eluded him) nor understand government reports even when read to him, let alone comprehend the intricacies of affairs of state.

Nguema was in like manner an extremely limited person. His lack of aptitude for mental effort and study during childhood, his intellectual shortcomings, his broken Spanish, and his utter naiveté about the outside world destined him for minor clerical work in the Spanish civil service. He acquired *emancipado* status, the key to any socioeconomic advancement, in 1950 only after four unsuccessful attempts at the qualifying tests, and then through overt favoritism on the part of the Spanish authorities. Subsequently promoted to administrative posts beyond his native abilities, Nguema became the somewhat uncomprehending but willing pawn of Spanish expatriate interests trying to secure continued privileged status in the postcolonial era. After independence, Nguema struck back at his puppeteers with decrees leading to the exodus of Spaniards from Equatorial Guinea. He then presided over the cultural, economic, political, and administrative regression of the country down to the level of his own limited intellect and understanding.

Both Bokassa and Amin excelled in the martial arts and frequently boasted of their proficiencies in this area. Bokassa fully deserved his twelve citations for bravery in combat during World War II and France's struggles in Indochina, notwithstanding his idiosyncratic penchant for wearing all his medallions and decorations on a special, over-sized tunic. A truly courageous officer under fire, Bokassa was transformed into a cruel and insecure potentate after he became president. He tortured and executed his main military competitor, Colonel Alexandre Banza, who had masterminded the original coup d'état. He fell into the habit of handwhipping servants, aides, even cabinet ministers, and, later, foreign journalists; he adored fawning behavior; and he boasted of his leadership in the brutal assaults on Bangui's prison inmates (1972) and schoolchildren (1979).

Observers lauded, ad nauseam, Amin's prowess, stamina, and combative initiative: He was Uganda's boxing champion for nine years and retired undefeated. Yet during the 1969 assassination attempt on President Milton Obote, Amin revealed a cowardly streak, and his personal command of the Ugandan Army during the Tanzanian invasion in 1979 was considerably less than inspiring.

By contrast, very little is known about Nguema in this context, although it appears that he never boasted of his physical powers (if only because he had many medical problems); nor was he personally involved in, or even present at, the thousands of deaths either directly ordered by him or committed under his aegis. Reportedly extremely squeamish, Nguema could not stand the sight of blood and brutality; and when "reminded" of the reality of the liquidations going on in his land, he would become morose and withdrawn.

Nguema was also odd-man-out in terms of the cult of sexual masculinity that developed around both Bokassa and Amin. The sexual proclivities of the latter two were voracious, and they boasted about their exploits. Large stocks of pornography were found in both their residences after the coups that toppled them. Bokassa virtually institutionalized his womanizing. His widely known and trumpeted assignations disrupted the traffic in the capital several times a day: Each time he left his palace to visit a mistress, the police had to stop all cars on the road to let his motorcade pass. He unabashedly installed his mistresses, including a favored Romanian dancer, in state houses and assisted them in setting up petty enterprises. His formal consort, known as "Empress" Catherine after his coronation, owned a fashionable boutique in downtown Bangui and held a total monopoly during 1978–1979 over school uniforms, which were produced by another of Bokassa's mistresses—a fact that triggered the 1979 student riots and his ultimate downfall.

A curtain of darkness descended over Equatorial Guinea in 1969, when few foreign observers were allowed into Malabo (as Santa Isabel was renamed); hence little is known about the exploits of Nguema, except that he preferred mulatoo women and was sexually extremely jealous. In at least two documented cases, he ordered the liquidation of all former lovers of his current mistresses (a rather lengthy process in one instance). And the fact that Nguema left no progeny (unlike Amin and Bokassa, who sired dozens of children) has been alluded to as holding some importance in explaining his morose predisposition.

All three tyrants commenced their advance to the summit of their careers, civilian or military, with the approach of independence and the tremendous pressures for at least symbolic Africanization. None was regarded as suitable for the positions to which they were invariably promoted, and colonial officials were not blind to their shortcomings. Evan Bokassa, technically suited to lead the fledgling army of the Central African Republic, was viewed as temperamentally unmatched for the task. Yet, within the context of approaching independence, all three were catapulted to senior positions. Policies of localization took precedence over objective qualifications: They zoomed from promotion to promotion, leaping within a few years from the rank of noncommissioned officer to chief of staff, from junior civil servant to cabinet minister. Amin, for example, moved in six years from the rank of effendi (subofficer) to colonel—an advance normally requiring eleven to seventeen years of service, assuming suitability, technical proficiency awards, and attendance at staff college training courses of varying durations in which Amin could not have possibly participated, let alone passed.

All three future heads of state also benefited overtly and covertly from the assistance of expatriate groups anxious to preserve their privileges after independence. Amin, for example, was consistently given the benefit of the doubt by his British superiors. He was viewed as an ideal platoon sergeant and never regarded as "officer material"; but Uganda's urgent need for at least a few African officers at independence brought about his promotion from the ranks. His past servility to British officers, his gregariousness, his popularity with the troops (who were his true mental peers), his leadership qualifications as an NCO, and the general British preference for "warlike" northern ethnic groups assured him one of Uganda's two coveted officer slots.[10] Amin's routinized promotion could not possibly have been blocked after he broke the NCO "barrier." Within six years the illiterate Kakwa had become the chief of staff; the platoon leader was now in command of a large military machine. Throughout his rapid and steady progress to the summit, after each grudgingly given promotion, Amin was regarded as having definitely reached his terminal rank, only to be promoted again quite quickly. Although Amin was seen as unqualified for officerhood, British staff officers (and Obote, who provided the nationalist impetus) downplayed his intellectual and educational shortcomings, stressing that "experience" compensated for his absence of formal schooling.

Nguema likewise would have been destined for little more than a petty administrative career, were it not for the winds of change that began to ruffle even the stagnant outposts of Spanish colonialism in Africa. Expatriate interests played a much more direct role in the shaping of his future than was the case with Amin or Bokassa. With most of the budding Fang leaders in Río Muni in opposition to Spain, Nguema was "discovered" as a rare ally. Sponsored for, and assisted in obtaining, *emancipado* status, he was then promoted, again beyond his abilities of qualifications, to become Spain's "loyal Fang" in the National Assembly. Ironically, unlike Bokassa and Amin, who despite everything retained an adoratory fixation on the metropole (i.e., colonial master), Nguema harbored deep resentments against Spain. Regarded favorably by Madrid, the local administration in Santa Isabel, and the powerful expatriate economic community in Fernando Póo, Nguema was taken under the wing of an ambitious lawyer-entrepreneur, Antonio Garcia-Trevijano, and molded for the final drive to power. His early speeches ghost-written, his political stances literally typed out for him, and his political tactics laboriously defined and explained, Nguema was for all practical purposes the "creation of his colonialist masters."[11] When he finally broke away from these constraints, his chaotic actions in office eliminated the totality of the Spanish stake in Equatorial Guinea. Only Garcia-Trevijano—and the shady financial interests linked to him—retained a measure of influence in Malabo, and then only because of their provision to the beleaguered dictatorship of its sole cash revenues and luxury commodities.

Bokassa, too, cannot claim advancement on merit alone. Despite his valorous service in France's colonial wars, he served for seventeen years as a sergeant and was promoted because some indigenous officers were needed in the "pipeline" for leadership of the nascent Central African army. His proved bravery while under fire, solid pro-French credentials, and long service in the colonial armies were the grounds for his original promotion, there being fewer reservations in his case than in Amin's. By definition, this initial advancement ensured for Bokassa the eventual leadership of the armed forces. Reservations about his vain, bombastic, and essentially irresponsible personality, and his weaknesses in the area of organizational detail, were brushed under the carpet. In a country with tighter civilian control over the armed forces, or in a more professional officer corps, Bokassa might have performed an acceptable leadership role. But in the context of the Central African Republic, his flamboyant nature rebelled against the constraints of drab, uneventful garrison duty and petty accounting and economizing—which is what leadership of a 500-man force in stagnant Bangui was all about.

Extraconstitutional coups catapulted Bokassa, Nguema, and Amin to supreme power against a backdrop of socioeconomic stress, political void, and deflation of authority. Moreover, idiosyncratic and/or personal factors played a dominant role in all three upheavals. In unstructured, malintegrated societies with little political institutionalization and high levels of socioeconomic stress, personal motives for takeovers often possess important explanatory value in that they conform with empirical reality; yet they are obviously difficult to verify.[12] More complex socioeconomic reasons for coups often camouflage what is in essence a simple interplay of naked greed, fear, and lust for power—motivations all too often granted to civilian politicians but denied to military leaders. The fragmented African political context encourages bids for power, allowing a much greater role to ambitious personalities motivated in their quest for power by a host of particularistic considerations.

Nowhere was this more visible than during Amin's 1971 coup in Uganda, which was triggered primarily by fear. Under investigation for embezzlement and mismanagement of army funds, Amin was also directly implicated in the murder of a fellow senior officer who had mocked his cowardly behavior during the 1969 attempt at Obote's life. Quasi-secret recruitment drives for the armed forces in Amin's own ethnic area (against the express directives of President Obote), and the transfer of troops and officers personally loyal to Amin to units directly under his own control, had even raised doubts about his intrinsic loyalty. Already shunted from sole supreme command of the armed forces, Amin had also been fighting a losing battle to block the promotion of several well-qualified and better-educated officers who were clearly being groomed to replace him. A major confrontation with Obote on these and related issues was imminent; Amin's coup can thus be seen as a classic takeover motivated by simple fear of eclipse, if not imprisonment, of an individual who, without his uniform and the power it conferred, was almost literally a nothing and a nobody in Uganda.

In Bokassa's case the motives for the 1966 seizure may not be as well known, but personal factors certainly played a dominant role. On several previous occasions Bokassa had aggressively demanded a greater personal say in the military and political spheres. In 1965, for example, he had bulldozed the cabinet to ratify totally unscheduled and unbudgeted increases in military expenditures and, later, to give him the war portfolio. His personal flamboyance and natural propensity for a more "exciting" role than that of mere commander in chief of a minimal army in an isolated, small, insular state, from which fewer than a dozen weekly international flights departed weekly, were sharpened by the ulterior motives of his second-in-command. Finally, adding fuel to the situation was Bokassa's ongoing tug-of-war with the head of the *gendarmerie*. When the latter's intention to seize power was leaked out, Bokassa's preemptive action—within the zero-sum context of "winner takes all" in Bangui—could literally be predicted. Neither social, economic, nor political variables played any critical motivating role in Bokassa's or Amin's coup. Personal, highly idiosyncratic, basic human motivations catapulted them both to power, and under such conditions their administrations could axiomatically have been expected to reflect their personal idiosyncrasies, fears, and ambitions.

In the case of Nguema, the civilian "coup" took place within a convoluted series of events, all of which reinforced his hostilities and insecurities. An insensitive Spanish "slight" of the new Republic's symbols of independence provoked his innate anti-Spanish hostility; and a power interplay aimed at a parliamentary ouster of Nguema (heading a coalition in which his party was in a minority) helped to trigger his insecurity. The heavy-handed Spanish meddling arrogance that mobilized the country's elite against him and evoked his distrust of intellectuals led to his assumption of power and to the massive liquidations that followed.

Patterns of Repression and Political Decay

All three leaders institutionalized ruthless and vindictive personalist dictatorships and showed little sensitivity to human life after their seizures of power.[13] Nguema personally ordered the arrest of all his political rivals, real or imagined, immediately after he consolidated his authoritarian rule in 1969. Ondu Edu, Ndong Miyone, and countless others—a *Who's Who* of the anticolonialist phase in Equatorial Guinea—suffered indescribably brutal deaths within months after independence. Any criticism, however slight or untimely, let alone an act of opposition, was punishable by death.

Intellectuals were hounded while all schools, newspapers, and printing presses were closed down, not to open for a decade. Nearly the entire pre-independence cabinet perished, as well as half of all the subsequent Nguema ministers, two-thirds of the pre-independence National Assembly, and a large percentage of the senior and middle echelons of the civil service. These killings were over and beyond those routine deaths committed by the unaccountable army, and the additional thousands whose liquidation was approved by Nguema in Mongomo, by phone or by courier, on perfunctory petition by his subordinates for sentencing for minor (often baseless or erroneous) infractions of the civil code.

By the time Nguema was toppled, hardly a single intellectual remained in the country; fewer than a dozen technical school graduates survived the holocaust. Entire governmental spheres of activity vanished; literally a dozen ministries closed down, most under lock and key. Organized activity by the regime ended in most domains. In 1976, the last pitiful remnants of the higher-level civil service petitioned Nguema *en masse* (no single person dared to act as a spokesman) for a relaxation of the country's total isolationism that had feudalized society. Though handpicked by Nguema to replace those previously murdered, and in essence constituting the last backbone of the administrative services of the state, every one of the 114 petitioners was arrested, tortured, and brutalized, many never to be seen again.

Amin's colossal brutalities in office defy cataloging and need no review. As crimes against humanity they rival those of Nazi Germany; Amin's hands were literally bloodied by his countless murders. His disdain for human life was obvious early in his military career. During the Mau Mau rebellion in Kenya, his brutality in the performance of his duties—about which he actually bragged twenty years later at a shocked OAU Heads of State meeting—nearly got him cashiered from the colonial army. Indeed, right up to independence, his career and promotion prospects (dependent as they were upon British superiors) were at stake in the face of his cavalier disdain for human life. He was "forgiven" for various minor infractions essentially because "his heart was in the right place," as one colonial officer put it.[14] But he actually relished the utilization of brute force: Twice during the Obote era he suppressed local unrest with undue zeal, and the highly unnecessary murder of Brigadier Pierino Okoya, who had accused him of cowardice during the 1969 unrest, has also been laid at his door. After the 1971 coup, the real bloodbath began as Amin personally, or through his NCO cohorts, committed massive liquidations among all the strata of society, military as well as civilian.

Equally resentful of those who were better educated than himself (though delighted with honorary titles), Amin sought out and promoted his unlettered social peers to positions of power and authority in his new Uganda. A quasi-total purge of the officer corps—and not only its Langi and Acholi ethnic component, loyal to Obote—got rid of most of its graduates of foreign staff colleges. Amin's deep insecurity regarding his education reinforced him in his ethnic witchhunt and widened its swath of destruction. By 1976, the "new" Ugandan Army was very much a force of foreigners (composed of Nubians, Sudanese, Zairiens) largely led by ex-NCOs promoted to senior officer rank.

Intellectually bored with the political kingdom he had just seized, incapable of comprehending expertise, and unable to restrain his flights of fancy, Amin rapidly disposed of his cabinet and civilian aides, whose chatter, style, and forebodings were an enigma to him. Although the educational system itself was not dismantled, dwindling fiscal allocations and salaries caused many teachers and students simply to move into the bush, reverting to the cultivation of staple crops as a means of survival.

Bokassa's main weakness was vanity. Despite his secondary education and a certain cosmopolitan veneer, he too felt threatened, at least to some extent, by more qualified personnel, even as he craved their adulation and constant glorification. Projecting the image of an all-powerful patron-father, Bokassa quickly became vindictive when spurned. When his self-image was threatened or mocked, he lashed out with violence. Cries for mercy or signs of remorse never swayed Amin or Nguema; indeed, both took a seemingly perverse pleasure in condemning such supplicants. In contrast, pleas for forgiveness, couched in "true humility," reinforced the image of Bokassa as a benevolent "Papa Bok"—his favorite nickname—and hence were successful more often than not, irrespective of the crime. But although ministers guilty of embezzling millions of CFA (French Financial Community) francs were forgiven and even promoted to higher office in acts of "magnanimity," Bokassa headed the merciless and senseless beatings of prisoners who had been caught stealing in order to stay alive.

As father-patron of numerous schools and of the local university, Bokassa delighted in having them named after himself; other institutions, military camps, agricultural projects, and roads also bore his name, just as exercise books and, later, school uniforms bore his effigy. In 1979, his wrath was raised to the pitch of near-madness, not because of student unrest as such, but because "his" children had dared to riot against him. In fact, Bokassa brooked no opposition when in power, although he rarely physically eliminated his rivals or opponents. His bullying tactics and hand-whippings kept officials in line, but most learned in due time how to manipulate his vanity and escape his wrath. Indeed, it has even been suggested that the idea of establishing an empire (and Bokassa's coronation) had its origins in a flattering proposal by a cabinet minister trying to deflect the president's wrath.

Bokassa seems to have been the least bloodthirsty of the three tyrants, but this appearance is somewhat misleading. Although his killings were, indeed, greatly dwarfed in number by those in Uganda and Equatorial Guinea, a whole string of individual liquidations may be attributed to him virtually from the moment he seized power. Unreported at the time was the vicious settling of accounts after the 1966 coup d'état that led to Bokassa's assumption of power. The head of police, his prime rival, was eliminated, followed by a bout of selective killings and brutal clubbings of many individuals (expatriates not excluded) who had cast aspersions on his professional or intellectual limitations, including those who had openly laughed at his medallion-encrusted tunic during the Dacko civilian era. Throughout his reign he behaved ruthlessly toward his aides and intermittently sent those regarded as untrustworthy to face firing squads in distant garrisons. The senseless murder of the infant son of his recently executed son-in-law, Fidel Obrou (for a coup bid), was yet another manifestation of Bokassa's brutality.

Like Amin but unlike the squeamish Nguema, Bokassa was personally involved in many of these sadistic bouts. He tortured the hapless Colonel Banza (who was arrested for an amateurish plot) prior to his execution, and he was personally involved in the aforementioned beating of helpless prisoners in Bangui prison and in the widescale torture and killing of children during the 1979 school riots. Indeed, it was the gruesome evidence of Bokassa's personal participation in some of these latter brutalities both in prison and in his palace compound that finally swung a very reluctant France to engineer his downfall.

Also of passing interest is the fact that ritual cannibalism was practiced by two, and possibly by all three, dictators. Persistent rumors about Amin's proclivity in this respect were finally substantiated with the fall of Kampala to Tanzanian troops and the examination of Amin's house. Bokassa's participation in similar practices came to light in 1979; indeed, he had alluded to his involvement in numerous cryptic and sphinxlike quips, but no one took them seriously.[15] But in the case of Nguema, despite his large personal collection of human skulls (which conferred upon him magic powers), no evidence has yet emerged regarding his actual participation in the Fang fetish of the consumption of the vital organs of rivals. The documented instances of ritual cannibalism on the part of Amin and Bokassa strongly underscore their "cultural marginality"; they also go a long way toward viscerally illustrating the characteristics of absolute rule in these African states.

Moreover, all three tyrants implicitly or explicitly relied on soothsayers, sorcerers, and diviners to spread the myth of their omniscience and divine powers; and with the exception of Bokassa, they strongly interfered with organized religion in their own society. Amin had his own personal fortuneteller in constant attendance, and he claimed omnipotence, omniscience, and divine guidance in his state "policies." The "inspiration" for the expulsion of Uganda's long-resident Asian community, the "strategy" for the liquidation of South Africa, even the exact date and manner of his own death, were allegedly revealed to him in his dreams. Wily and cunning, Amin evaded literally dozens of ambushes and attempted assassinations, utilizing subterfuges, multiple vehicles and routes, and even a "double," thus further spreading the myth of his invincibility and divine foreknowledge of events.

Nominally a Muslim, Amin surrounded himself with Muslim and animist sycophants, tinkering with the internal array of power in Uganda's two main Muslim communities, appealed to the Arab world for technical, financial, and military assistance, and even secured a powerful Libyan military contingent at the time of the Tanzanian assault. In a country where religion was a sensitive issue, strongly polarizing society—and where Islam was a minority faith of less than 15 percent of the population—Amin did not cringe from persecuting and killing priests, favoring his Muslim brethren in the allocation of spoils of office, and ultimately sanctioning the murder of the Catholic bishop.

Despite his veneer of greater sophistication, Bokassa also frequented soothsayers, cryptically claiming omniscience and foreknowledge of everything going on in the country; he wisely refrained, however, from overly antagonizing the Church or from transferring some of his whims into the religious domain. In certain flights of fancy he, too, was to claim divine inspiration, although this was more in the nature of play-acting, similar to his habit of using the regal "we" in all addresses. Certainly his brief conversion to Islam (and adoption of an Arab name), and many of his "inspirations," were little more than cunning acts aimed at achieving dramatic publicity in the right circles. In the case of his conversion (in a country that had suffered severely from Arab slave raiders), when the expected Libyan financial "pay-off" was not forthcoming, Bokassa casually reverted to his old faith, promptly followed by his clownish "court," which had originally converted with the emperor.

Nguema, on the other hand, was almost totally immersed in the world of spirits. A master of traditional witchcraft, preoccupied with "centralizing" all magic in his own hands, after forcing the local clergy to insert references to his quasi-divine status in church liturgy, he rejected Christianity as unsatisfactory for Guinea and proclaimed the country "atheistic." When he had closed down churches everywhere (many were transformed into cocoa warehouses) and had incorporated the Malabo Cathedral into the presidential compound, missionary activity disappeared and Christian worship became a crime. Although Nguema adopted a myriad of titles, including "El Unico Miraclo" (The Sole Miracle), he made no effort to institutionalize his personalized faith, if only because of the almost total breakdown of administrative activity in the country and the virtual impossibility of implementing anything, anywhere.

After Nguema had withdrawn to his home village, his collection of skulls assured him awesome powers. He was best known to the masses as the incarnation of the tiger (an animal *not* found in Africa), and the fear of his omnipotence and immortality was so prevalent that foreign troops had to be assigned to guard him after his overthrow. Indeed, widespread apprehension over his vengeance after reincarnation was such that only a foreign (Moroccan) firing squad could be reliably charged with his execution.

All three dictators shunned expert opinion, distrusted or did away with cabinet meetings, ruled by personal decree, and brought about the ossification of political structures in their societies. Their immediate reference groups, their trusted lieutenants, were the sycophants, the self-seeking aides who were often unlettered. None of them embraced or enunciated any long-range policy or ideology. Nguema and Amin could hardly set any purpose or goal for states that were viewed as fiefs of human and material plunder. As for Bokassa, his excessive vanity, flights of fancy, and whimsical vacillations precluded either consistency in any policy or attention to detail and to day-to-day administration within the context of mass and wholesale plunder of state resources.

Still, although reference may be made to the "government" of the Central African Republic during the Bokassa era, it is quite difficult to employ that term with respect to the other two regimes. Uganda was more of a decentralized network of regional warlords who had absolute power over life and property in their domains, with Amin only very loosely, and only in certain areas, in control of his minions. And Equatorial Guinea was more of a traditional patrimonial society, run by an ad hoc coterie of family *mafioso*.

By no stretch of the imagination can Equatorial Guinea be said to have been "governed" by Nguema. Within twelve months of the establishment of his reign of terror, all traces of cabinet meetings, orderly government, and consistent policymaking had disappeared. The central regime came to be characterized by telephone edicts, inertia, and ad hoc decisions often at variance with one another. The few foreign observers to remain on the island noted the ghost-like appearance of the capital, and the closure, under lock and key, of many ministries and offices (intermittently including the Ministry of Foreign Affairs). Ill-at-ease in Malabo, Nguema soon withdrew to the mainland—first to Bata, where a new presidential palace was built for him, and then to the seclusion and tranquility of Mongomo in the interior. There Nguema held court, and his surrogate rulers could meet with "El Unico Miraclo" in his distant regional center—should they wish to hazard such potentially unpredictable encounters—to solicit policy directives. More often than not they would make the journey solely to resupply the presidential compound with drugs and scarce commodities, or to importune Nguema to release cash, often stored in suitcases, to pay troops and civil servants.

Surrounded by relatives, civil and military aides, and aging village elders, and protected behind barbed wire by crack Eastern-bloc security forces, Nguema would reminisce for hours around a campfire about the "good old days" before the onset of modernity. Delegations would sometimes wait on Nguema in Mongomo for days, until he decided to deal with the real issues at stake, often perfunctorily and with evident distaste. Eventually such consultations dwindled in number, with everything but the most sensitive issues dealt with briefly over the phone or wireless. Rational decisions concerning either public administration or foreign policy were all functionally superfluous in a subsistence-cum-slave economy kept in line by random terror and administered by a family *mafioso* in the context of a regime that had renunciated all other aspects of twentieth-century social, economic, and political activity. Although the disappearance of governmental structures and policymaking evolved over time and was especially obvious after 1971–1972, for ten long years Equatorial Guinea suffered under a system of unmitigated lawlessness, terror, arbitrary murder, rape, theft, and slavery under the ad hoc control of a recluse in faraway Mongomo who left the details of day-to-day administration to his family and ethnic cohorts.

Uganda likewise cannot be said to have been truly "governed" by Amin. The process of decay there never advanced to the same degree as in Malabo, and until the very last day a number of state organs were operational in Kampala. Some were actually quite active as well, although Amin would brook no opposition and personally beat up ministers and civil servants who disputed his "facts." Yet, much that passed as policy in Kampala was contradictory and unattainable. There did exist a measure of deliberation about societal goals. But this deliberation did not occur through formal structures; nor were there any mechanisms to ensure their effective implementation or supervision. As Amin was incapable of grasping complex matters and could neither communicate nor concentrate, he was acutely uncomfortable in formal meetings that he was unable to preside over or conduct and soon did away with his technocrats and advisory bodies. Policymaking, when not adopted on the spur of the moment out of a gut reaction to the triggering event, took place informally, and sometimes at great length, within the context of Amin's reference groups. Initially, Amin turned to his NCO cronies, now promoted to senior military officers, and to his rank-and-file orderlies, Nubi and Sudanese drinking companions, and Kakwa kinsmen; later, in a more structured manner, he consulted the so-called Supreme Command Council, which merely grouped together his more trustworthy ex-NCO commanders who expressed viewpoints unadulterated by the processes of Western socialization. Much like Nguema, who sat for hours by the campfire discussing "state policy" with tribal leaders who had never left Mongomo, Amin sat for hours with his intellectual peers tossing about ideas and policies that were forgotten, unrecorded, and irrelevant because they were unimplementable.

The brutal image of the Ugandan dictatorship also camouflaged the reality of a highly splintered and regressive quasi-anarchic socioeconomic setting over which Amin only nominally exercised power. Although a central regime existed in Kampala, with ministries, public servants, and at times even routinzed processes of decisionmaking, Amin never truly controlled the periphery. The writ of the civil service probably did not extend more than 50 miles from the Kampala-Entebbe corridor, except when personally enforced by Amin and especially when accompanied by military force.

The bulk of the country was actually under the real control of highly autonomous military units based in garrison towns and for the most part living off the land. Unruly, intermittently in open rebellion over the nonpayment of their salaries, and perpetually half-drunk (beer being the only item regularly supplied by the army headquarters), these formations controlled life and property in their territorial segments and were the ultimate fount of all activity and authority. Amin had encouraged this trend early in his reign, when he had very emphatically proclaimed the supremacy of the lowliest military orderly over even cabinet ministers, if civilian. The warlord mentality and disdain for civilian administration (particularly for "outsiders") were thus reinforced in the officer corps. It is not surprising that few Kampala edicts were enforceable outside the immediate core of central control, given both the highly anarchic nature of "administration" in post-coup Uganda and the unwillingness of the much-intimidated and only intermittently paid civil servants in distant districts to test Amin's directives face to face with brutal and totally unaccountable local military commanders and trigger-happy soldiers—especially since loyal military commanders were more precious to Amin than administrators.

The Ugandan economy was also very much beyond the control of Amin. The big Asian-owned tea estates rapidly became unproductive (just as the cocoa plantations promptly collapsed in Malabo), as did much of the service sector and cottage industry. Many commercial enterprises were expropriated from the Asians and then left abandoned after having been milked dry by Amin's cohorts. Coffee growers evaded government purchasing structures, smuggling their crop into Kenya in exchange for consumer goods; many converted their fields from cash to staple crops in order to physically survive; others relocated away from roads, modern centers, and garrison towns in order to avoid marauding military units. The economy of Uganda not only came to a near-halt under Amin; it also shifted to more traditional crops, modes of production, and marketing as these were suddenly more relevant to survival.

As previously noted, the operational modality of dictatorship in the Central African Republic was somewhat different. The reasons for this are crucial in that Bokassa could easily have been an Amin. The regime structures under Bokassa never truly decayed or functionally disappeared because they were increasingly harnessed to provide the emperor with an enhanced and more gratifying role, status, and prestige. Bokassa's motivations for seizing power were different from those of the other two tyrants; his quest for personal role-expansion, psychological self-gratification, adulation, prestige, and glory axiomatically precluded, and was antithetical to, the nihilism and anarchy implicit in, or stemming from, the political style and modality of rule by Nguema and Amin.

Although Bokassa, too, may not have had a very clear conception of his role once in power, he was much more acculturated to Western norms. Moreover, modernization, organization, and administration were intrinsic prerequisites for his greater self-fulfillment as president. Yet the severe socioeconomic constraints besetting the acutely isolated and globally insignificant Central African Republic precluded any appreciable enhancement of Bokassa's status and prestige. As the novelty of his new role wore off, the ennui resulting from his frustrating limitations grew. An ex post facto analysis of the Bokassa era from this conceptual perspective clearly reflects a continuum from early policies that were not much different from those of the preceding Dacko regime (self-gratification through "good government") to dramatic flights of fancy and whims, whereby the state became merely the backdrop for the adulation of Bokassa and the stage for the enactment of his private fantasies.

Grandiose, counterproductive, and wasteful policies were pursued. Radical shifts in strategy and ideology followed one another in bewildering succession; in 1976–1977 alone, the Central African Republic changed from a capitalist state to a socialist state to an Islamic Republic to an empire replete with a Napoleonic coronation. Sycophants had a field day in Bangui. Increasingly all the state coffers and national resources (notably diamonds and ivory) became the private preserve of the emperor. Even when Bokassa retreated to his "ancestral home" after his coronation in order to set up his "imperial court," replete with courtiers, head of protocol, and ministers, the day-to-day administration of the empire was not relinquished to his cabinet and the prime minister in Bangui, the new constitution notwithstanding.

Bokassa's eccentricities were at all times abetted and encouraged by his entourage. His lack of concern for the concrete and the possible and his gross flights of fancy were but continuations of his pre-coup inclinations, and these traits were encouraged by a coterie of sycophants. They were rotated with regular periodicity to allow others a chance at the plunder implicit in state office. At no time, however, was Bokassa ever out of touch with reality, as could be said of Nguema and, at times, of Amin as well. A telling fact is that while insisting that all offices and enterprises in the country should display his favored photograph (in his oversized medallion-encrusted tunic), he still made its *sale* in Bangui or its dispatch abroad (for curiosity value) a civil crime, well aware of the guffaws it widely elicited. Swayed by whim into dramatic actions (declaring for Islam or scientific socialism, setting up Air Centrafrique, breaking with the Customs Union for Central Africa, etc.), he was nevertheless able to see error and take corrective action. Though he allowed his ministers a free reign to milk the state dry, Bokassa was meticulous in ensuring that none of them became either too greedy or too powerful, and he rapped the knuckles of those whose self-enrichment schemes were likely to foment societal unrest. At times, he even announced misleading "policy changes" so that he could observe his Cabinet rushing to adulate or imitate his "innovations."

Bokassa's "policies" in office were, above all, wasteful. Certainly they were less humanly destructive, culturally regressive, or institutionally void than those of Amin or Nguema. The forced adulation and egocentric policies with all their institutional trappings were inevitably less destructive than either the brutal socioeconomic regression in Equatorial Guinea or the murderous ethnic-religious supplanting of societal strata in Uganda; the human costs of Bokassa's tyranny were consequently correspondingly lower. Although his authority ultimately rested on the control of the forces of repression, he was not prevented from establishing a clientelist network of sycophants beholden to him. Day-to-day administration continued in Bangui, and most Centrafricans suffered little from the presence of a tyrant on the throne. Their lives were economically harsh, no doubt; but the country was accustomed to poverty and austerity. At least it was devoid of the constant hazards of instant arrest and arbitrary death characteristic of Kampala and Malabo.

On Physiology and Psychology

Dictatorships and authoritarian systems have always attracted scholarly attention, just as social unrest, revolutionary change, and political instability are often the focus of more intensive analysis than stability and democracy. There are cogent reasons for this. Although libertarian democracy came of age in much of Europe during the twentieth century, this era can also be described as one of totalitarianism and authoritarianism, genocide and racial conflict. Statistically, at least, more people live under authoritarian regimes, and patterns of violence and instability are more prevalent, than ever before.

Within this context, the emergence of idiosyncratic personalist dictatorships, especially when accompanied by wide-scale societal violence and brutalization, clearly invites analysis. Systemic institutionalized violence, routine massacres, brutal liquidations, and reigns of terror may be merely alternative means of social control in the absence of political legitimacy and authority within which insecure dictators pursue their goal of paramount power. After all, inefficient and socioeconomically wasteful though they may be, selective terror and indiscriminate political murders were recognized techniques of stabilizing authoritarian rule long before Machiavelli codified his maxims in *The Prince*. But an ongoing period of random terror that virtually brings a nation to its knees is so counterproductive as to be axiomatically aberrant in terms of the quest of absolute power itself, and it inevitably raises questions about the mental state of the tyrant in office. Societal terror of this dimension, which often acquires a *leitmotif* of its own, may be not merely a technique of social control but also a symptom of personality disorders or physical maladies that are manifesting themselves in socially combative, vengeful, sadomasochistic, or nihilistic policies that ravage the polity.

Marginal men may, indeed, tend to overutilize the repressive means of social control at their disposal. Catapulted to power by greed, fear, avarice, or ambition, they tend to view authority as stemming from the barrel of the gun, and they perceive power solely in its brute physical sense, aware of their own insignificance "without the gun." Megalomania, the "bully-syndrome" writ large, the "little man" catapulted to the heights of power, who can now, with impunity, lord it over those who had hitherto bossed or mocked him—all these are not new conceptualizations, and they certainly have explanatory value. But the nature and dimensions of the incredible bestiality and human carnage levied against the populations of Equatorial Guinea and Uganda by Nguema and Amin, and the bizarre idiosyncracies of Bokassa in the Central African Republic, demand additional perspective. Alternate or supplementary explanations beyond the purely political and sociological need to be garnered to account for the roots of the terror unleashed by these three tyrants. Otherwise, how are we to account for the liquidation, in the most frightful manner possible, of as many as 300,000 people?

Numerous studies in recent years have persuasively offered psychological insights into and explanations of complex political behavior, including styles of leadership.[16] The combined focus of "traditional" social analysis and psychohistory or political psychology accounts for much of the incisiveness of many contemporary studies of world leaders. Although little empirical research in this vein has been conducted by

Africanists, sufficient *suggestive* data have accumulated with respect to the personalities of the three dictators in question as to place some of the antecedent analysis in a better perspective.

Nguema is an excellent case in point. Acknowledged (even before his atrocities had become routinized) as one of Africa's most demented rulers, as an "unsophisticated man . . . completely unprepared to cope with the complexities that have been thrust upon him,"[17] Nguema nurtured an inferiority complex that manifested itself in utter servility to perceived superiors, in arrogance and domineering behavior toward those beneath him, and in a hatred of and desire for vengeance against those better educated and more socially privileged. With the arrival of independence, Nguema was afforded the opportunity to vent his pent-up grievances against a modern world he little understood and was greatly threatened by. No other explanation, whether sociological or political, better accounts for his virtual extermination of the entire educated class in Equatorial Guinea, his personal edict against using the word *intellectual* in any context, and his very real rejection of the twentieth century.

"Unbalanced, inconsistent and unpredictable,"[18] Nguema engaged in behavior characterized by "periods of lucidity interspersed with uncontrollable violence."[19] He had a medical history of treatment in Spain for certain undisclosed diseases, the divulgence of which was prohibited by Spanish censorship laws and still remains classified. He was progressively deaf to the point of having to scream during his speeches just in order to hear himself, refusing the use of any hearing aids. His physical movements were jerky and progressively uncoordinated, triggering speculation about a host of possible afflictions—including brain damage, allegedly the reason for his medical trips to Spain. Nguema regularly consumed various drugs (such as *bhang, iboga* [hallucinogenics], and *hashish*), the effects of which were visible in the pupils of his eyes, in his totally disconnected speeches, and in his bizarre personal actions and occasional states of acute disassociation. Ridden with fear of vengeance by his dead victims, Nguema often conducted one-sided dialogues with them, fuelling the local consensus that he was "medio-loco," or "half-mad."[20] He was always an introverted loner, unable to form close personal relationships or to reach outside his egocentric world, and only intermittently concerned with the issues of his fellow human beings. Although many questions have been raised as to Nguema's actual sanity, no authoritative published diagnosis exists. Like nearly everything that transpired during much of his dictatorship, the Spanish *materia reservada* classification (lifted only partially in 1974) shielded the tyrant from outside scrutiny.

By contrast, a surplus of testimony about the state of health of Idi Amin has been provided by medical practitioners and specialists, some of whom personally treated him at one time or another.[21] The most authoritative reference work on Africa notes that Amin suffered from hypomania—"a mental state in which thought processes are speeded up,"[22] resulting in alternating cycles of frenetic energy followed by general nervous collapse. Such patterns of behavior were, indeed, observed in Amin when phases of acute hyperactivity (several mass meetings a day, exhortations, socioeconomic "innovations," foreign denouncement, confrontations with the military, and so forth) were followed by weeks of total withdrawal, inactivity, and absence from the public eye, raising speculation as to the possible success of one of the many ambushes on his convoys. References have also been made to Amin's manic-depressive attacks,[23] the after-effects of untreated syphilis, and other physical or mental maladies. The variety cited rather boggles the mind, for surely Amin could not have suffered from all these disorders.

Other scholars have declined to delve into the possible repercussions of Amin's alleged maladies on his leadership style and personality traits, notwithstanding the richness of the suggested data,[24] because they feel that the standard sociological interpretations are more than adequate. His idiosyncrasies, biases, cruelty, force-orientation, and other aberrations are correlated with his formative values and socioeconomic origins, and his other traits—hyperactivity, manic outbursts of temper, and so on—are viewed either as secondary in importance or as derivatives of his nonintegrated ego. Thus, Amin's behavior can be directly linked to his Kakwa background, marginally lower-class, uneducated origins, lack of personal roots or family home-life, and malintegrated and nonsocialized ego. Thus viewed, this "not even semi- . . . at most sub-Westernized" soldier advanced through life relying on his burly physique and innate cunning,[25] retaining nonsublimated prejudices and resentments against broad societal classes as a result of real or perceived slights. As Amin was intellectually unsuited for managerial or executive tasks—at best an "ideal foreman"[26]—his actions, once he attained power, were the predictable reaction of the "common man's gut feeling and bias."[27]

The violence and brutality that characterized the Amin era are "normal" manifestations of the "bully syndrome," in which brute force becomes the operational modality of the "little man" thrust into a position of paramount power, dragging in his wake an entire class-cohort of those who were similarly marginal. Unable to cope with the nuances of the Westernized elite because of socialization deficiencies, Amin reverted to the behavior and company of his true peers—the drivers, orderlies, guards, and NCOs. "Politics" in Kampala became a barracks-room activity.

There is very little authoritative analysis about the possible roots of Bokassa's idiosyncrasies. Reference has been made to an alleged head wound suffered during the Indochina campaigns, but the evidence is hardly conclusive, and no observer has suggested that this explains Bokassa's erratic behavior. Scholars have alluded to his excessive emotionalism, his wild moodswings, and a complex amalgam of personality traits. He has manifested extreme vindictiveness and great personal cruelty, but these traits were rarely alluded to in the French press, which also suffered from censorship laws.[28] (Some new data were revealed at his 1987 trial.) Indeed, observers who know him best suggest that he has been subject to fits of virtual madness during which he loses total control over his senses and over rational thought, and that these occurrences became progressively more frequent.[29] His aborted Napoleonic-style "return to the throne" in 1983, for example, may well have been nothing more than play-acting; but what is one to make of his actual October 1986 return to Bangui and his submission to a spectacular public trial?

Observers have also noted Bokassa's extremely heavy drinking (a case of virtual alcoholism according to some), bountiful sexual proclivities, wild flights of fancy, play-acting, and need for self-gratification. All of these traits, in combination with his megalomaniac coronation as Emperor *à la* Napoleon, suggest a maladjusted personality, but they are not as deviant from the accepted norm as are those of the other two dictators. In addition, policymaking did not break down in Bangui as it did in both Malabo and Kampala. Bokassa's fiscal excesses and whims cannot compare in magnitude to those in Equatorial Guinea and Uganda, where routine printing of paper currency "solved" the problem. And although the latter option may well have been palatable to Bokassa had it been available,[30] much of his profligate spendings were subsidized either by France (as with the coronation) or by resident French expatriate groups. Neither do Bokassa's killings and liquidations compare in magnitude (if murder can ever be compared purely statistically or otherwise) with the routinized butchery in Kampala and Malabo. Socialized to some extent to Western middle-class norms, exposed to the wider world through overseas service, and personally quite sophisticated, Bokassa emerges as an "average" man set loose on an open stage that allowed him not only to fulfill his wildest fantasies and dreams but also to play out his individualistic idiosyncrasies—including a decided streak of cruelty.

The Legacy of Dictatorship

Despite their different personalities, policies, and political styles, Nguema, Amin, and Bokassa left their societies awesome legacies. Beyond the 300,000 dead and 200,000 still in exile (mostly Hispano-Guineans),[31] countless individuals physically and mentally maimed, and a legacy of interethnic hatreds unleashed by the rule of terror, the three dictators pulverized whatever semblance of political legitimacy had existed in the center.[32] They destroyed the social glue that held together their multi-cleavaged societies; they uprooted large segments of the population, forcing them into exile or active opposition, and they left behind such terrible burdens as economic collapse, bankruptcy, social strife, and political decay, which time alone may not necessarily heal.

The "liberation" of Equatorial Guinea, Uganda, and the Central African Republic—in the latter two cases, by foreign force of arms—brought a sigh of relief that the madness had been evicted and the nightmare ended; but a host of monumental problems remained. In Malabo, of course, dictatorship still reigns supreme. A less murderous, more venal, twentieth-century *caudillo* dictatorship has replaced Nguema's demented rule.[33] There is now a concrete reason for the social repression (plunder) and a few restraints on terror (if only due to considerations of cost-effectiveness). In Kampala and Bangui, despite efforts by successor regimes to bring about social and economic reconstruction, *more* societal tumult (including terrorism and guerrilla warfare) has occurred than under either Amin or Bokassa. Incredibly, there has even been talk in both capitals of the "good old days" under the latter two tyrants. Along with more credible sources of opposition to the new administration in Kampala, "Brigadier General" Moses Ali and his "liberation" force of ex-Amin brigands offered their services to the nation they had just brutalized; whereas Bokassa, encouraged by indications of possible interest in the Central African Republic in a Napoleonic-style comeback, nearly risked the firing squad in 1983 (though, as noted, his attempted return to the throne may have been nothing more than theatrical play-acting).

Although post-liberation developments in the three countries are largely outside the scope of this study, clearly the carnage of a decade or more of dictatorship has fundamentally constrained efforts at developing a new political order. In each case, an analysis of socioeconomic reconstruction efforts dramatically underscores the three conclusions that will be further expanded in the individual case studies.

First, antecedent social, political, economic, and religious (in the case of Uganda) cleavages have survived; indeed, they have become further entrenched. There has been no "leveling effect," no inward collapsing of cleavages, subsequent to the ravages of the dictatorial era that afflicted all segments of society equally. Not even through their massive devastation of humanity have these three tyrants brought about any possible steps toward unity among survivors. The characteristic ethnic/regional cleavage in all three countries has remained intact, as has the religious (Catholic-Protestant) tug-of-war in Uganda specifically.

Second, in a varying but distinctly visible manner, the dictatorships shattered the basic social inertia that had hitherto loosely bound these syncretic societies to the authority of weak political centers. The reimposition of the most fundamental parameters of "public and political order"—to use Zolberg's phrase[34]—has been axiomatically the first task embarked upon by the successor regimes, but it has not been attained since the fall of the tyrants. If the very legitimacy of the state in Uganda, Central African Republic, and Equatorial Guinea was under question or attack previously, it is certainly as insecurely anchored today. Even Yoweri Museveni, whose successful guerrilla warfare catapulted him to power and dramatically changed Uganda's prospects for the better, faces fundamental divisive challenges to the territorial integrity of the country.

Finally, incipient class consciousness appears to have taken root. Two outcomes of the massive socioeconomic dislocation in these three societies have been their atomization and proletarianization. No doubt abetted by the natural evolutionary processes that are taking place in many parts of Africa, such atomization and proletarianization have produced larger and more stridently militant, class-conscious, and ideologically motivated urban pressure groups, as well as more easily mobilizeable rural elements.

These developments have coincided with prolonged periods of acute austerity necessitated by the policies of socioeconomic reconstruction in Kampala and Bangui and by the venal plunder in Malabo; they have also caused considerable unrest, strife, and (in Uganda) ethnic massacres and rebellions. Ultimately, they portend not just instability but also grassroots pressures for fundamental socioeconomic change; already an array of willing leaders are espousing "revolutionary" goals. This potential long-term instability and ultimate radicalization of society may in essence be the true legacy of Amin, Nguema, and Bokassa. The following three chapters will trace the specific socioeconomic factors in Equatorial Guinea, Uganda, and the Central African Republic that allowed the emergence of dictatorship, its unique style in each case, and the nature of the societal problems inherited by the successor administrations.

Notes

1. Aristide R. Zolberg, *Creating Political Order: The Party-States of West Africa* (Chicago: Rand McNally, 1966). See also his equally seminal article, "The Structure of Political Conflict in Africa," *American Political Science Review* (June 1968).

2. See, in particular, Fred Hayward's insightful analysis in "Political Participation and Its Role in Development: Some Observations from the African Context," *Journal of Developing Areas*, vol. 7 (1973).

3. *West Africa* (London), January 28, 1985.

4. See, inter alia, T. O. Odetola, *Military Regimes and Development* (London: George Allen & Unwin, 1982); and Claude Ake, "Political Integration and Political Stability," *World Politics*, vol. 19, no. 4 (July 1967).

5. Amos Perlmutter, *Modern Authoritarianism* (New Haven, Conn.: Yale University Press, 1981), p. 170.

6. Ibid., p. 1.

7. An oligarchy, junta, or clique would, by definition, negate the personal element of dictatorship as here defined.

8. The concept of an "imperial" modality of rule is a necessary category in any analysis of authoritarian rule in Africa. Most current typologies do not provide a truly adequate fit for the empirical reality of African case studies. For one useful typology, see Robert H. Jackson and Carl G. Rosberg, *Personal Rule in Black Africa: Prince, Autocrat, Prophet, Tyrant* (Berkeley: University of California Press, 1982).

9. See Gordon Matate, "Exit Africa's Triad of Tyrants," *Africa* (London, November 1979), pp. 12–18.

10. The second appointment was given to Shaban Opolot, who, shortly after the showdown between Obote and the *kabaka*, was dismissed from the army and placed under house arrest.

11. *Africa Research Bulletin: Political, Social, and Cultural Series* (September 1979).

12. See Samuel Decalo, *Coups and Army Rule in Africa: Studies in Military Style* (New Haven, Conn.: Yale University Press, 1976), Chapter 1.

13. All three also exchanged state visits, signed treaties of friendship, and lauded each other's accomplishments. See *West Africa* (London), October 1, 1973, and January 27, 1976.

14. Interview in Nairobi, July 21, 1980.

15. *West Africa*, January 5, 1981.

16. For a good introduction to this methodological issue, see Fred I. Greenstein, *Personality and Politics: Problems of Evidence, Inference, and Conceptualization* (New York: W. W. Norton, 1975); and Greenstein, "Personality and Political Socialization: The Theories of Authoritarian and Democratic Character," *Annals of the American Academy of Political and Social Science*, no. 361 (1965), pp. 81–95. See also E. Victor Wolfenstein, *The Revolutionary Personality* (Princeton, N.J.: Princeton University Press, 1967); Fred I. Greenstein and Michael Lerner, *A Source Book for the Study of Personality and Politics* (Chicago: Markham, 1971); and Paul M. Sniderman, *Personality and Democratic Politics* (Berkeley: University of California Press, 1974).

17. *New York Times*, March 25, 1969.

18. Robert af Klinteberg, *Equatorial Guinea, Macias Country* (Geneva: International University Exchange Fund, 1978), p. 46.

19. René Pélissier, "Equatorial Guinea: Autopsy of a Miracle," *Africa Report* (May–June 1980), p. 10.

20. Klinteberg, *Equatorial Guinea*, p. 46.

21. Colin Legum (ed.), *Africa Contemporary Record, 1972–73* (New York: Africana Publishing Co., 1973, p. B270); *The Times* (London), October 25, 1972; Colin Legum, "Behind the Clown's Mask," *Transition* (Accra, October 1975–March 1976); and *The Observer* (London), May 1, 1977.

22. Legum (ed.), *Africa Contemporary Record, 1972–73*, p. B270.

23. David Martin, *General Amin* (London: Faber & Faber, 1974), p. 248.

24. This tug-of-war between sociological and psychological explanations of social behavior is an integral part of contemporary political science. For details on some of the controversy surrounding this issue, see Greenstein, *Personality and Politics*.

25. Ali Mazrui, "Racial Self-Reliance and Cultural Dependence: Nyerere and Amin in Comparative Perspective," *Journal of International Affairs*, vol. 27, no. 1 (1973), p. 114.

26. Interview in Nairobi, July 23, 1980.

27. Ibid.

28. *Africa Research Bulletin* (December 1983).

29. A number of French correspondents have provided extremely insightful analyses of Bokassa's rule; see for example, *Le Monde* (Paris), June 6, 1979.

30. Currency control was lodged in Paris and in the regional central bank for the French equatorial states.

31. According to Klinteberg (*Equatorial Guinea*, p. 55), the Hispano-Guineans constitute "the largest percentage of any nation to have gone in exile."

32. See *West Africa*, August 13, 1979.

33. Lieutenant-Colonel T.O.N. Mbazogo was not only Nguema's right-hand man and part of the family *mafioso* but also his prime executioner as *gauleiter* of Fernando Póo.

34. Zolberg, *Creating Political Order*.

2 Francisco Macias Nguema
Tyrant of Equatorial Guinea

Few African states are as little known abroad, or have remained as isolated from the mainstream of African political developments, as Equatorial Guinea.[1] Although it was "discovered" and explored as early as the fifteenth century, the country's geographical configuration (a small undeveloped enclave in the equatorial rainforest, and scattered offshore islands), coupled with its colonial status as one of Spain's few African possessions, have kept the territory very much in the esoterica backroom of African Studies. Despite a per capita income and gross national product at independence (1968) level with that of Ivory Coast,[2] Equatorial Guinea became a minor fulcrum of interest only with the consolidation of President Francisco Macias Nguema's dictatorship.

Nguema was the last of the continent's three personal dictators to be overthrown, and the only African leader ever to be tried, sentenced to death, and executed for criminal acts while in office. By the time his brutal reign came to an end, Equatorial Guinea had been ravaged beyond recognition. The originally vibrant country and rich plantations were in shambles. Half of the population had fled the country to live as destitute refugees in neighboring countries. The entire educated class and most of the early nationalist leaders, clergy, and politicians had either been liquidated or were likewise in exile, most in Madrid. The country's educational system and all social services were practically nonexistent, routinized territorial public administration was a thing of the past, and much of the surviving adult population (especially in Fernando Póo) was shackled to a system of slave-labor akin to the colonial one criticized by the League of Nations more than forty years earlier.

It is difficult to assess the prospects for a return to normality in this much brutalized country. The young military junta that supplanted Nguema was overwhelmingly drawn from family relatives and former

MAP 1 Equatorial Guinea

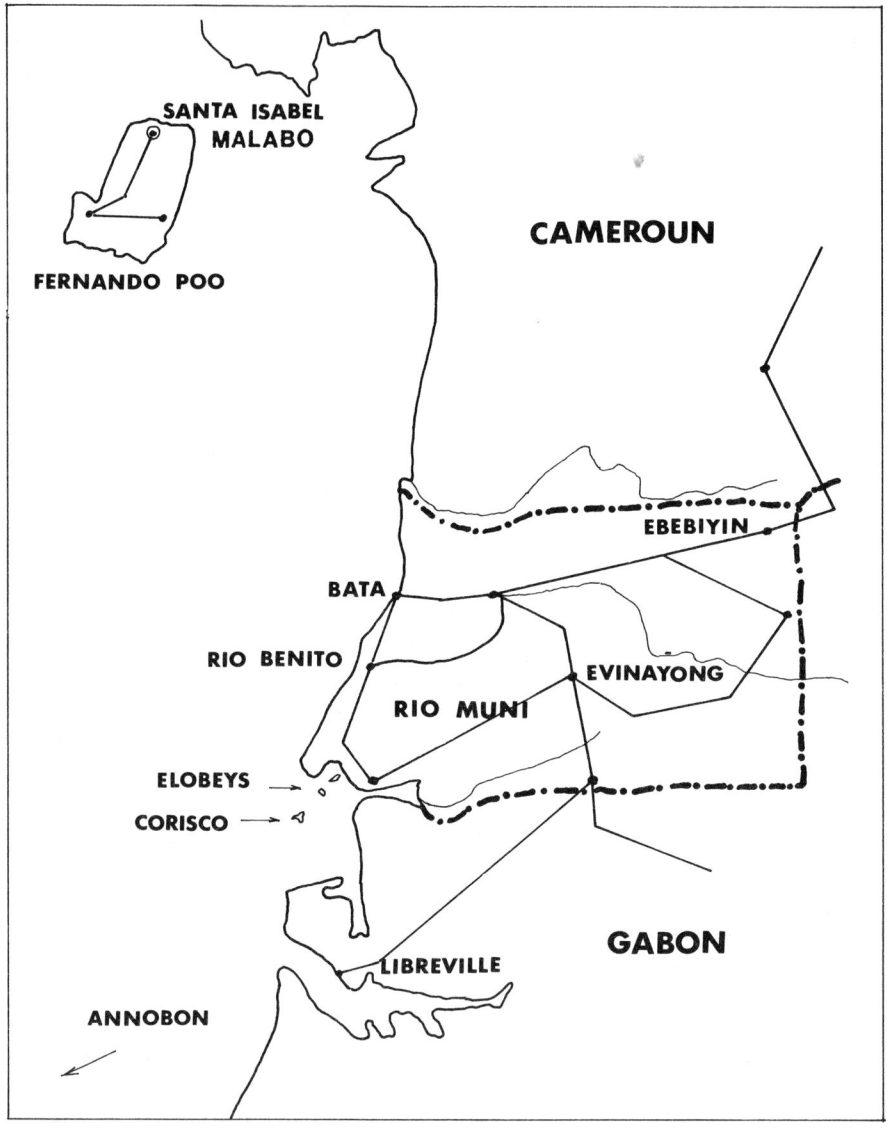

key lieutenants. The new president—Colonel Teodoro Obiang Nguema Mbasogo—is Nguema's own nephew and, as military commander of Fernando Póo, was the chief executioner of the regime. Although Nguema was the fulcrum of much of the madness that permeated Equatorial Guinea, culpability for the brutal atrocities is equally shared by all those in power today. Indeed, the crimes for which Nguema was placed on trial after his capture specifically related only to his *first* five years in office (1969–1974), inasmuch as the entire military junta accusing him shared direct, possibly greater, culpability in the killings of the *last* five years of his reign.

Nor is the current junta, or Mbasogo himself, either repentent or fundamentally concerned with much more than making the new dictatorship in Malabo more cost-efficient, personally lucrative, and less repugnant abroad. Consequently, the level of violence in the country has declined significantly, a measure of civil administration and rational economic planning has returned to Malabo, and the slave labor battalions are more properly forced labor units. But dictatorship still reigns supreme in this much ravaged land.

Socioeconomic Background

Formerly known as Spanish Guinea and one of Spain's few African colonies,[3] Equatorial Guinea comprises the mainland Río Muni province, the main island of Fernando Póo (with the Republic's capital, Santa Isabel) some 28 miles off Cameroun, the Egoué estuary islets of Corisco, Elobey Grande, and Elobey Chico off the coast of Gabon, and the small island of Annobon some 400 miles south of Fernando Póo.[4]

Río Muni is by far the largest province, encompassing 10,038 square miles, dwarfing the 779 square miles of Fernando Póo, which is nevertheless the socioeconomic core of the country. The other islands are of little importance. The largest, Annobon, is barely 7 square miles in size, and most of its population of 1,500 (1960) had been farmers and fishermen before being forcibly drafted to work on Fernando Póo's plantations.[5] In the 1970s, Annobon's population was sharply decimated by a virulent cholera epidemic that Nguema refused to arrest. Corisco, 6 square miles in size, and the Elobeys, less than 1 square mile each in size, have even smaller populations. Except for the fact that exploration for suspected offshore oil deposits is proceeding in their immediate vicinity (whetting Gabonese interest in them), the tiny islets have not figured at all in the social and economic life of Equatorial Guinea.

Despite its small size and population (245,000 in 1960),[6] Equatorial Guinea has been as plagued by acute regionalism and sharp ethnic cleavages as other larger African entities. Much of its internal competitions and frictions stem from the mismatched union of the backward mainland Río Muni with Fernando Póo, and the neglect of the former during much of the turpid Spanish colonial era.

On virtually every dimension—size, population, ethnicity, economic mainstays, mode of production, per capita income, social evolution, levels of education, even topography—the two provinces are poles apart.[7] Fernando Póo with its volcanic cones, crater lakes, inaccessible gorges, and rich lava soils is in total contrast to the monotonous flat physical relief and poor soils of Río Muni. By the turn of the century Fernando Póo was already a rich settler colony despite its modest size (45 miles long and 22 miles wide), in sharp contrast to Río Muni, where very few Europeans ever settled. By independence, the island was dotted with no fewer than 1,900 Spanish *fincas* (plantations). Many estates encompassed up to 5,000 acres; in 1962 the 300 largest Spanish *fincas* controlled more than 150,000 acres of land, whereas the biggest 1,600 African farmers (many grouped into cooperatives) controlled fewer than 17,500 acres. By contrast, Río Muni was not under effective Spanish control until the second decade of the twentieth century; utterly neglected until 1939, it was economically opened up through the operation of expatriate companies given timber concessions in the enclave.[8] The political shackling of the socioeconomically advanced, Westernized but numerically weak Bubi and Creole populations of Fernando Póo to the less developed but more numerous Fang of Río Muni has been at the root of many of the tensions of the country.

Fernando Póo—originally called Formosa, or "the beautiful"—was visited in 1471-1472 by Fernao do Po, after whom it was later renamed. The islands, and sovereign rights over the mainland between the Niger and Ogoué rivers (stemming from the 1494 Treaty of Tordesillas that partitioned Africa and Latin America between Portugal and Spain), were ceded to Spain in 1778 in exchange for the latter's renunciation of territorial claims in Brazil. Spain's half-hearted attempts to occupy and colonize its new dominion were cut short by yellow fever epidemics that forced its withdrawal from the island in 1781.

In 1827, Britain leased naval bases at Clarence (later Santa Isabel) and San Carlos Bay for use by its antislavery vessel patrols off the West African coast. A large number of liberated slaves were subsequently offloaded in Fernando Póo, and others were later shipped to the island from Jamaica and Sierra Leone. (The heterogeneity of Fernando Póo's population was further compounded by the island's use as a penal colony for Cuban convicts.)[9] An agreement to sell the island to Britain (for £60,000) was not consumated due to a patriotic public outcry in Madrid. Somewhat reluctantly, Spain reestablished its tenuous presence in Fernando Póo in 1844. By then, Spain was a burnt-out third-rate power with neither the will, skills, nor resources to build a global empire; it was not until fifty years later, in 1898, that Spain exerted total effective control over the small island.[10] Madrid's utter lack of interest in its equatorial colony was reflected in both the very miserly budgetary allocations granted the island (until the Primo de Rivera dictatorship) and the very high turnover of its disinterested *Gobernadores Generales*—fully sixty-five of whom governed the island between 1865 and 1910.

By the turn of the century, moreover, Spain's territorial claims to the mainland (i.e., the contemporary Cameroun and Gabon) were totally unrealistic, especially as they had never been buttressed by even a token physical presence. Politically and militarily weak (with the Spanish-American War disencumbering it of most of its other colonial possessions), Spain was forced to relinquish all but a small fragment of its original claims to the mainland. The Río Muni enclave was the final "settlement" on its original claims, primarily granted to Spain by the other colonial powers as a labor "reserve" for its plantations on Fernando Póo. Effective occupation of the enclave was not completed until the late 1920s, and Río Muni's economic development did not really commence until 1939.[11] As one scholar has noted, "The history of Spain in the Gulf of Guinea is the story of a state which, through ineptitude, poverty of resources, dearth of initiative, internal antagonisms, foreign defeats, and a distinctively Spanish assortment of vices, completely failed to carve itself a piece of the African pie."[12]

The main indigenous people of Fernando Póo are the Bubi, descendants of pre-fifteenth century migrations from the Cameroun mainland.[13] The Bubi arrived in several waves and originally were ethnically close to the Fang. At the time of the Spanish occupation they lived in sedentary, decentralized villages, owing only nominal allegiance to King Moka at Riabbo. Early Spanish efforts to recruit labor among the Bubi for the first cocoa plantations were strongly rebuffed, forcing the colonial power to look to the mainland for manpower. Probably not the first occupants of the islands, the Bubi were in due course decimated by a variety of diseases introduced by the Spaniards. Although only a few thousand survived at the turn of the century, by 1960 their numbers had again risen to around 15,000. Resentful of the unificationist political evolution of Spanish Guinea that had made them a minority in their own island and linked their future with that of the Fang of Río Muni, the Bubi were the most pro-Spanish ethnic group in the colony, pressing for continued colonial links if only out of the fear of a Fang "takeover." Like the Creoles, the Bubi were among the most socioeconomically advanced ethnic groups in Equatorial Guinea, and most of the territory's early administrators and teachers were of Bubi origins.

Fernando Póo has also been the home of some 4,000 "Fernandinos" (descendants of liberated slaves), who constituted an extremely important middle class through the 1920s and were the richest Creole community in West Africa. Originally landowners, or the much-favored foremen of absentee Spanish plantation owners, the Fernandinos later established a quasi-monopoly over the free professions.[14] But traditionally the *largest* group on the island has been made up of foreigners, especially Nigerian contract laborers. Until their mass repatriation in 1975–1976 (due to abuses under Nguema), the roughly 45,000 Nigerian plantation laborers (mostly Igbo, Ibibio, and Efik) had been the cornerstone of much of Fernando Póo's prosperity.

By contrast, very few foreigners, African or European, have established themselves on the mainland. The largest group in Río Muni are the Fang, who constitute more than 80 percent of the enclave's population of 183,000.[15] Under indirect military pressure from the Adamawa emirates in the interior of Cameroun in the latter part of the nineteenth century, the Fang fanned southward, subjugating, expelling, or assimilating most of the original inhabitants they encountered.[16] Split into a number of clans, the Ntumu Fang are in general found north of the Río Benito, and the Okak Fang are south of it. The core Fang "heartland" is the Woleu Ntem district in Gabon, which has acted as a powerful magnet upon Río Muni's Fang populations.

Also referred to as Pahouin or Pamué, the Fang are an upwardly mobile and aggressive people. Originally regarding farming (as opposed to hunting and trading) as a demeaning "female" occupation, many Fang nevertheless moved into agriculture in the 1930s and 1940s with the introduction of coffee cultivation. Others moved into the modern cash economy and, after some resistance, provided labor for the (hardwood) timber concessions round the Campo, Benito, and Muni rivers. Their sense of identity, cultural integrity, and ethnic unity was profoundly affected by the impact of colonialism, and a number of revivalistic movements sprang up among the Fang aimed at a national reassertion and unification. The disorientation of Fang traditional life following the colonial impact has been especially documented by Georges Balandier for Gabon[17] and has been observed in the Río Muni context as well.[18] The *Elar ayong* movement in the 1920s and 1930s, in particular, was regarded as subversive of colonial authority by both France and Spain. Indeed, a French official sent to investigate the movement in Gabon noted that "it is certain that once their regroupment is entirely finished . . . they will form a kind of government presided over by an elected official . . . an entity capable of governing itself. It would be organized democratically and would arrive at the stage foreseen by article 75 of the Charter of the United Nations . . . which gives them the right to demand their independence."[19] A variety of other syncretic quasi-religious sects that sprang up in the 1950s were likewise heavily suppressed because of their fundamental challenge to European rule. Such was the case with the Bwiti secret cult, a leopard-society with ritual sacrifices and antiwhite overtones that integrated Christian concepts with ancestral rites, which replaced the former Biéri cult of ancestor worship suppressed by the Spanish in Río Muni.[20]

Spanish colonial rule in Equatorial Guinea was oppressive, culturally paternalistic, and suffused with puritanism and middle-class value-biases.[21] And, as one observer has commented, "among all the modern colonizations in Africa, it appears that one can give the Spaniards the record for police vigilance, even if there are other serious contenders in this domain."[22]

Commencing in 1904, the legal code of the territory was based on the *patronato de indigenas* ("patronage of the natives"), which made the indigenous population virtual legal minors who could neither sell their lands nor conduct commercial transactions of more than 2,000 pesetas in value. Subject to customary law, rather than to the Spanish civil code, they were also forced to undertake onerous corvée labor on European cocoa plantations in partial payment of their annual taxes.[23] Originally applied only on Fernando Póo, the *patronato de indigenas* was in due course extended to Río Muni in an effort to syphon mainland labor into the island's plantations. Fang resistance to plantation labor and their tendency to return to Río Muni to set up their own (coffee) farms, coupled with the similarly strenuous resistance among the Bubi, virtually ensured the island's heavy dependence upon foreign labor for its economic development.

Lack of adequate indigenous manpower has always been a major constraint on the Fernando Póo economy. This has been especially true of the labor-intensive but highly productive cocoa sector. As early as 1905, a Spanish-Liberian treaty provided the island with imported manpower from the mainland. The availability of Liberian contract labor dramatically declined in 1927 following widely publicized revelations of conditions tantamount to slavery under which manpower was recruited by Monrovia and employed in Fernando Póo. (As early as 1899, in fact, persistent breaches of labor contracts and neopeonage conditions on Fernando Póo had prompted the British consul general to recommend a total embargo on recruitment of labor from the British West African colonies.)

After pledging reforms and experimenting with Camerounian workers, Nigerian labor became the staple of the island's plantations for the next thirty-five years. As Nigerian migrant labor on the island at times exceeded the total indigenous population, affecting language, culture, and food habits, Fernando Póo was a veritable melting pot of cultures and influences; one scholar referred to it as "ethnically becoming an appendage of Eastern Nigeria."[24] In 1975–1976, however, this source of supply also came to an end; after years of callous abuses of their labor contracts including nonpayment of salaries by the Nguema regime, the Nigerian government repatriated most of its nationals, leading to the total collapse of Fernando Póo's economy.[25]

In mid-1959, Spanish colonialism finally began to shed some of its more oppressive characteristics. On July 30, for the first time ever, a *civilian* was appointed to head the colonial administration, which until then had been the exclusive preserve of admirals of the Spanish Navy. The territory was also "promoted" to the status of an integral part (province) of Spain; its name, The Spanish Territories of the Gulf of Guinea, was changed to Spanish Equatorial Guinea and the *patronato* system was scrapped. With the population now, in theory, made up of full-fledged Spanish citizens, they were granted the right to send six representatives to the Cortés in Madrid.[26] The first elections *ever* in Spanish Guinea took place in 1960, and in December of that year three Hispano-Guineans took their seats in the Cortés.

The 1959 reforms were in part motivated by Spain's desire to regain international respectability in a rapidly decolonized world and to obtain allies and leverage in its dispute with Britain over Gibraltar. A marked step-up in fiscal allocations for educational and socioeconomic projects in Equatorial Guinea accompanied the colonial reforms, with per capita expenditures for state services rising above those in metropolitan Spain and thus possibly attesting to a "serious attempt to make up for past neglect."[27] Finally, in 1963, Spain granted local autonomy to Equatorial Guinea, setting the stage for the emergence of indigenous competitive politics.

Basic Features of the Economy

The economy of Equatorial Guinea rests almost entirely upon the production and export of cocoa, coffee, and timber (see Table 1), all of which have consistently been adversely affected by shortages of both skilled and manual labor.[28] With the mass exodus of most Spanish landowners and entrepreneurs in 1968–1969, and the onset of Nguema's rudderless dictatorship and the repatriation of Nigerian manpower in 1975–1976, the economy collapsed, production levels, productivity, and exports plummeted (see Tables 2 and 3), import-export trade reverted to primitive barter exchanges, and internal commerce came to an abrupt halt. Equatorial Guinea never regained a semblance of its pre-indepen-

Table 1
Equatorial Guinea: Exports, 1970

Commodity	Value[a]	% of Total Exports
Cocoa	1,136.6	65.3
Coffee	421.5	24.2
Timber	149.4	8.6
Other	33.4	1.9
Total	1,740.9	100

[a]Figures are in millions of pesetas.

Note: The economy of Equatorial Guinea collapsed in 1971 and no more recent reliable statistics exist.

Source: Compiled from International Monetary Fund, "Equatorial Guinea," Surveys of African Economies; vol. 5 (1973), p. 341.

Table 2
Equatorial Guinea: Cocoa Exports, 1970–1978

	Exports (thousands of tons)[a]
1970–1971	30
1971–1972	22
1972–1973	12
1973–1974	12
1974–1975	12
1975–1976	11
1976–1977	8
1977–1978[b]	6

[a]All figures are estimates.
[b]Although data from 1979 on are not cited here, in 1984 an estimated 8,400 tons of cocoa were being exported, compared to the low point of 5,000 tons in 1980.

Source: Africa Research Bulletin, Economic Series (April 1974 and May 1978).

dence production levels and relative prosperity. Despite the overthrow of Nguema in 1979 and a significant amount of foreign aid since that time, the economy remains in a shambles. As the roots of the economic collapse are inextricably related to the policies of the Nguema dictatorship, they will be analyzed in a greater detail in that connection.

Table 3
Equatorial Guinea: Foreign Trade, 1973–1977

	1973	1974	1975	1976	1977
Imports	32	35	23.8	14.8	12.8
Exports	36	36	23.8	14.5	17.8
Balance	−4	−1	−	−0.3	−5

Note: All figures are estimates, in millions of dollars.

Source: Colin Legum (ed.), *Africa Contemporary Record 1978–79* (London: Holmes and Meier, 1979).

Of the country's three main exports, cocoa is by far the most important, accounting in 1970 (the last "normal" year) for 66 percent of Equatorial Guinea's exports. Introduced in Fernando Póo from Brazil (via Sao Tomé) in 1854, cocoa immediately became the mainstay of the economy. In 1910, that small island was already the world's tenth largest producer of cocoa, steadily improving its ranking and introducing the crop in turn to Ghana and Nigeria. Indeed, Fernando Póo accounts for about 90 percent of the country's output; its rich volcanic soils, high humidity, and heavy rainfalls have contributed to the production of cocoa of outstanding quality on what were once considered the world's best cocoa groves. Subsidized by Spain, Equatorial Guinea's entire crop traditionally has been exported to the metropole to be used in the preparation of confectionary. Subsequent to its falling out with Spain, Equatorial Guinea entered into a series of barter arrangements, especially with Eastern Europe; the 1975 cocoa crop, for example, went mostly to East Germany, and that of 1976 to the USSR, China, and Cuba.

Annual cocoa production figures have fluctuated sharply, ranging from 35,000 to 45,000 tons in the pre-independence period. The 1970 expropriation of the plantations and their redistribution to Fang elements loyal to Nguema resulted in an immediate decline in production to 22,000 tons. Neglect, lack of efficiency, lack of capital, and manpower shortages all brought about further production declines; and with the repatriation of Nigerian contract labor, production levels plummeted again and remained stagnant at between 3,000 and 8,000 tons. Despite the virtual enslavement of up to 60,000 Bubi and Fang farmers from all over the country, cocoa exports have remained severely depressed. After the 1979 coup d'état, Spanish agronomists examined the state of the groves and expressed doubts as to whether they could be revived to pre-1969 levels. Today, fully nine years after the overthrow of Nguema, and despite important infusions of capital and technical assistance, what were once the finest cocoa plantations in the world remain in an acute state of decay.

The country's second main commodity, coffee, is grown mostly in Río Muni rather than in Fernando Póo. Prior to independence, the enclave exported an average of 6,000 tons of poor-grade coffee, largely cultivated on small family plots. Together with large amounts smuggled in from Gabon, the entire crop was exported to Spain, providing 24 percent of Equatorial Guinea's foreign exchange.

As coffee is a stable crop produced by large numbers of sedentary farmers, production levels did not collapse to quite the same extent with the onset of the Nguema era. After a bad harvest in 1968 (1,800 tons), production stabilized at around 4,800 tons per year. Malabo made few efforts to spur a greater output. The poor quality of the crop resulted in low producer prices, hardly an incentive for more intensive cultivation. Severe population dislocations also played a role in depressing production levels. And the acute paucity of consumer goods in the country reversed traditional patterns of smuggling of Fang traders, who now started bringing their produce into Gabon. Notwithstanding the depressed state of coffee production in Río Muni, their *relative* value to foreign exchange–starved Equatorial Guinea has gone up dramatically. Indeed, in the latter years of the Nguema era the meager foreign revenue generated by Fang coffee farmers in Río Muni very much sustained the regime in Malabo.

Timber is Equatorial Guinea's third most important export, bringing in 9 percent of the republic's cash earnings. Logged almost exclusively in the mainland's extensive rainforests, the largely Spanish timber concessions produced 300,000 metric tons of hardwood lumber a year prior to independence, all of which was exported to the metropole. A highly mechanized and capital-intensive sector, Río Muni was set to embark upon a major expansion of logging operations. Extremely poor race relations in the concessions and friction between the haughty Spanish companies and the newly independent government in Malabo played a major role in precipitating the 1969 crisis that led to the exodus of Spanish people from their former colony. Although a number of expatriate concessions continued to operate in Río Muni throughout the Nguema era (virtually the only foreign entrepreneurial presence in the country), exports of timber steadily declined after 1970 to minimal levels.

No economic statistics exist on post-independence Equatorial Guinea. Existing data either are painstakingly pieced together from foreign sources (and hence are likely to be incomplete) or are nothing more than rough guesstimates. Equatorial Guinea's trade balance, commodity exports, staple food production levels, monetary supply, budgets, and other fundamental fiscal details have simply not been compiled, let alone published, since independence. As the International Monetary Fund drily noted in its attempt to assess levels of budgetary outlays in the country, "No information is . . . available on the structure of expenditure and revenue."[29] For all practical purposes, a dark curtain fell over the republic with the rise to power of the regime of Macias Nguema.

Prelude to Independence

René Pélissier has observed that, in 1968, "the two provinces of Guinea were less prepared for unified independence . . . than they were when autonomy was granted over four years ago."[30] The country's societal cleavages, politicized by a large number of aspiring leaders, produced a very splinterized political arena that was exacerbated by separatist movements on Fernando Póo and abetted by the local Spanish administration and *finca* landlords.

Although some Bubi and Fernandino leaders were politically active from the outset, most of the early political movements in Equatorial Guinea were overwhelmingly dominated by Fang elements and were preponderantly based in Río Muni. The more sophisticated population of Fernando Póo remained largely apathetic, uninvolved in the movement for political emancipation, and, later, solely concerned with rejecting the proposed linkage of the island's political evolution with that of the mainland enclave. In 1967, with independence on the horizon, separatist Bubi and Fernandino political parties briefly emerged—with overt Spanish backing—to contest the forthcoming elections on anti-independence planks. These were in many ways the first popular political stirrings in Fernando Póo.

Until a few years before independence, the political scene in Spanish Guinea was suffused with heavy-handed official repression and intimidation, which forced most Fang political aspirants into self-exile in Cameroun and Gabon. Indeed, until 1963, political activity was banned in the colony and Spain did not recognize any of the parties that had formed. Because of this political repression, the various nationalist movements that sprang up were in essence narrow elitist underground groupings within the colony itself, and their leaders were mostly in exile abroad. At the same time, the colonial administration, tightly linked to Spanish propertied elements and with major financial interests in Fernando Póo, exerted constant pressure on Madrid to slow the island's political evolution "in order to save the substantial profits which the government, through its preferential cocoa prices, secured for them personally."[31]

The first nationalist movement to emerge in Equatorial Guinea was set up in Port Iradier (Río Muni) in June 1959 to oppose that year's change in status of the colony to that of a metropolitan department of Spain. The party was formed by Atanasio Ndong Miyone, a former catechist (self-exiled in Libreville) and son-in-law of Gabon's President Leon Mba;[32] most of its support was drawn from Fang straddling the border and from Río Muni refugees in Gabon. Eventually expanding by absorbing other splinter groups, the party—originally called Movimento Nacional de la Liberacion de la Guinea Ecuatorial (MNLGE)—became known as MONALIGE. The party suffered from acute factionalism and had a militant wing that in 1964 called for immediate independence and the nationalization of Spanish assets in the colony. Despite its popularity, the party lacked drive and momentum because of Ndong's leadership from abroad and the schisms within its own ranks. One of its early members was the then little-known Macias Nguema, a civil administrator from Río Muni with shifting political loyalties who in 1968 successfully challenged Ndong's leadership. MONALIGE was the main opposition in the colony to the collaborationist MUNGE, which emerged in 1964 to take control of the transitional Autonomous Republic.

Chronologically speaking, the second main party to be established in Equatorial Guinea was set up by a Bubi lawyer, Luis Maho, who played a role in numerous other movements as well.[33] The party, which had antecedents going back as far as 1947, developed in 1959. It was known at that time as the Cruzada Nacional de la Liberacion de Guinea Ecuatorial (CNLGE). The grouping collapsed in 1962 as a result of internal factional splits, and the bulk of its membership merged with a splinter party set up that year by Pastor Tarao Sikara (a key Bubi chief and mayor of Santiago de Baney) to form MPIGE (Movimento pro-Independencia de la Guinea Ecuatorial). In 1969, the latter unsuccessfully campaigned for the immediate independence of Fernando Póo and union with Cameroun.[34] It was not only as unstable as its chronological antecedents but also acutely factionalized. Some of its followers transferred their allegiances to the neo-Marxist Idea Popular de la Guinea Ecuatorial (IPGE), while most eventually joined MONALIGE.

The third and only ideologically distinct and militant party to emerge in Spanish Guinea was IPGE, founded in 1962 (or 1959, according to some) by José Perea Epota, a former trader in Chad. Based in Cameroun, and financially subsidized by official circles in Yaoundé, IPGE eventually split into two wings. The most radical (and illegal) segment, led by Epota, remained in Cameroun (later Congo) from which it tried to direct the popular struggle against Spanish colonialism. The more moderate wing, led by Clemente Ateba, made its peace with Spain and was legalized; having established itself in Río Muni, it held subsequent elections in Equatorial Guinea.

Despite the great degree of fission and fusion in the political scene, a unified nationalist movement never emerged in Equatorial Guinea. The deep schism between the two territorial segments of the colony triggered completely different and mutually antagonistic popular responses to the process of decolonization. And in Río Muni, personal competitions and factionalism, which stemmed in part from clan divisions internal to the Fang community in the enclave, ensured the continued splinterization of the anticolonial forces.

A pragmatic centrist grouping did emerge in Río Muni, however. Directly encouraged and financially supported by the local Spanish administration, it brought together a number of splinter groups and political aspirants willing to collaborate with, rather than oppose, Spanish rule.[35] Formed in Bata just prior to the 1963 referendum on the new Basic Law and proposed provincial autonomy, the party was headed by Bonifacio Ondu Edu, a former catechist and member of several of the aforementioned political formations, including MNLGE. Following the referendum, numerous defeated politicians of various persuasions joined the bandwagon of the moderate Movimento de Union Nacional de la Guinea Ecuatorial (MUNGE), and the party's organizational edge, financial resources, and Spanish "connection" assisted its victory in the subsequent 1964 municipal elections. In terms of the constitutional evolution of the colony, the latter elections were of crucial importance because they directly determined the composition of both the new eighteen-man National Assembly of Equatorial Guinea and its Governing Council (i.e., cabinet). Ondo, who was elected mayor of the key Río Muni town of Evinayong, consequently became president of the Council, and MUNGE formed the government of the transitional Autonomous Republic.

Despite the apparent emergence of the pragmatic-opportunistic MUNGE as the new center of gravity in Equatorial Guinea, its electoral strength was both ephemeral and quite misleading. The results of the referendum of December 15, 1963 (see Table 4), clarified the issue in that they vividly underscored the irreconcilable cleavages within the colony that were becoming more intense with the approach of independence. The referendum triggered an unusually high turnout, with more than 74 percent of those on the electoral rolls exercising their right to vote. Although only 38 percent of those voting rejected the proposed devolution of power that ushered in local autonomy and set the colony on the road to independence, the aggregate results camouflaged not only the deep fissures between the two territories but also those internal to the Fang community itself.[36]

The split was complex, dividing the Fang population along traditional clan lines; it also reflected the differential external (Gabon-Cameroun)

Table 4
Equatorial Guinea: Referendum of December 15, 1963

Region	Votes Cast	For	Against
Fernando Póo	12,500	5,340	7,150
Río Muni	82,317	53,940	28,387
Total	94,817	59,280	35,537

Source: Official data.

pulls on the community. The voting results clearly set off the Fang from the Playeros; the islands from the mainland; and in Fernando Póo, the Bubi from the non-Bubi. In Río Muni, for example, part of the littoral populations and the Fang-Okok south of Río Benito, who gravitate strongly toward the Fang "heartland" in Gabon, voted for the constitutional changes. By contrast, the Fang-Ntumu, ethnically tied to their kinsmen in Cameroun, were much more swayed by the rejectionist call of IPGE. In Fernando Póo, Bubi fears of encroaching domination by the Fang, and by the more populous mainland in general, produced a clearcut (66 percent) rejection of the Basic Law, signifying a desire to retain the tighter "protective" link with Spain. At the same time, most of the minorities on the island (Fernandino and non-Bubi in general) voted *for* the Basic Law reforms, swayed more by the perceived advantages of greater local autonomy from Spain. Five years later, virtually the same divisions were visible in the voting on the referendum that was to usher independence into the colony.

In October 1967, under increasing pressure at the United Nations over its delaying tactics, Spain convened a Constitutional Conference in Madrid to determine the nature of the ultimate devolution of power. Invited to the conference were representatives of all the parties in Equatorial Guinea, including recently formed separationist factions in Fernando Póo. The conference was a stormy and acrimonious one. All the territory's internal divisions—ethnic, regional, and personal—again came clearly into the open. Utterly deadlocked on all basic issues, the conference had to be adjourned. As one Hispano-Guinean forcefully argued during the sessions, "Equatorial Guinea does not exist except on paper; it is an artificial creation, in reality two territories."[37]

In April 1968, the Constitutional Conference was reconvened and a Spanish-devised constitutional formula was rammed through. Presented for popular ratification in the August 1968 referendum, the new Basic Law established a unitary state with constitutionally entrenched regional autonomy for each territorial entity and a disproportionate political weight and representation for Fernando Póo. Notwithstanding these attempts to assuage the island's fears of a Fang "takeover," the Basic Law was widely criticized in Fernando Póo, where separatist sentiments came to the surface. Demonstrations in Santa Isabel called for "Independence, yes, but *without* Rio Muni," and the majority of the 41,197 votes against the new constitution (constituting 35 percent of the total vote) were cast in Fernando Póo.

The sharp polarization of opinion in Equatorial Guinea during the Constitutional Conference and approaching independence also saw the erosion of Ondu Edu's power base, the disintegration of MUNGE, and the slow rise to prominence of Nguema. Emulating the worst of the Spanish colonial vices, the Ondu Edu Cabinet was riddled with corruption and nepotism, and characterized by the ostentatious lifestyle of its ministers and their administrative incompetence. Moreover, the transitional government's attempt to preserve its monopoly of power until the country was "politically, culturally and economically" ready for independence[38] made it vulnerable to more nationalist and anticolonialist political planks.

Personally selected by a Spanish entrepreneur, Antonio Garcia-Trevijano (who was seeking economic preeminence in the colony),[39] Macias Nguema seemed the ideal candidate to be groomed for power to replace the discredited Ondu Edu. At the time the rather inept and servile minister of public works and leader of a militant segment of MONALIGE, Nguema began receiving both financial backing and tactical advice from Garcia-Trevijano and other Spanish backers who perceived possibilities of personal post-independence economic empires.

Grouping around him not only dissident elements of all political parties in Equatorial Guinea but also politicians shut out of positions of importance by the Ondu Edu regime, Nguema and his Spanish backers commenced their bid for power. Originally called the Secretariado Conjunto, and later simply Grupo Macias, the rather undistinguished and amorphuous grouping of marginal political aspirants and malcontents was Nguema's springboard to office. Vociferously attacking the entire political establishment (Ondu Edu, Ndong Miyone, Pastor Sikara, etc.) as unfit to govern the country, Nguema rapidly became a force to be reckoned with. Although he never elicited broad support (especially in the towns) for his policy planks (which were ghost-written by his Spanish backers), Nguema's antigovernmental invectives nevertheless found receptive ears.

In the aftermath of the constitutional referendum of 1968, presidential elections were held in Equatorial Guinea. None of the candidates secured the absolute majority required to win in the first ballot. But Nguema, concentrating his fiery speeches on villages, chiefs, and the Fang countryside (speeches largely ignored by his opponents) emerged as the leading contender. He secured 36,716 votes as opposed to Ondu Edu's 31,941 and Ndong Miyone's 18,223. (The latter two campaigned on the MUNGE and MONALIGE labels, respectively.) Ondu Edu's arrogant refusal to form an electoral compact with Ndong Miyone was a tactical mistake that led to the latter's withdrawal in favor of Nguema, who promised him the Foreign Ministry. In the subsequent ballot, Nguema emerged victorious. Fewer than three months later, the first arrests and killings of intellectuals commenced with the brutal liquidation of Ondu Edu himself. Having fled to Gabon in fear for his life, Ondu Edu had been extradited and lynched in prison in January 1969 after being tortured, mutilated, blinded, and left without medical attention for a week. The next month witnessed the clash with Spain that triggered the frenzied exodus of most expatriates from the newly independent state as well as the descent of an iron curtain (entailing total censorship, etc.) over Equatorial Guinea.[40]

The Events of 1969 and the Onset of Dictatorship

According to one observer, Equatorial Guinea savored freedom for less than four months, and even then human rights were already being progressively curtailed; "real independence did not last more than 145 days, from October 12, 1968 to March 5, 1969."[41] The traumatic incidents of February–March 1969 brought about the repatriation of nearly all colonists from the country, freeing Nguema from a host of inhibiting internal and external constraints; in like manner, the first brutal executions during this period psychologically opened the floodgates for the massive killings that subsequently ravaged the country.

The 1969 crisis erupted on February 25, 1969, in the midst of Nguema's tour of Río Muni after his discovery that Spanish installations in Bata were still flying (as in colonial days) *three* Spanish flags, the symbol of Spanish sovereignty. At the root of what might have been but a minor diplomatic incident was the fact that independence had changed nothing in Equatorial Guinea. The haughty demeanor of the expatriates remained unabated; the economy was still completely controlled from abroad; colonial officers remained in their former posts, insensitive of the *de facto* independence of the country. And Nguema's feelings of acute unease in the "hostile" Bubi capital, Santa Isabel, were driving him into combative postures.

Indeed, Nguema's visit to Bata was primarily aimed at consolidating his power base in Río Muni. His authority over the multiparty Cabinet was none too secure. Some of his own ministers, whether personally ambitious or disenchanted with Nguema's uninspiring political style and pro-Spanish subservience, were conniving in his parliamentary ouster. With only nine of the National Assembly's thirty-five seats under his party's control, such an upheaval was a distinct possibility; some of his own cronies and Spanish advisers were actually nudging him to adopt a more authoritarian posture lest he lose control over the fluid political power-balance.[42] Within this context, the sudden spectacle of the symbols of Spanish sovereignty flying, as in times immemorial, was one affront too many.

Lashing out with a vitriolic speech critical of Spanish colonialism in general and of Spanish expatriates in particular, Nguema ordered that the offending flags be removed. The Spanish consul general refused to lower the flags. The situation subsequently got rapidly out of hand. Unemployed youth (the self-styled "Macias Youth") rampaged through Bata roughing up expatriates. In the process of disturbances on the timber concessions, a Spanish foreman was killed in Río Benito. Fearing further violent incidents the resident Spanish ambassador then issued an order to the still Spanish-officered Guardia Civil to cordon off the country's airports and guarantee the safety of all means of communication. Nguema retaliated by demanding the ambassador's recall to Spain and the evacuation of all Spanish security personnel from the country, to be replaced by a United Nations peacekeeping force. At the same time, he imposed a state of emergency in Equatorial Guinea.[43]

The imbroglio and Nguema's inflammatory speeches aroused the resident Spanish community's worst fears—a Zaire-style massacre of expatriates—and many of the 7,000 Spaniards in Equatorial Guinea began streaming out of the country. On March 3, 1969, Foreign Minister Atanasio Ndong and UN Ambassador Saturnino Ibongo, returning from a visit to Madrid, tried to prevail upon Nguema to soothe the situation. When the latter refused to listen to their counsel, the two allegedly rallied their supporters in Bata and staged a coup attempt.[44] The power-gambit failed, and both were brutally murdered by Nguema loyalists a few days later. In a major settlement of accounts that singled out Bubi politicians in particular, more than 200 arrests were made, including the Bubi president of the National Assembly (Pastor Tarao Sikara) and the Bubi mayor of Santa Isabel (Armando Balboa). Most of those arrested were never heard from again.

The developing internecine struggle in the country provided the last impetus for the Spanish exodus. by the end of March 1969, fully 92 percent of the Spanish community had fled Equatorial Guinea. Barely 60 (of the original 1,500) remained in Río Muni, and only a few hundred (of 5,500) in Fernando Póo. Virtually all Spanish civil administrators, teachers, technicians and professionals, and most plantation owners and shopkeepers departed. With the Spanish exodus, more than 15,000 local workers instantly lost their jobs as servants, clerks, store attendants, and manual laborers. In the general economic paralysis that followed, trade and commercial activity greatly contracted, the entire tertiary (service) sector collapsed, the money economy shrank dramatically, customs duties and tax revenues plummeted, and the civil administration and social services in Equatorial Guinea ground to a halt. None were to revive to any degree during the remainder of the Nguema era. Indeed, with the eventual similar exodus of Nigerian contract labor from Fernando Póo in 1974–1975, the socioeconomic decay of Equatorial Guinea was complete.

The Spanish exodus of 1969 traditionally marks the onset of Nguema's reign of terror. The constitution was soon suspended and all political parties were forcibly merged into Nguema's. Large numbers of Fang from Río Muni were recruited to staff administrative vacancies in Santa Isabel. In due time forced labor began to be employed to keep some of the cocoa plantations of Fernando Póo operational, thus further changing the basic demographic characteristics of the island as thousands of additional Fang were imported from the mainland. According to Robert af Klinteberg,[45] Equatorial Guinea had become the Dachau concentration camp of Africa, as forced labor, routine wanton killings, and brutal liquidations became an integral part of life.

Profile of a Dictator

"A proud, mercurial and unsophisticated man . . . completely unprepared to cope with the complexities that have been thrust upon him"—such was the characterization of Nguema by the *New York Times* during its observation of the tumultuous events of 1969.[46] The same source, after referring to a speech in which Nguema lauded Hitler as one "who intended to free Africa," added that "no one doubts his devotion to the country, but he has failed to create a government relevant to Guinea's problems."[47] Can this be the same leader who was described by other scholars as Africa's Caligula,[48] as a "paranoid, cruel megalomaniac,"[49] as "an envious, embittered scourge of intellectuals"[50] who created in Guinea a system of "deliberate cultural regression not unlike that of Nazi Germany"?[51] The two contrasting images of Nguema are not inconsistent, however, inasmuch as his brutal nature manifested itself only after political power was securely his following independence.

Francisco Macias Nguema was born in Oyem in the Woleu Ntem province of Gabon on January 1, 1924. His father, a Fang of the Esengui ("Father of the Gorilla") clan, was reportedly a much-feared sorcerer.

Nguema (who Hispanicized his original name, Msié) was raised in Nyasanyong in the district of Mongomo, which he regarded as his true home and where, in his latter years, he spent most of his time.

As a youth, Nguema had "no talent for study"[52] and was barely socialized by either church or school. Not particularly intelligent, he sat four times for the crucial qualifying examinations for a civil service career and *emancipado* status, passing only in his last attempt, in 1950, as a result of overt Spanish favoritism.

Subsequently a petty administrative orderly in the Forestry Department of the Ministry of Public Works, Nguema served in the Bata, Río Benito, and Mongomo districts. In the latter instance (in his home district), he served as an administrative assistant-interpreter, a position he utilized to advance his own interests. Relying on his role as sole intermediary between the unsophisticated local population and the Spanish administration (especially in legal matters at court), he extracted bribes and kickbacks from the peasantry (in exchange for his "interceding" on their behalf) while ingratiating himself in the eyes of his Spanish superiors by his "hard work" and abject servility.

Nguema was viewed by the colonial administration as an essentially apolitical, pliable, and trustworthy collaborator (at a time when Spain was hard-pressed to find loyal allies within a Fang elite mostly in self-exile and in opposition to continued Spanish colonialism); as a consequence, his career prospects suddenly brightened in the 1960s. Groomed and promoted by mercantile interests in Río Muni for higher office, Nguema was appointed *alcalde* (mayor) of Mongomo in 1963. Within the Spanish administrative system this appointment automatically made him both a member of the Río Muni (deliberative) Assembly and a deputy from Río Muni to the General Assembly in Santa Isabel. His status within the extremely limited collaborationist political elite of Spanish Guinea in 1964 gained him entry into Ondu Edu's Autonomous Government, as minister of public works.

"Very much the creation of his colonialist masters"[53] Nguema advanced in his career "not through his own merits but entirely through Spanish patronage."[54] Despite the fact that he joined a number of political formations that were either banned or harassed by the colonial authorities, Nguema himself was never arrested. As a contributor to the *Africa Research Bulletin* noted, Nguema was "seen by the Spanish administration as a trustworthy collaborator, always eager to please, and easy to handle because of his intellectual shortcomings."[55]

In 1967, with the approach of independence, Nguema fell under the sway of Antonio Garcia-Trevijano, a Spanish lawyer and entrepreneur who "regarded Macias as the ideal blunt instrument for his own ambitions."[56] Nguema's ambitions were sharpened, his political campaigns were subsidized, his "goals" and "platforms" were defined, and even some of his speeches were prepared by Garcia-Trevijano. In 1968, the effort bore fruit when Nguema defeated the other presidential contenders on the second ballot. Extremely telling, however, is the fact that one of the Río Muni districts that Nguema did *not* carry in the elections was his own home-district of Mongomo, *whose population had experienced at first hand his "leadership" for five years.*[57]

Although Nguema rose to the pinnacle of power on the back of Spanish colonial and expatriate interests, his pliable, servile facade camouflaged a host of resentments. In retrospect it is clear that Nguema, no doubt seething over his having been manipulated for so long by others, bore a deep hatred for the Spanish colonial administration and expatriates who had previously humiliated him as an *indigene*, and who later belittled him by acting as if they completely owned him.

Although those who had assisted his rise to power did in the end inherit an economic empire in Malabo, it was a minuscule one, emasculated beyond recognition from the rich plum they had anticipated. And the economic spoils that came their way were due less to gratitude for their former aid than to the fact that they constituted the dictator's sole lifeline to the outside world that shunned him.

Moreover, Nguema harbored deep resentments against those more educated and sophisticated than he was, and against whom he had had to compete so strenuously most of his life. Already as a young adult he had developed an inferiority complex vis-à-vis "foreigners and educated persons" that took the form of excess servility toward those socially superior to him and haughty arrogance toward those beneath him.[58] A marginal, malintegrated person who had managed to rise to the apex of power, Nguema ordered vindictive purges and liquidations that decimated most of Equatorial Guinea's intellectual strata. Indeed, so deep was his hatred for the educated that he even prohibited the use of the word *intellectual* in Equatorial Guinea and promptly fined his own minister of education when the latter used the term in his presence at a Cabinet meeting.[59] Within a few years of his rise to power, all libraries in the country were closed at his express orders, and "book and press publishing became extinct activities."[60] Education and intellectuals were viewed as the "greatest problem facing Africa today. They are polluting our climate with foreign culture."[61] Nonetheless, one of the 45-odd honorific titles Nguema adopted as president was "Grand Master of Education, Science, and Culture." His bias against formal education was perhaps most obviously manifested when in 1973 he conferred a medical degree, and the post of hospital director, to a football player and Macias Youth stalwart who had no knowledge whatsoever of medicine or administration.

Most observers trace Nguema's inferiority complex to his humble origins, intellectual limitations, and personal humiliations prior to attaining *emancipado* status. But Klinteberg also suggests that Nguema suffered a sense of loss of manhood status due to his inability to procreate. "For a Fang . . . if he does not have wives and children, he is considered a non-entity, a nobody, an object of condescension and ridicule. . . . Not regarded as a man by his own people . . . his desire for recognition and love takes on the preposterous expression of his mania for titles and the personality cult he has created."[62] Not only sterile, he also had difficulties establishing stable emotional relationships; he was married three times and had many casual liaisons, exhibiting a peculiar penchant for mulattos. In the case of his last wife he ordered the meticulous hunting down and killing of all of her previous lovers; he also ordered the murder of the husbands of the women he coveted.

When Nguema was executed on September 29, 1979, the firing squad charged with the task was composed of Moroccan troops on loan to the government. The charisma of Nguema's supernatural powers permeated all strata of society, including the army itself, and troops feared that if they participated in his execution he would return in the form of a tiger to hunt them down.[63] (The tiger, an animal *not* found in Africa, was nevertheless the symbol, or "talisman," of Nguema's party, and "El Tigre" was one of Nguema's popular nicknames.) Hated throughout the country, Nguema was nevertheless venerated and dreaded for his "magic" and control of the tiger. This visceral fear of Nguema's spiritual powers was best expressed by one of Klinteberg's informants: "You may be against Macias as long as the sun shines, but in the night you have to be for him."[64] Nguema constantly and consciously built up the image of his awesome supernatural powers; at least half of the fourteen plots that he claimed to have crushed during his reign were probably fictitious—invented in order to "prove" his invincibility. Mass unquestioning belief in his occult powers, which permeated all strata of society, was a core pillar of his rule of terror in Equatorial Guinea.

It is indeed difficult to comprehend Nguema's lengthy dictatorship in Equatorial Guinea without a proper awareness of his unerring utilization and manipulation of traditional beliefs and religion, including sorcery and witchcraft, both to prop up his "legitimacy" and to terrorize the population into immobile submission. The son of a venerated sorcerer in a society (Fang) where ancestor worship, syncretic cults, and witchcraft still play a major role to this day despite overwhelming (95 percent) nominal affiliation to Catholicism, Nguema skillfully exploited traditional beliefs to build up his supernatural credentials. Collecting in his home in Mongomo a veritable "arsenal" of skulls of the most potent powers, Nguema also tapped all other clan sorcerers of their powers, "concentrating" their magic in his own hands. He revived elements of the hitherto suppressed Bwiti and Biéri secret cults, and he utilized clan leaders and elders, as well as itinerant Mvet praise singers, to spread the dread of his magical powers throughout society.

Inevitably Nguema spread his control over organized religion and the Church in Equatorial Guinea. His occult powers were formally canonized in Church sermons by forced references to him as "the Only Miracle" and even the contention that "there is no God other than Macias." Constant adulatory praise of Nguema in Church liturgy was the *sine qua non* condition for continuation of Christian worship in the country. One popular slogan all priests were forced to reiterate in all Church services—at the pain of immediate arrest—was that "God created Equatorial Guinea thanks to Papa Macias. Without Macias Equatorial Guinea would not exist."[65] In due time, however, even this abject fealty to Nguema's omnipotence was insufficient to the dictator.

After constant harassment of Church clergy and speeches decrying the alien nature of Christianity, a series of edicts in November 1974 and April 1975 banned all religious meetings, funerals, and sermons and forbade (as part of an authenticity drive) the use of Christian names. Virtually all churches were subsequently closed under lock and key, or were converted into warehouses for cocoa. The Santa Isabel Cathedral— previously absorbed into the mushrooming presidential compound that soon encompassed much of the center of the city—became an arsenal for armaments arriving from Eastern Europe. Foreign clergy were systematically expelled; local ones were effectively silenced, many arrested, some liquidated. And in May 1978, Equatorial Guinea officially became Africa's first "atheistic" state[66]—without protest from either the Vatican or Spain. Indeed, officially between January 1971 and August 1974, informally until Nguema's demise, all news and every item of information on developments in Equatorial Guinea were regarded by Madrid as falling under the odious *materia reservada* censorship classification that prohibited *any* mention of the country in the local press.

As with Idi Amin, Jean-Bedel Bokassa, and a few other highly idiosyncratic African leaders, the question has inevitably been raised regarding Nguema's mental health. According to the leading authority on Equatorial Guinea, René Pelissier, in a view supported by several Spanish scholars, Nguema had been mentally deranged all along. "Periods of lucidity interspersed with uncontrollable violence,"[67] frenzied hyperactivity followed by physical prostration, and morose withdrawal suggestive of hypomania[68] rendered Nguema's behavior highly unpredictable. Medically treated in Spain at least four times (twice, rumor had it, for possible brain tumor)[69] subsequent to a prolonged undisclosed illness in the 1950s, Nguema was also progressively deaf and visibly manifested acute, jerky, uncoordinated movements suggestive of a nervous disorder. He regularly consumed large quantities of hallucinogenics such as *bhang* (hashish) and *iboga* (a local stimulant), the effects of which were clearly visible in his pupils and in his bizarre outbursts.[70]

"Unbalanced, inconsistent and unpredictable, with a pathologically psychic incongruity which provokes his outbursts of unusual violence, interrupted by periods of equilibrium and lucidity which must be related to a sense of bitter resentment arising out of a latent inferiority complex"—such was the diagnosis provided by Garcia Dominguez, who knew Nguema well between 1972 and 1974.[71] Klinteberg notes that all of the Guineans who had escaped into exile abroad regarded Nguema as literally mad, affected (as he seemed to them) by the phases of the moon and ridden with fear of impending vengeance by his dead victims (especially Ondu Edu and Atanasio Ndong), with whom he sometimes carried loud and lengthy monologues.[72] "Victim as well as perpetrator of his deeds, unlearned but shrewd, dynamic but without direction, ruthless but not sadistic, sensitive, lonely, haunted"—such was Klinteberg's final assessment of "Africa's Caligula," who for eleven years devastated both a nation and a state, personally ordered the liquidation of at least 1,000 people, was directly responsible for the murder of maybe 50,000 more, and drove into exile up to one-third of the country's population.

Equatorial Guinea Under El Unico Miraclo

Whatever motivations originally impelled Nguema to seek the pinnacle of political power, once he had attained it virtually all his actions in office were punitive, destructive, and negative. Hardly any action or "policy" was either progressive or beneficial to Equatorial Guinea or its people, although Nguema was to claim credit at his trial in 1979 for a host of developmental improvements, including the construction of nonexistent schools and hospitals. All edicts emanating from Malabo, Bata, or Mongomo—all leadership "initiatives"—were regressive, leading to stagnation, destruction, and moral decay. Increasingly in his latter years, Nguema withdrew morosely to the privacy of his own personal world at his fortified Mongomo "bunker," leaving day-to-day control of the country to a family *mafioso* made up of his kin and clan. There is more than literary eloquence in the comment of one observer that "after 1969 Equatorial Guinea slowly dropped out of the world."[73]

Naive, with only a rudimentary grasp of matters of state or economics, Nguema never formulated a cohesive policy, a set of national goals, or for that matter any developmental ideology. His "policy" speeches, both at home and abroad, were lengthy, rambling rantings. Bellowing forth in disjointed and incoherent thought sequences, he harangued his audiences on a variety of totally unconnected and often irrelevant themes. Switching from Fang to Spanish and back again, improvising as he went along, shouting loudly (in order to hear himself, as he refused to use hearing aids though progressively deaf), he was often also under the influence of drugs. Interestingly enough, his erratic speaking style and intellectual shortcomings had been clearly visible even prior to independence and his rise to power. For example, following his rambling incoherent speech at the United Nations in 1967 (engineered by Garcia-Trevijano to give his protégé international exposure), "what Macias wanted may not have been very clear to the Conference; but it was evident that he wanted it very strongly."[74]

His world outlook—if he ever really had one—was "confused, unknown, undefined," and his actions at the helm of the nation were "a marasme of pragmatism of the moment"[75]—fundamentally, just the gut reactions of a leader accustomed to selfishly personalizing everything without concern for wider societal consequences. Nothing better illustrates Nguema's lack of concern for the repercussions of his actions than the events leading to the 1975–1976 repatriation of Nigerian plantation labor from Fernando Póo; the withdrawal of foreign contract labor from the island spelled the economic doom of Equatorial Guinea, possibly more so even than the prior exodus of Spanish expatriates from the country.

The frenzied departure of Spanish *finca* owners and other entrepreneurs had shattered the economy and administration; at one stroke, they excised the major repository of technical skills and capital in the country. Paradoxically, the resultant fall in exports and state fiscal receipts, which was directly traceable to the European exodus, did not immediately create budgetary chaos. Administrative posts vacated by expatriates went unfilled or were staffed by Fang personnel at much lower salaries than budgeted. Levels of imports also plunged with the removal of the most highly consummatory strata in Equatorial Guinea.

The administrative backbone of the new state was shattered, however. The 1970 budgetary estimates—the last issued under the Nguema regime—could not even be prepared until after the end of the budget year in the absence of statisticians and economists in the country. Fiscal accountability, never a distinguished characteristic of Spanish colonial rule, totally vanished as the presidency spread its control over all aspects of social, economic, and political life in the country. State shops took over the distributive function from the departed private traders; operating with minimal stock and eventually no supplies whatsoever, most simply closed down as the last vestiges of the modern money economy disappeared. Trade and commerce were replaced by barter; cash crops gave way to staple food crops, which were more vital for physical survival; and urban life became fundamentally unproductive—as well as dangerous. By the early 1970s, even the international trade of Equatorial Guinea was largely based on barter agreements, with the occasional shipload of supplies arriving in the country distributed solely to the governing elite and its security personnel. In Madrid, Garcia-Trevijano exerted a quasi-monopoly over Malabo's foreign trade, in the process amassing a huge personal fortune. When finally stripped of his Spanish citizenship by Madrid, he had acquired an Equatorial Guinean diplomatic passport and continued acting as the country's most important external emissary.[76]

The valuable cocoa plantations on Fernando Póo had been taken over by the state with the departure of most of their Spanish owners. Although the groves were the country's major economic resource, they were grossly abused and their upkeep was ignored. They were still tended by Nigerian contract labor, but the economic anarchy that soon characterized Malabo led to major violations of the laborers' terms of service. Very erratically paid, and in due course treated virtually as slave-labor, these workers were repatriated by Nigeria, which by the mid-1970s could no longer ignore the scandalous conditions on Fernando Póo.

Historically, Nigerian labor in Fernando Póo had been much abused;[77] but with the emergence of the Nguema dictatorship, workers were actually beaten, molested, even murdered, and were denied virtually all of their contractual benefits, including wages.[78] In 1971–1972, some ninety-five Nigerians were brutally killed when they dared to demand payment of their back wages prior to sailing back to the mainland;[79] and in the subsequent year, up to 20,000 disgruntled cocoa workers left for home, most with large unsettled wage claims. By 1974, the Nigerian government could no longer tolerate the abuse of its citizens on the island and refused to renew its labor recruitment treaty with Equatorial Guinea; continuing reports about the constant brutalization of Nigerian labor on Fernando Póo even triggered a powerful domestic outcry for the invasion and occupation of the island. Moreover, Nguema's utterly uncontrollable security forces, combined with generally unsettled conditions in Equatorial Guinea, had already caused incidents involving the Nigerian diplomatic personnel who staffed one of the very few embassies to remain on the island. In 1975, consequently, the Nigerian government decided to repatriate all of its nationals from the island.[80]

With the withdrawal of Nigerian manpower, cocoa production again declined, further contracting state income. At independence averaging between 35,000 and 45,000 tons per year, and after the Spanish repatriation between 10,000 and 22,000 tons, production had fallen to around 8,000 tons by 1977 and dipped to 3,000 tons in 1979. Nguema, by now a recluse in Mongomo, briefly mounted a patriotic drive to enlist local labor to tend the cocoa groves. When his efforts failed to produce more than a thousand volunteers willing to work for their bare sustenance, Nguema ordered the forced recruitment of 2,500 males from each of the country's ten districts. The recruitment drives drove tens of thousands into refuge in Gabon and Cameroun, increasing the ranks of the Hispano-Guinean self-exiled community abroad.

More than 20 percent of the country's population was eventually dragnetted into the work brigades. Abused by their guards, molested, beaten, and at times wantonly murdered, the labor battalions were essentially "food-for-work" units that succeeded only in preventing cocoa production from collapsing completely—but they did nothing to revive the cocoa groves as a whole.

In 1977, Klinteberg visited Malabo and reported that it was virtually a ghost town. It was "strikingly depopulated," giving the impression of "a place hit by war or the plague";[81] nearly all its shops were permanently closed down, as were most of its native market stalls, its post office, and numerous ministries (e.g., the Ministries of Education, Construction, Agriculture, and Health). The sight of a moving vehicle in town was a very rare occurrence, and trade and commerce were virtually nonexistent. The shelves of the few shops still open were bare. Goods arriving on the few ships still calling at Malabo sold out promptly and at exorbitant prices. For example, Cuban sugar, when available, retailed at US$12 a kilogram, Chinese beer at $10 a bottle, and eggs at $1 each.[82]

Per capita income had dropped from $170 in 1967 to an estimated $70 in 1975. Fishing, which once added valuable protein to the diet of the population, was no longer officially permitted; most boats and canoes had been destroyed by the regime in its attempt to prevent both smuggling and escapes from the island. The interior of Fernando Póo also looked deserted; up to one-third of the population of Equatorial Guinea had fled Nguema's rule.[83] Air links with the outside world, never very developed, were now at the level of only three flights a week—the twice weekly Aeroflot link with Douala and the weekly Iberia flight to Madrid. A few ships called at Malabo, and imports were held at minimal levels. Yet despite the hardships imposed on populations accustomed to relying on certain imports from overseas, mass starvation was avoided. The island's rich fertile soil and heavy rainfall allowed for the relatively easy cultivation of subsistence crops, to which most city folk had reverted in order to survive.

But by far the most striking characteristic of Equatorial Guinea under Nguema was the reign of unmitigated terror that descended on the country with the repatriation of the last Spaniards. Commencing with the murder of Ondu Edu, and in earnest with the liquidations accompanying the 1969 crisis, the killings in Equatorial Guinea were systematic and gruesome. Frightful details—rivaling in brutality and inhumanity, though not in numbers, those in Amin's Uganda—have been fully documented elsewhere.[84] Hundreds of people were ordered liquidated by Nguema personally, and thousands were condemned to execution in his capacity as chief judge. Living "on the margin of international society in a suffocating atmosphere of suspicion"[85] and mutual spying, "almost anybody [could] be arrested for anything."[86] Alleged crimes were unverified even by cursory examination of the evidence; those accused were simply thrown into jail, with a request tendered to Nguema for the punishment to be meted out. This punishment was often the death penalty, invariably executed with inordinate brutality. And although many of Nguema's death sentences affected Bubi leaders and intellectuals in general, in the final analysis Fang and Bubi alike suffered the brutal ravages of the Nguema era. As one observer put it, "[Nguema] practices racial non-discrimination in his choice of people to be eliminated."[87]

Practically the entire budding leadership of the 1960s was liquidated by Nguema. The list of those executed includes 11 ministers of the Autonomous Republic, some of whom were also among the 10 liquidated of Nguema's original 12-member cabinet. After 1968, an additional 22 cabinet ministers perished, as well as two-thirds of the deputies of the 1968 National Assembly and 37 senior officers of the security services and high civil service.[88] Desite a total news blackout during Nguema's reign, a total of 619 formal executions were confirmed as of the mid-1970s, when the prisons were bulging with as many as 5,000 political prisoners.[89] Estimates of those who lost their lives during the Nguema era vary, but the number ranges between 50,000 and 80,000;[90] the "cottage industry Dachau of Africa"[91] simply continued its gruesome slaughter with little criticism from the outside world.

The liquidations were often casual and unannounced, although at times they were given profuse publicity. On June 13, 1974, for example, an "attempted coup" from within the prison of Bata was widely publicized. In all, 114 prisoners were involved. At the subsequent trial many "gave testimony," although the government had previously announced that all had committed suicide when the conspiracy was discovered. The epidemic of "suicides" spread as the regime began arresting family members and even mere acquaintances of the original 114 plotters.[92] In 1975, Bosio Dideo, vice-president of Equatorial Guinea, and scores of others were rounded up and ruthlessly killed when Nguema was informed that a poster bearing his effigy had been anonymously mutilated in Malabo. Their execution was widely publicized as a "lesson" to all other "antisocial" elements in the country. And in December 1976, all 100 top civil servants who had petitioned Nguema en masse for an end to

Equatorial Guinea's policy of isolationism were arrested and tortured; many were never seen again.[93]

The liquidations in Equatorial Guinea triggered an outflow of skilled manpower and intellectuals. It has been estimated that, by the time Nguema was deposed, not a single university graduate remained in the country. As economic conditions harshened, especially with the establishment of forced-labor battalions in the cocoa groves of Fernando Póo, a second outflow commenced—this time made up of common farmers and workers. This emigré community is, as Klinteberg put it, "the largest proportion of any nation ever to have gone into exile."[94] *Conservative* estimates in the mid-1970s placed the number of Hispano-Guineans in Gabon at 80,000, in Cameroun at 30,000, and in Spain and Nigeria at 6,000 and 5,000, respectively.[95] Since then, these numbers have increased significantly, with only a few refugees returning to Equatorial Guinea after the 1979 coup d'état.

Despite the constant outrages committed in Equatorial Guinea, most foreign governments continued to maintain cordial relations with Malabo, and some even moved to exploit Nguema's economic hardships to their advantage. Spain, wishing to protect its future interests in the former colony, went out of its way to impose the *materia reservada* classification on all news from Guinea; trade and aid, including budgetary subsidies (and ransoms for those of its nationals who were at times arrested), continued unabated during most of Nguema's lifetime. Agencies of the United Nations likewise continued their local aid programs without demur, despite the inhuman repression clearly visible to their representatives in the country. Indeed, so important was this source of aid to cash-starved Malabo that the Nguema dictatorship in its last years was largely sustained by the fiscal infusions of the United Nations Development Program (UNDP) into the country.

As Spain's influence declined in Malabo, other powers moved in. French interests, in particular, sought to establish a monopoly over Río Muni timber and expended much effort in this direction. After the crude rupture in Guinea's relations with the United States in 1976, France remained the only Western European country with a diplomatic presence in Malabo. Indeed, apart from France, the only resident embassies in Equatorial Guinea were those of neighboring states (Nigeria, Gabon, Cameroun) and Communist states (Soviet Union, China, East Germany, and North Korea).

The most visible foreign presence in Equatorial Guinea after 1969 was that of the Communist bloc of nations. By late 1970, the country had established friendly relations with the Soviet Union and North Korea, and diplomatic relations later proliferated with other such states. Important naval and trawling rights were granted to Moscow, which promptly dispatched a large fishing fleet to its new base in San Carlos. Part of the fleet's catch constituted the staple food of the forced labor camps on the cocoa plantations. A large (400-strong) Chinese technical assistance team was based in Río Muni, engaged mostly in roadbuilding, while a somewhat smaller Cuban mission provided Nguema with his praetorian guard and trained his security forces. All of these personnel, including the Soviet fishing fleet, were withdrawn from Equatorial Guinea after the 1979 coup, at the request of the successor regime.

Equatorial Guinea's relations with neighboring states were acutely strained throughout Nguema's reign. Harboring large numbers of refugees, these states were quite aware of conditions in Equatorial Guinea—if only through their diplomatic personnel in Malabo. Nonetheless, they all adopted a scrupulous hands-off policy out of solidarity with their sister African state. Nigeria, as previously noted, was driven to the edge of rupturing relations with Nguema over the abuse of its contract laborers on Fernando Póo, and relations with Gabon were at times stormy. In the latter case, Gabon's unilateral appropriation of several uninhabited sandbanks in the Ogoué estuary (when Libreville extended its territorial waters in 1972 to 100 miles) triggered talk of war, but the tension abated. The fact, however, that oil deposits are suspected in the disputed area (as well as near some of Equatorial Guinea's islands) may cause flare-ups in the future.[96]

Patterns of Control and Repression

Although at the outset Nguema maintained a semblance of "government" in Malabo, by 1973 most structures in the country were moribund, and all pretense of routinized decisionmaking had been dropped. The country had become Nguema's personal fiefdom. All decisions, verdicts, pronouncements, and appropriations, from the most trivial to the most momentous, were issued directly by him. Nguema personally screened the infrequent requests for visas from foreigners abroad and personally authorized the issuance of passports and foreign currency allocations to Hispano-Guinean diplomats and officials requiring travel overseas on state missions. Indeed, all the domestic and foreign currency in Equatorial Guinea was stored in a pile of suitcases in Nguema's house in Mongomo, to be released only at his discretion. Authority started and ended with Nguema. As his own minister of the interior was fond of saying (until he fled for his life), "once you needed a certificate of baptism to enter Heaven; now all you need is the card from PUNT [Nguema's party]."[97]

Although a cabinet of sorts did exist at the outset, it rarely met, especially after the early 1970s, if only because most of its members were dead or in prison by then. Some ministries existed on paper only (with their buildings permanently closed down), while others carried on the pretense of "operating" even though they lacked a budget, were paid very irregular salaries, and indeed had no mandate to make the most minute decision or policy. In July 1973, the new constitution abolished regional autonomy and fused executive, legislative, and judicial powers in Nguema's hands for life. In the absence of structures, legal codes, or the sort of pragmatic give-and-take that prevails even in authoritarian regimes, the political system that evolved in Equatorial Guinea was based solely on arbitrary, supreme, personal power. "Government" totally atrophied; most state and municipal services simply ceased to exist. The money economy disappeared, to be replaced by barter and a primitive subsistence economy. Forced labor, isolationism, sociocultural regression, and personalism became the distinctive hallmarks of Equatorial Guinea.

Notwithstanding a number of amateurish civilian plots and minor mutinies by disgruntled military elements (and a bizarre ill-fated seaborne invasion financed by the American author John Forsythe), the Nguema dictatorship survived for eleven long years. Its eventual collapse was not the consequence of a massive groundswell of popular opposition; nor did it result from the disenchantment of the armed forces (Nguema's ultimate power prop) with the system of repression. Rather, as elsewhere in Africa,[98] the regime was overthrown only when it began to threaten the interests—and safety—of Nguema's key lieutenants.

The lengthy survival of dictatorship in Equatorial Guinea was rooted in (1) its ruthless use of terror, which pulverized the will to resist by its random arbitrariness and casual brutality; (2) the liquidation or hounding into exile of all educated people and potential sources of opposition; (3) the complete isolation of the country from outside influences or scrutiny; (4) the skillful manipulation and magnification of Nguema's widely attributed supernatural powers, which terrorized into immobility large segments of the traditional society; (5) the regime's total control of literally all commodities and patronage in Equatorial Guinea, a fact that glued Nguema to his cohorts; and (6) Nguema's personal and kinship network in the security forces, which maintained his partners in the mayhem that was ravaging Equatorial Guinea tightly under control.

The country's 3,500-man security services force (composed of the Militia and the Civil Guard) was corrupt, barely literate, and acutely unruly. Only intermittently paid and thus for the most part living off the land, this iron fist of internal colonialism was primarily engaged in political surveillance and repression. Thoroughly purged of its former Bubi and Fernandino personnel in 1969–1971, most of the subsequent officers and personnel were either relatives of Nguema, kinsmen from Mongomo, members of the Esengui clan, or Río Muni Fang. The strength of this very unruly force, despite its professional inefficiency and its rudimentary materiel (its acute scarcity of live ammunition accounted in part for the brutality of the executions committed in the prisons), was more than adequate to cow the population into submission.

The officer corps, like the upper echelons of the civil service, were linked to Nguema by ties of blood and kinship, and personally beholden to him for their well-being and even physical survival. All economic privileges in the country—money, property, scarce drugs, imported foodstuffs, and luxury items—were distributed to a very restricted circle of Nguema sycophants and supporters in the civil service and security forces, often only on the very rare occasion when a cargo vessel docked at Malabo or Bata.

Thus Nguema's rise to power was not just a Fang takeover, although the Bubi in Fernando Póo perceived it as such. Rather, an Esengui political stranglehold was established. At its core was a veritable political dynasty—a dynasty that continues to rule despite Nguema's execution.

Any list of Nguema's relatives who were appointed to key governmental and security positions reads like a *Who's Who* of the clan. The regime's number-two man, Colonel Teodoro Obiang Nguema Mbosogo, was a devoted nephew who in 1975 became commander of the National Guard, military commander of Fernando Póo, and secretary general of the Ministry of Defense, becoming in effect the dictatorship's prime executioner. Other nephews included Daniel Oyono Ayingono, chief of National Security and former minister of defense; Mo Maye, secretary general of the armed forces; Micha Nsué, commander of the Presidential Guard; and Ela Nseng, personal aide de campe of the dictator and civil commander of Río Muni. Clara Osa, one of Nguema's wives (who escaped to Cameroun in 1973), served as director of (the nonexistent!) Pharmacies; Eugene Ntutumu, an uncle, was for a long time the powerful governor of Río Muni; Evuna Owono Asangono, a maternal relative, was Equatorial Guinea's Representative to the United Nations; and Nguema's own stepbrother and the latter's son were appointed in 1979 president of the (fictitious) Supreme Court and minister of the Sûrété, respectively. Among Nguema's cousins were Bonifacio Nguema Esona, the foreign minister and vice-president of the Republic; Masié Ntutumu, the minister of the interior and the police, exiled in 1976; Feliciano Oyono, secretary of the PUNT party; Mba Onana, commander of the Second Company of the National Guard; and Florencio Maye Ela, naval commander of Bata—and these were only *some* of the most prominent posts staffed by direct relatives of the president of the republic.[99]

Largely a law unto themselves, the security forces could denounce, arrest, harass, rape, or murder virtually anyone not of the core Nguema political strata; and even when the occasional "error" was made, no retribution ever visited them. Travel was prohibited throughout the country without a *credencia* permit, usually granted only for labor purposes; army checkpoints on all roads ensured mobility control; possession of canoes or boats was prima facie evidence of treason; and Nguema periodically ordered his forces to round up suspected opposition elements and "teach them a lesson." Thus, for example, when the director of statistics published rather low demographic estimates in 1970 that threatened Nguema's self-esteem (by underscoring the insignificance of his fiefdom), Nguema had him dismembered to "help him learn to count";[100] and before each state visit abroad, a few political prisoners would be routinely executed to dissuade any conspiracy from forming.

Constantly in fear of the secession of Fernando Póo (which, accordingly, was much more severely controlled) and uncomfortable as a mainlander on the island that had traditionally resisted his rule, Nguema increasingly withdrew to his heavily fortified "bunker" in Nyasanyong, leaving the day-to-day running of his fiefdom to his young family lieutenants. After appropriating much of downtown Malabo into the presidential compound, and later building a $12 million presidential palace in Bata (replete with a $4,400 bed), Nguema by the late 1970s had withdrawn to a bare concrete dwelling in his home village, protected by searchlights, barbed wire, and 200 hand-selected troops and Communist-bloc security personnel.

Nguema rarely visited Fernando Póo, "enemy" territory, and only occasionally Bata, and the primitive and parochial Mongomo became for all practical purposes the state seat of Equatorial Guinea. It was here, and not in the opulent newly constructed Central Bank in Bata, that the state's foreign and domestic fiscal reserves were casually stored, rotting on the mud floor of a closet room or stuffed Mafia-style into cheap presidential suitcases. It was here, at the periphery of the state, that the entire pharmaceutical stock of the country was kept, stingily released while thousands suffered or died unnecessarily for want of drugs. (As noted, a cholera epidemic in 1976 decimated the population of Annobon, while Nguema turned down even international offers of medical help.)[101] Here too were kept state treaties and confidential documents, haphazardly piled on chairs and desks. It was here, in dense tropical jungles, that cabinet ministers and military officers came for their infrequent sessions with Nguema, and that "state policy" was hammered out.

And it was in Mongomo, in his home village, that Nguema may have made the best impression on his real social peers. According to refugee reports, Nguema (when not on drugs) carried out lengthy and convivial conversations with village elders and common farmers around the campfire in Mongomo. He truly felt comfortable and at home here, away from the responsibilities of high office. The day-to-day "administration" of Fernando Póo was left to his nephew, Colonel Obiang, and the somewhat less heavy-handed "administration" of Río Muni was left to his vice-president and military commander of the province. When these two officers combined against him, Nguema was to lose his fiefdom and his life.

The Fall of a Dictator

Within the existing context of the power hierarchy in Equatorial Guinea the coup of August 3, 1979, was very much a family affair, an internal settling of accounts. It was engineered by the 33-year old Obiang, "one of the pillars of the regime of terror,"[102] who meticulously recruited into the conspiracy against his uncle nearly all of Nguema's civil and military lackeys except those personally attending the dictator in Mongomo.[103]

Although the new military junta to seize power pledged a host of reforms and placed the fallen dictator on trial for his crimes, the prime motives for the upheaval were hardly altruistic, and the regime that emerged from the ashes of the antecedent one was not less dictatorial. Indeed, the criminal charges leveled against Nguema were specifically related only to his first five years in power, that is, to the years prior to the 1975 elevation of Obiang to the post of *gauleiter* of Fernando Póo (and of its infamous Black Beach charnel house prison); thus the new junta is equally—and more directly—responsible for the very same misdeeds. During the public trial, attended by delegates of the International Commission of Jurists and attested to as "fair," Nguema was crudely silenced whenever he attempted to refer to post-1975 events.

The motives of the key plotters of the coup deserve close analysis, for the etiology and morphology of military rule in Malabo are inextricably intertwined, indicating the true limits of what may be expected of the contemporary Obiang dictatorship.

By all accounts, the falling out among the family *mafioso* ruling Equatorial Guinea occurred spontaneously in mid-1979 against a background of growing disenchantment with the *material* benefits of high office under Nguema's idiosyncratic, austere, and stingy regime. By then, Nguema's summary detentions and liquidations had begun to cut a swath of destruction within the inner circle of his own hitherto loyal cronies and relatives. This destruction specifically triggered a personal vendetta between Nguema and Obiang, and directly threatened Nguema's allies in the security services by underscoring their own vulnerability to the murderous whims of the dictator.

In June 1979, six officers of the National Guard made the always unpredictable journey to Mongomo to importune Nguema to release funds from his suitcases for the security service officers who had not been paid salaries for several months. For this impertinence all six were summarily shot. Among them was Obiang's younger brother, whose execution shattered the former's fealty to his uncle. During the same period, moreover, Nguema was beginning to discover plots within the military, a fact that caused significant unease among his key aides. Several officers were already in prison, including Captain Salvador Ela, formerly a trusted lieutenant. And Obiang himself had been personally humiliated by his uncle (in March 1979) when forced to undertake manual work in the Mongomo plantations.

Forewarned that Obiang was no longer reliable, Nguema ordered the governor of Río Muni to mount a naval sortie against Fernando Póo. But Obiang had alredy forged a broad anti-Nguema coalition out of all the dictator's relatives in the armed forces and retaliated by declaring Nguema deposed and by advancing against Mongomo. Loyalist troops, directed by Cuban and North Korean officers, resisted for several days but eventually melted into the bush. After setting fire to most of the country's fiscal reserves, Nguema escaped (with two suitcases of foreign currency) but was captured on August 18, 1979.

After considerable debate among the young putschists as to whether to place Nguema on trial, exile him, or intern him in a psychiatric ward, the former course of action was agreed upon. Two efforts to liberate Nguema punctuated the brief trial that commenced on September 24 and ended a few days later with the death sentence for a limited list or proven crimes. (For example, the court accepted the proof of 500 murders of an original indictment specifying his culpability in 80,000 liquidations.) Nguema consistently rejected all murder charges against him, claiming (with an obvious allusion to Obiang) that he had been "the Head of State, not the chief of a jail."[104] On September 29, eleven years to the day after his election as president of Equatorial Guinea, Nguema and six of his most brutal aides and prison commanders were executed by a Moroccan firing squad, part of the new praetorian guard of the Obiang regime. Not a single local soldier was willing to shoot at the former president, whose supernatural powers were still considered intact, out of fear of his dreadful vengeance after reincarnating in the form of a tiger. Long after his death, Nguema's ghost was believed to remain a potent force in Equatorial Guinea.[105]

The Second Republic and the Obiang Dictatorship

The very first pronouncements of Obiang affirmed a commitment to the UN Human Rights Charter and pledged a host of reforms, including freedom of religion, an end to arbitrary arrest, the release of political prisoners, and a pro-West foreign policy. Responsibility for ushering in the reforms was explicitly lodged in the military—a point periodically reiterated throughout 1987. As one observer noted, "The military will oversee everything and will always be at the head of the country even if there are civilians in the government," as "for eleven years politicians have made a mess of everything."[106]

The immediate aftermath of the coup did, indeed, see both a major relaxation of the acute terror and an end to the international isolation of Equatorial Guinea that had so characterized the Nguema era. The harassment of religious worship ended, a number of schools were reopened, plans for the country's first university were announced, and even a weekly government newspaper was inaugurated. Massive shipments of food and medicine began to reach the devastated country from abroad, in due course obviating the need for all visitors to bring with them ample supplies of food and water for the duration of their stay. Water and electricity services began to operate (albeit only sporadically) for a few hours a day. The fishing treaty with the Soviet Union was allowed to lapse, personnel at the latter's embassy was pared down from 100 to 12, and the Cuban military mission was withdrawn. And to symbolize the reunion of the metropole with the wayward former colony (relations were ruptured between 1977 and 1979), King Carlos of Spain paid a state visit to Malabo in mid-December, followed by the pope in 1982.

In the economic domain, expatriate elements were actively courted by the new junta in Malabo. French interests in particular converged on Río Muni to expand their operations in the lucrative timber sectors of the mainland. But efforts to rapidly revitalize the former economic mainstay of the country proved futile: Spanish experts who flew in to assess the damage of eleven years of decay found the cocoa groves in "an unimaginable state of chaos,"[107] requiring up to a decade of labor-intensive care before they could regain their productivity. The regime's offer to return the plantations to their former Spanish landlords in exchange for rehabilitation of the groves (i.e., a virtual recolonization of the economy) found few takers. By 1979, the plantations were producing less than 6,000 tons of cocoa. Despite Nigeria's agreement to resume (limited) recruitment of contract labor for the island, the groves continued to be tended by the same chain-labor gangs as those in Nguema's days. The effort and risk of relocation to the by-now primitive conditions of Malabo appealed to very few expatriates. As late as 1987, despite major infusions of capital and technical expertise from the European Economic Community (EEC), productivity was increased to only 11,000 tons of cocoa.

Moreover, few expatriates could avoid the fact that, notwithstanding the jubilation over Nguema's ouster, an equally dictatorial system had installed itself in Malabo. Apart from the six executions of 1979 (including those of three of the most sadistic prison wardens), virtually the entire terror hierarchy of yesteryear was very much intact. As a correspondent for *Africa Confidential* put it, "although the head of the snake has been cut off, Equatorial Guinea is still left with the same snake. . . . The Old Guard survives at every level of government. . . . Macias killed so prolifically that it is difficult to evade the stark conclusion that anybody who survived under him in a position of any influence was more than a passive witness to the excesses of his regime."[108] A year after the coup, the UN Commission on Human Rights starkly warned that the junta would have to be viewed as little more than "a military dictatorship unless efforts are made to . . . promote democratic procedures."[109] By 1983, the Madrid newspaper *El Pais* concluded that conditions in Equatorial Guinea were "as bad [as] or worse" than those in 1978.[110]

Certainly arbitrary arrest and wanton murder had greatly diminished in the country, but not forced labor, heavy-handed repression, or massive institutionalized corruption. Starved of sources of corruption during the long Nguema isolationist interregnum with the opening up of the economy to global trade, investments, and large-scale humanitarian aid, the entire military apparat became a sieve of corruption and embezzlement. Between 1979 and 1981, a total of $36 million in aid reached Equatorial Guinea from Spain and the IMF—an amount roughly equal to $150 per inhabitant. Much of this aid was misappropriated. By 1983, Spain as well as certain international agencies were formally warning Malabo that their aid efforts would be discontinued unless the funds reached their intended targets. If during the Nguema era military officers largely lived off the land (and in the case of Obiang, commander of Fernando Póo, lodged in the only operational hotel in Malabo), by 1983 luxurious military estates and plantations were sprouting up on the island.

The regime's blanket amnesty for all refugees, and appeals for Hispano-Guineans to return home and help in the reconstruction of the country, fell on deaf ears. A few thousand people did return, but within months the stark conditions at home had driven them back to Spain or Gabon. Their exile abroad had greatly opened up their horizons and politicized them. The minimal human rights prevailing in Equatorial Guinea and the reforms pledged by Obiang were viewed as totally inadequate. Indeed, the Supreme Military Council's Spanish acronym—CMS—was pejoratively referred to abroad as standing for *Con Mongomo Siempre* ("Always with Mongomo"), an allusion to the unchanged power base of the junta. With the awareness that little had truly changed in Malabo, refugee political movements began to proliferate. In 1983, both a government-in-exile and a wall-to-wall Coordinating Junta made up of all opposition movements were formed in Madrid.

Although Obiang slowly "civilianized" his cabinet, meticulously including a number of Bubi ministers (in 1985, even a Bubi prime minister was appointed), there was little sharing of power in Malabo. In 1982, a referendum gave the country a constitution that, "on paper at least, is one of the most liberal in Africa,"[111] and in 1983 a deliberative assembly was set up. But these measures reduced neither Obiang's concentrated power (he had appointed the majority of the 120-man Assembly) nor the top-heavy preponderance of Fang elements in the administration and government.

The original junta that came to power in 1979 was overwhelmingly composed of Nguema's relatives, most from the Esengui clan and Mongomo region. Many of those who had coalesced behind Obiang's conspiracy in 1979 fell by the wayside. His two vice-presidents, Salvador Ela and Florencio Maye Ela (both of whom had led the revolt in Bata), were quite early shunted into ambassadorships to China and the United Nations. Other relatives (e.g., Mba Onana and Nguema Essono Nchama) were given local sinecures or purged completely. With the concentration of power in Obiang's hands, conspiracies and coup bids began to erupt periodically. Most plots were triggered by the growing intra-elite splits within the armed forces created by the continued stranglehold over the country of members of the Esengui clan, or as a result of the political ambitions of specific key officers within the highly fluid context of Malabo. Discontent with Obiang was more generalized, however, as evidenced by the large numbers of officers and troops involved in these power bids, by the dangerous mutiny of the Bata garrison in January 1985, and by the "family plot disguised as a coup d'état"[112] that erupted in July 1986. Both the mutiny and the family plot (which were suppressed by the Moroccan Presidential Guard) had complex motivations; in part they represented opposition to Obiang's foreign policy, which had progressively wrenched Equatorial Guinea into the French orbit.

To an increasing degree, the new Socialist administration in Madrid refused to stabilize the oppressive junta in Malabo either by making budgetary subventions (including payment of the salaries of the by-now 1,000-man Moroccan force) or by pegging the worthless *ekwele* to the Spanish peseta. Moreover, constant revelations in the Spanish press of the involvement of the entire ruling junta and Obiang himself in the massive embezzlement of Spanish fiscal aid created powerful pressures in Madrid to reexamine its commitments to its former colony. In June 1983, these and other tensions between the two countries brought about Obiang's demand for the evacuation of all Spanish security personnel—a fact that triggered (as in 1969) a mini-exodus of the small (350-person) Spanish expatriate community.

The friction between the two countries brought about Obiang's quest for a firmer economic and military patron than the equivocal and vacillating Spain. France's proven military "reliability" in times of domestic crisis in Francophone African states no doubt appealed to the severely beleaguered Obiang. But entry into the French orbit carried other important economic advantages as well. Specifically, joining the Franc Zone meant that the *ekwele* would be pegged to the CFA franc, not to the weak peseta; and with currency convertibility and common customs tariffs with its main neighbors, the illicit outward movement of agricultural produce from Río Muni would be significantly halted, thereby vitalizing official exports and state revenues.

French economic interests, present in Río Muni for the duration of the Nguema era, were encouraged to develop a larger role in the mainland economy after Obiang seized power. As French interests and trade rapidly increased, so did Obiang's desire for full integration within the Francophone community of African states. In 1983, Equatorial Guinea joined the UDEAC (the local customs union of French Equatorial Africa) and, in 1984, became the only non-Francophone member of the Franc Zone; the twin acts signified the penultimate eclipse of Spanish influence in Equatorial Africa.[113] Bubi refugee elements abroad strongly deplored these new international affiliations, well aware of the lack of sympathy in French circles toward separatist sentiments in Africa. To most non-Bubi Hispano-Guineans, the prospect of faster economic reconstruction under French benevolence carried with it the possibility that the current regime would evolve from a harsh personal dictatorship to a somewhat more flexible authoritarian system.

Equatorial Guinea's integration into French Africa, as well as the introduction of the CFA franc in January 1985, did relieve several economic pressures. In particular, France increased its involvement in the exploitation of Río Muni's timber resources, exports of which exceeded 100,000 cubic meters per year. But little of any consequence transpired on Malabo, whose cocoa plantations remained neglected, producing barely 11,000 tons of cocoa per year.

Currently, unlike the case of Uganda and the Central African Republic, a post-mortem of dictatorship in Equatorial Guinea is not possible. Dictatorship still reigns supreme in Malabo—no longer the highly capricious, half-crazed murderous dictatorship of Nguema, but the more venal cost-conscious dictatorship of Obiang. Society and economy are no longer ruthlessly pulverized, regressed, or allowed to stagnate; rather, they are venally exploited and plundered for gain. The country is economically bankrupt and nearly totally dependent on foreign aid. A quasi-monopoly of all import-export trade is in the hands of a company owned by Obiang and his immediate family. The regime continues to be sustained by the "well-paid and frequently rotated Moroccan Guard . . . rather than . . . [by] the loyalty of its own troops or the popularity of its ambitious President."[114] Health and educational services remain primitive. In 1984, a cholera epidemic swept Malabo unchecked, and the few schools that were reopened operate with unpaid teachers and without writing supplies or texts in any language. Although in 1985 Equatorial Guinea became Africa's thirty-first state to sign the UN Charter of Human Rights, the civil rights of Hispano-Guineans are extremely limited, possibly the least protected relative to the status of such rights elsewhere, except in South Africa. (Paradoxically, a stream of South Africans has begun to enter the country since 1985, some allegedly to mount an intelligence network against West Africa.)[115] Constant intimidation, harassment, and unprovoked clubbings (of locals and expatriates) still take place in the capital, as does wide-scale forced labor and somewhat overzealous (though limited) executions of convicted plotters. As a correspondent for *Africa Contemporary Record* noted in 1984, "one of Africa's worst regimes has been replaced by one . . . whose track record is bad, and getting worse."[116] The clothes of the emperor may be different, but the modality of rule—personal dictatorship—is very much intact in Malabo.

Notes

1. Paradoxically, there are some excellent bibliographical guides to, and biographical compendia of, the (mostly) Spanish research on this country. In particular, see the compilations of Max Liniger-Goumaz—namely, *Guinea Ecuatorial: Bibliografia General*, 2 vols. Berne: Commission Nationale Suisse pour l'Unesco, 1976); *Historical Dictionary of Equatorial Guinea* (Metuchen, N.J.: Scarecrow Press, 1980); *La Guinée Equatoriale: Un Pays Méconnu* (Paris: Editions l'Harmatlan, 1980); and "Guinea Ecuatorial—population, Bibliographie," *Journal de la Société des Africanistes*, vol. 42, no. 1 (1971), pp. 195–206. See also Sanford Berman, *Spanish Guinea: An Annotated Bibliography* (Washington, D.C.: Multen Library of the Catholic University of America, 1961); and S.K. Rishworth, *Spanish-Speaking Africa: A Guide to Official Publications* (Washington, D.C.: Library of Congress, 1972).

2. See "Les institutions Monetaries de la République de Guinée Equatoriale," *Banque Central des Etats de l'Afrique de l'Ouest*, no. 186 (July 1971), p. 1.

3. The other such colonies are the former Rio de Oro (Spanish Sahara), which is currently battling for its separate independence, and the Ceuta and Mellila enclaves on the Moroccan coast.

4. The names of Fernando Póo and Annobon were changed in 1971 by Nguema to Macias Nguema Biyago (or Bioko) and Pigalu, respectively; and the capital, Santa Isabel, was renamed Malabo. In 1980, the post-Nguema junta reversed all the name changes, but both maps and professional literature use the various names interchangeably.

5. See S.V. Peris Torres, "La isla de Annobon," *Archivos del Instituto d'Estudios Africanos*, no. 57 (January 1961). See also Liniger-Goumaz, *Historical Dictionary of Equatorial Guinea*, pp. 7–8. For Corisco, see ibid., pp. 42–43, and for the Elobeys, see ibid., pp. 54–55.

6. This is the only reliable census estimate available. The massive population dislocations of the 1970s make any subsequent extrapolations hazardous.

7. For comparative figures, see Juan Velarde Fuentes, "El Plan de Desarrollo economico y social de Fernando Poo y Rio Muni," *Archivos del Instituto de Estudios Africanos*, vol. 28, no. 71 (January 1966), pp. 12, 13, 14. One example might be in order: In 1968, per capita income stood at $40 in Río Muni versus $280 in Fernando Póo.

8. See I.X. de Aranzadi, "Rio Muni ayer y hoy," *Guinea Española*, vol. 62, no. 1598 (Santa Isabel, 1965); E. Arrojes Gomez, "Los territorios españoles del Golfo de Guinea," in *España en Africa* (Madrid: Instituto de Estudios Africanos, 1950), pp. 19–32; T. Martinez Garcia, *Fernando Poo* (Santa Isabel: Instituto "Claret" de Africanistas, 1968); E. Sandinot, "Guinea Ecuatorial española," *Cuadernos del Ruedo Ibérico*, nos. 13–14, (Madrid, July–September 1967).

9. See I.K. Sundiata, "A Note on an Abortive Slave Trade: Fernando Poo 1778–81," *Bulletin d'IFAN*, vol. 34, no. 4, (Dakar, October 1973), pp. 793–804, and "The Importance of Fernando Poo: Humanitarians and Africans" (Paper presented at the African Studies Association meeting, Boston, 1976). See also R.T. Brown, "Fernando Poo and the Anti–Sierra Leonean Campaign 1826–34," *International Journal of African Historical Studies*, vol. 6, no. 2 (1973), pp. 249–264.

10. See René Pélissier, "Fernando Poo: Un archipel hispano-guinéen," *Revue Française d'Etudes Politiques Africaines*, no. 33 (September 1968).

11. See A. Mangongo-Nzambi, "La délimitation des frontieres du Gabon 1885–1911," *Cahiers d'Etudes Africaines*, vol. 9, no. 33 (1969); I.X. de Aranzadi, "Rio Muni ayer y hoy," *Guinea Española*, vol. 62, no. 1598 (Santa Isabel, 1965); A. de Unzueta Yuste, *Guinea Continental española* (Madrid: Instituto de Estudios Africanos, 1944); J.P. Yaniz, "La Guinea Ecuatorial española: de la occupation a la independencia," *Historia y Vida*, no. 84 (Madrid, 1975).

12. Sanford Berman, "Spanish Guinea: Enclave Empire," *Phylon*, vol. 18 (October 1957).

13. Antonio Ayemi, *Los Bubis en Fernando Poo* (Madrid: Direccion General de Marruecos y Colonias, 1942); E. Gori Molubuela, *Etnologia de los Bubis*

(Madrid: Instituto de Estudios Africanos, 1955); A. Martin del Molino, "Origen del pueblo Bubi de Fernando Poo," *Guinea Española*, vol. 60, no. 1569 (Santa Isabel, 1963); Conte de Castillo-Fiel, *Notas para un estudio antropologica y etnologico del Bubi de Fernando Poo* (Madrid: Instituto de Estudios Africanos, 1949).

14. See I.K. Sundiata, "The Fernandinos: Labor and Community in Santa Isabel 1827–31" (Ph.D. thesis, Northwestern University, 1972). See also Sundiata, "The Importance of Fernando Póo."

15. The other groups in Río Muni—the Benga, Komba, Bujeba, and Lenga—encompass few members, are less developed than the Fang, and have played a minimal role in the evolution of the colony. See A. de Unzueta y Yuste, "Etnografia de la Guinea Española, los Bengas," *Estudios Geograficos*, vol. 6, no. 19 (May 1945); L. Baguena Corella, "Sobre los grupos humanos de la Provincia Española de la Guinea," *Africa* (February 1957), pp. 16–26; H.R. Alvarez Garcia, *Leyendos et mitos de Guinea* (Madrid: Instituto de Estudios Africanos, 1951).

16. Pièrre Alexandre, "Proto-histoire du groupe beti–bulu–fang," *Cahiers d'Etudes Africaines*, vol. 5, no. 20 (1966); Pièrre Alexandre and Jacques Binet, *Le Groupe dit Pahouin (Fang–Bulu–Beti)* (Paris: Institut International Africain, Presses Universitaires de France, 1958); I.X. de Aranzadi, *En el bosque fang* (Barcelona, 1963); A. Panyella Gomez, "El individuo y la Sociedad Fang," *Archivos del Instituto de Estudios Africanos*, no. 46 (Madrid, September 1958); A. Panyella Gomez, *Esquema et etnologia de los Fang-Ntumu de la Guinea Española* (Madrid: Instituto de Estudios Africanos, 1959).

17. See Georges Balandier, "Social Change Among the Fang of Gabon," in his *Sociology of Black Africa* (New York: Praeger Publishers, 1955).

18. Berman, "Spanish Guinea."

19. Cited in Brian Weinstein, *Gabon: Nation-Building on the Ogoué* (Cambridge, Mass.: MIT Press, 1966), pp. 58–62.

20. Antonio de Veciana Vilaldach, *La Secta del Bwiti en la Guinea Española* (Madrid: Instituto de Estudios Africanos, 1958); and M. Pinillos de Cruells, "Guinea Española: la secta del Mbueti," *Africa*, vol. 86 (February 1949).

21. See Philippe Decraene, "Le Putsch de Guinée Equatoriale," *Revue Française d'Etudes Politiques Africaines* (September–October 1979), pp. 30–31.

22. See Pélissier, "Fernando Poo ou la politique de l'insularité," *Revue Française d'Etudes Politiques Africaines*, no. 36 (December 1968), p. 88. See also his "Guinea Equatoriale: au seuil de l'independence," *Revue Française d'Etudes Politiques Africaines* (October 1968), pp. 16–19.

23. A. Iglesias de la Riva, *Politica indigena en Guinea* (Madrid: Instituto de Estudios Africanos, 1947); H. Altozano Moraleda, "El patronato de Indigenas de Guinea: institucion ejamplar," *Archivos del Instituto de Estudios Africanos*, vol. 40 (March 1957).

24. Pélissier, "Le Mouvement nationaliste en Afrique espagnole," *Revue Française d'Etudes Politiques Africaines* (July 1966), p. 124.

25. For additional background, see Nigeria, Legislative Council, "Report on Employment of Nigerian Labourers in Fernando Poo" (Lagos, Sessional Paper No. 38, 1929); I.K. Sundiata, "Prelude to Scandal: Liberia and Fernando Poo, 1880–1930," *Journal of African History*, vol. 15, no. 1 (1974), pp. 97–112; S.O.

Osoba, "The Phenomenon of Labour Migrations in the Area of British Colonial Rule," *Journal of the Historical Society of Nigeria*, vol. 4, no. 4 (1969); Nigeria, Legislative Council, "Parliamentary Delegation to Fernando Poo and Rio Muni," (Lagos, 1957); M. Mveng, "Notes sur l'emigration des Camerounais à Fernando Poo entre les deux guerres mondiales," *Abbia*, no. 23 (Yaoundé, September–December 1969); and Bolaji Akinyeni, "Nigeria and Fernando Poo 1958–1966," *African Affairs*, no. 276 (July 1970), pp. 236–249.

26. In 1938, a Spanish decree provided the theoretical grounds for the political emancipation of culturally assimilated colonial subjects, but only 150 individuals in Spanish Guinea were able to benefit from this reform. For a discussion of the evolution of Spanish colonial philosophy, see G. Heraud, "Aperçu sur l'organisation des territoires espagnols d'outre mer," *Revue Juridique et Politique*, no. 8 (July–September 1954); *España en el Africa Ecuatorial* (Madrid: Instituto de Estudios Africanos, 1964); "La Guinee Espagnole," *Revue Française des Sciences Politiques*, vol. 13, no. 4 (September 1963).

27. See Robert af Klinteberg, *Equatorial Guinea, Macias Country* (Geneva: International University Exchange Fund, 1978), p. 10. See also Pélissier, "Spain's Discreet Decolonization," *Foreign Affairs* (April 1965), and his "Spanish Guinea: An Introduction," *Race*, vol. 6, no. 2 (1964), pp. 122–123.

28. See J. Fuentes Velarde, "Problemas de empleo en la Guinea ecuatorial," *Revista de Trabajo*, vol. 6, no. 2 (1964); and R. de Cossio y de Cossio, "Problemas que afectan la estractura economica de la Guinea continental española," *Africa*, vol. 21 (July 1964). See also International Monetary Fund, "Equatorial Guinea," in *Surveys of African Economies*, vol. 5 (Washington, D.C.: IMF, 1973), pp. 314–353; International Bank of Reconstruction and Development, "The Economy of the Republic of Equatorial Guinea," International Development Association Report No. AW-37a (November 27, 1972); A.E. Kobel, "La République de Guinée Equatoriale: Ses resources potentialles" (Ph.D. thesis, University of Neuchatel, 1976).

29. *Surveys of African Economies*, pp. 320–321.

30. Pélissier, "Uncertainties in Spanish Guinea," *Africa Report* (March 1968), p. 16. For discussions of the early nationalist movements, see the three previously cited articles by Pélissier, "Fernando Poo," "Le Mouvement nationaliste," and "Spanish Guinea: An Introduction"; see also Pélissier's "Political Movements in Spanish Guinea," *Africa Report* (May 1964).

31. Pélissier, "Fernando Póo," p. 85.

32. Miyone later married the widow of Cameroun's radical leader, Felix Moummié.

33. For Maho's biography as well as that of others, see Liniger-Goumaz, *Historical Dictionary*.

34. Pélissier, "Spanish Guinea," p. 124.

35. Pélissier points out that the party's program itself was prepared by a Spanish civil servant. See Pélissier, "Uncertainties," p. 20.

36. See L. Beltran, "L'Afrique d'expression espagnole: la région autonome de la Guinea equatoriale," *Etudes Camerounaises*, vol. 10, no. 5 (Kinshasa, September–October 1967), pp. 48–50; see also Pélissier, "Political Movements,"

pp. 6–7, as well as the map illustrating the split in Río Muni, in Pélissier, "Le mouvement nationaliste."

37. See Ramon Garcia Dominguez, *Guinea: Macias, la ley del silencio* (Barcelona: Plaza & James, 1976), p. 111.

38. See Decraene, "Le Putsch," p. 35; and Pélissier, "Fernando Poo." See also *Africa Research Bulletin*, Political Series (January 1965); and Rafael Fernandez, *Guinea: Materia Reservada* (Madrid: Sedmay Ediciones, 1976).

39. For discussion of Garcia-Trevijano's role after independence, see Fernandez, *Guinea: Materia Reservada*, pp. 217–220.

40. See Pélissier, "Guinée Equatoriale: embuches sur la voie de l'independence," *Revue Française d'Etudes Politiques Africaines* (October 1967), pp. 13–17; and "Guinée Equatoriale: Les Debuts de l'Independence," *Afrique Contemporaine* (November–December 1968).

41. Klinteberg, "L'Enfer de la Guinée Equatoriale," *Revue Française d'Etudes Politiques Africaines* (July–August 1979), p. 131.

42. See, in particular, Robert C. Gard, "Equatorial Guinea: Machinations in Founding a National Bank," *Munger Africana Library Notes*, no. 27 (October 1974), p. 41.

43. For accounts of this crisis and subsequent events, see Pélissier, "Guinea Equatoriale: la crise," *Revue Française d'Etudes Politiques Africaines* (April 1969); *Africa Research Bulletin*, Political Series (April 1969); *New York Times*, March 24, 1969; *West Africa*, March 15, 22, 1969; and Legum (ed.), *Africa Contemporary Record 1969–70*. See also Fernandez, *Guinea*, pp. 105–127; and Dominguez, *Guinea*, pp. 178–216.

44. There is *still* no consensus as to whether an actual coup attempt or an amateurish plot became the pretext for the arrest of Ndong. For the contrary position and a good overview, see Liniger-Goumaz, "La République Guinée Equatoriale—une independence à refaire," *Afrique Contemporaine* (September–October 1979), pp. 8–21.

45. Klinteberg, *Equatorial Guinea*, p. 55.

46. *New York Times*, March 25, 1969.

47. Ibid. For the precise 1967 speech on Hitler, see Klinteberg, *Equatorial Guinea*, Appendix 1, p. 84.

48. "Moderner Caligula," *Der Spiegel*, December 27, 1976, pp. 67–68; "The Man the Churches Call the Caligula of Africa," *Times Review* (London), December 29, 1974, p. 6.

49. Liniger-Goumaz, *Historical Dictionary*, p. 92.

50. *Africa*, no. 34 (June 1974).

51. Klinteberg, *Equatorial Guinea*, p. v; Liniger-Goumaz, *Historical Dictionary*, p. 84.

52. See Klinteberg, *Equatorial Guinea*, p. 43. And for bibliographical data, see Pélissier, "Equatorial Guinea: Autopsy of a Miracle," *Africa Report* (May–June 1980); and Liniger-Goumaz, *Historical Dictionary*, pp. 92–95.

53. *Africa Research Bulletin*, Political Series (September 1979).

54. Pélissier, "Equatorial Guinea: Autopsy," p. 10.

55. *Africa Research Bulletin*, Political Series (September 1979).

56. Klinteberg, *Equatorial Guinea*, p. 44.
57. Ibid., p. 46.
58. Liniger-Goumaz, *Historical Dictionary*, p. 92.
59. Ibid., p. 93.
60. Pélissier, "Equatorial Guinea: Autopsy," p. 11.
61. As cited in *Africa* (June 1974), p. 22. See also *Africa Research Bulletin*, Political Series (September 1979).
62. Klinteberg, *Equatorial Guinea*, pp. 49, 50.
63. *Africa Research Bulletin*, Political Series (October 1979).
64. Klinteberg, *Equatorial Guinea*, p. 54.
65. See *Le Monde*, July 11, 1975; *West Africa*, October 6, 1975; and Pélissier, "Les suicides de Papa Macias," *Revue Française d'Etudes Politiques Africaines* (March 1975), p. 14.
66. See Klinteberg, p. 52. See also *Africa Research Bulletin*, Political Series, (September 1979).
67. Pélissier, "Equatorial Guinea: Autopsy," p. 10.
68. Ibid., p. 11; Dominguez, *Guinea*, pp. 26, 36.
69. Klinteberg, *Equatorial Guinea*, p. 47.
70. Dominguez, *Guinea*, p. 57.
71. Ibid., p. 36, as cited in Klinteberg, *Equatorial Guinea*, p. 46.
72. Klinteberg, *Equatorial Guinea*, p. 46.
73. Ibid., p. 23.
74. Ibid., p. 44.
75. Dominguez, *Guinea*, pp. 26, 29.
76. See Liniger-Goumaz, "La Republique," p. 17.
77. See S. Cronje, "Equatorial Guinea—The Forgotten Dictatorship" (London: Anti-Slavery Society, 1976); Klinteberg, *Equatorial Guinea*.
78. "The Cocoa-Slaves of Fernando Poo," *The Guardian*, November 21, 1976.
79. *New York Times*, November 13, 1972; *Sunday Times* (London), February 1, 1976.
80. See *West Africa*, January 26, 1976; February 1, 1976; *The Times* (London), January 14 and 20, 1976; February 6, 1976; August 26, 1976; *Africa Research Bulletin*, Political Series (February 1976); *Le Monde*, January 13, 1976, p. 3; "La Guinea equatoriale et les travailleurs nigerians," *Marches Tropicaux*, January 2, 1976; "Life on Devil's Island," *Africa* (June 1974), pp. 21–22.
81. Klinteberg, *Equatorial Guinea*, p. 27.
82. Ibid. See also "Equatorial Guinea: Nguema's Chamber of Horrors," *New African* (February 1976); and "The Horror of Equatorial Guinea," *West Africa*, October 16, 1978. For an economic overview, see *West Africa*, November 22, 1976.
83. See Klinteberg, *Equatorial Guinea*, pp. 27–28.
84. See, among others, Cronje, "Equatorial Guinea," pp. 21–24; and Klinteberg, *Equatorial Guinea*.
85. *Jeune Afrique*, November 2, 1974.
86. See Klinteberg, *Equatorial Guinea*, p. 32. See also "Equatorial Guinea: Silence Is Dangerous," *Africa* (February 1979).

87. Pélissier, "Les suicides de Papa Macias," *Revue Française d'Etudes Politiques Africaines* (March 1975), p. 16.
88. See, inter alia, International Commission of Jurists, *The Review* (December 1974 and December 1978), as well as "Life on Devil's Island," *Africa* (June 1974). See also Liniger-Goumaz, "La Republique"; *London Times*, August 10, 1977; and Peter Enahoro, "Tyranny in Equatorial Guinea," *Africa* (August 1976).
89. Liniger-Goumaz, *Historical Dictionary*, p. 84.
90. *West Africa*, August 13, 1979.
91. Klinteberg, *Equatorial Guinea*, p. 55.
92. Cronje, "Equatorial Guinea," p. 23 and passim. See also Pélissier, "Les suicides."
93. *Le Monde*, December 20, 1976.
94. Klinteberg, *Equatorial Guinea*, p. 55.
95. See *Le Monde*, January 24, 1976, November 28, 1975, November 2, 1976; *The Times* (London), December 18, 1976; *West Africa*, August 23, 1976.
96. See Pélissier, "Guinée Equatoriale: mourir pour Corisco," *Revue Française d'Etudes Politiques Africaines* (October 1972). See also *Africa Confidential*, July 22, 1972; and Colin Legum (ed.), *Africa Contemporary Record 1972–73* (London: Rex Collings, 1973).
97. Klinteberg, *Equatorial Guinea*, p. 16.
98. See Samuel Decalo, *Coups and Army Rule in Africa: Studies in Military Style* (New Haven, Conn.: Yale University Press, 1976), Chapter 1.
99. See "Népotisme," in Liniger-Goumaz, *La Guinée Equatoriale: Pays Méconnu* (Paris: Harmattan, 1980).
100. Ibid., p. 290.
101. *Africa Research Bulletin*, Economic Series (March 1977).
102. Liniger-Goumaz, "La Republique," p. 20.
103. For the best description of this event, see Liniger-Goumaz, *La Guinée Equatoriale*. See also *Le Monde*, August 25, 1979, and August 29, 1979; *Africa Research Bulletin*, Political Series (September 1970); Decraene, "Le Putsch"; Pélissier, "Equatorial Guinea: Autopsy."
104. *West Africa*, October 1, 1979.
105. See *Jeune Afrique* (July 1980); and *The Observer*, May 25, 1980.
106. *West Africa*, August 27, 1979.
107. *West Africa*, August 20, 1981; Pélissier, "Equatorial Guinea: Autopsy."
108. "Equatorial Africa: A Coup Dissected," *Africa Confidential*, October 17, 1979.
109. *Africa Report* (May–June 1980), p. 33.
110. Cited in *West Africa*, June 13, 1983.
111. *Washington Post*, September 7, 1982.
112. *Le Monde*, July 26, 1986; Tikum Mbah Azonga, "Assertions and Denials," *West Africa*, August 4, 1986.
113. See Tikum Mbah Azonga, "Breaking New Ground," *West Africa*, February 3, 1986.
114. Legum (ed.), *Africa Contemporary Record 1985–86*, p. B222.
115. See Eddie Momoh, "Equatorial Guinea: Mr. Botha's Long Hand," *West Africa*, November 30, 1987.
116. Legum (ed.), *Africa Contemporary Record 1983–84*, p. B373.

3 Idi Amin

The Brutal Reign of the Iron Marshal

Located at opposite ends of the continent, maritime Equatorial Guinea and insular Uganda at first glance may appear to have little in common. The two countries differ markedly on virtually every dimension—size, diversity of population, precolonial history, traditional forms of social organization, economic potential, and recent political evolution. Moreover, though hardly at the mainstream of regional or external influences, Uganda (known to British colonists as the "Pearl of Africa") was never the stagnant, isolated geographical backwater that Equatorial Guinea was. British colonialism, despite its indignities and exploitation, was infinitely more enlightened in comparison to the oppressive authoritarian paternalism of Spanish colonial rule. And although the transition to independent statehood was complicated in Kampala by the acute fragmentation of society and of the indigenous elites, Britain did not attempt to unduly arrest or retard the process as did Spain, both directly and indirectly, in Santa Isabel.

Notwithstanding these and numerous other differences between the two countries (including the enhanced role of the world of spirits in Equatorial Guinea), the Nguema dictatorship that emerged in Santa Isabel was in essence quite similar to the brutal tyranny that sprang up in Kampala under Idi Amin. True, the personalities of the two tyrants were quite different, as were their idiosyncrasies—and their individual preoccupations once they seized power clearly reflected this fact. But the unique modality of rule in both countries—personal dictatorship—was identical. The awesome personal concentration of power, its arbitrary and ruthless use for purposes of personal self-gratification, the utter absence of state policy and goals, the total pulverization of all strata of society for the duration of the dictatorial interregnum, and the sheer magnitude of the resultant socioeconomic devastation of both societies certainly set the two countries apart from the rest of the continent. And

MAP 2 Uganda

the legacy of their recent brutal past continues to haunt the two countries to this day, playing havoc with efforts at national reconstruction.

Ugandan Social Dynamics

Uganda is a relatively small, insular country astride the equator that encompasses 91,000 square miles and a population estimated at just over 15 million people. Largely a profusely vegetated 4,000-foot-high plateau (a fact that accounts for Uganda's moderate climate), the country includes within its boundaries the 17,000-foot Ruwenzori Mountains, the western escarpment of the Great Rift Valley, and the source of the Nile River. Although to the north and northeast soil conditions tend to be poor, the land in general is very fertile. This is especially true of the region around Lake Victoria (the heart of the Kingdom of Buganda). The fertile soil, together with the district's high rainfall, has made the area the economic and demographic core of the country.

Geographically at the juncture of a multiplicity of cultural influences, historic migratory patterns, and distinct lifestyles, Uganda is extremely diverse. Its population is composed of some 40-odd ethnic groups, fully

MAP 3 Uganda's Major Ethnic Groups

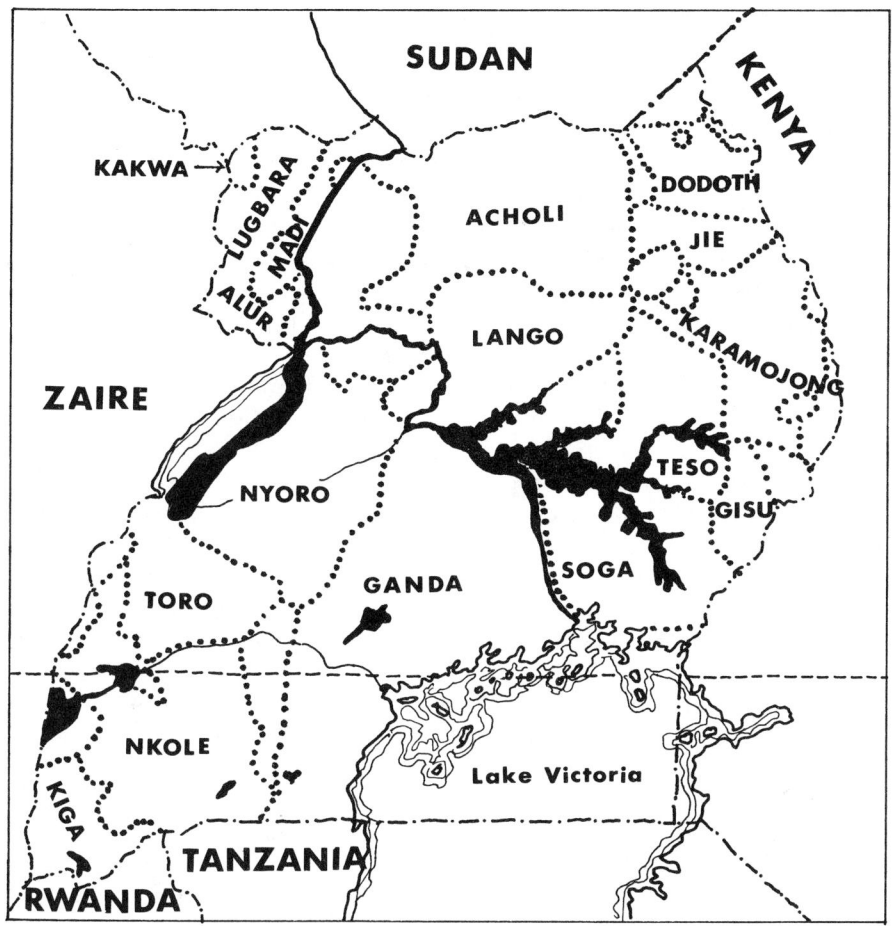

10 of which number more than 600,000 people each. The country is devoid of any single large ethnic core that could have provided a stabilizing anchor; much of its social fluidity and political volatility stems from this acute diversity of peoples, cultures, and lifestyles.

Uganda's population is normally grouped in terms of each ethnic group's appurtenance to a number of African linguistic families: Bantu, Eastern Nilotic, Western Nilotic, and Central Sudanic.[1] The Bantu-speaking groups constitute two-thirds of the population and are found in a thick arc around Lake Victoria in the southern part of the country. Among the Eastern Bantu peoples are the Baganda, who number 17 percent of the population and are Uganda's largest ethnic group. Settled heavily along the northwest rim of Lake Victoria, and primarily made up of agriculturalists, Ganda farmers produce the country's key cash crops—coffee and cotton. At the time of the arrival of British influence in the Lake Victoria area, their kingdom, Buganda, was a powerful, centralized, quasi-feudal monarchy in the process of an aggressive territorial expansion. The establishment of a tacit Anglo-Bugandan alliance secured for Buganda total supremacy in the region, as Bugandan forces acted as surrogate conquerors of Uganda for the British. In the process, Buganda acquired major advantages in the new colony, not least of which was separate protectorate status. Both the capital (Kampala) and the main commercial center (Entebbe) were located within Buganda, and the former was shortly to be connected with the outside world via the railroad from Mombasa (Kenya). Virtually the first schools, hospitals, roads, and commercial ventures were set up in Buganda, a fact that in due time gave the region the highest literacy and income levels in the country.

Sophisticated in its political structures, proud of its culture and achievements, upwardly mobile, and adaptable to the new European influences, Buganda rapidly transformed itself into the most modern segment of the new colony. This modernization did little, however, to undermine the legitimacy of the "kabaka" (king) or the quasi-divine concept of kingship in general.[2] Continuing their surrogate role for the British as in the past, a majority of the colonial administration soon came to be staffed by Ganda. Their language became the *lingua franca* of the country, much to the resentment of both the historical enemies in the south and the recently conquered peoples in the north.

The Western Bantu-speaking groups include the Banyoro, whose turn-of-the-century defeat at the hands of Buganda came as a result of the entry of British power on the side of Buganda. At the time, the kingdom of Bunyoro was the most ancient and most powerful in the region,[3] with most of the other Bantu groups (e.g., the neighboring Banyankole and Batore but *not* the Basoga)[4] in a tributary relationship to either Buganda or Bunyoro. Bunyoro's defeat led to the absorption by Buganda of rich Banyoro-populated territories—the origin of the "Lost Counties" dispute that so poisoned relations between the two until it was resolved in Bunyoro's favor by President Obote's post-independence referendum. The Banyoro are found northwest of the Baganda. Like the latter, and indeed like most other Bantu groups, the Banyoro are sedentary farmers, with a tight social organization and quasi-sacred monarchy.

Despite their traditional competitions and rivalries, the Bantu ethnic groups are sharply set apart on practically every socioeconomic dimension from the Nilotic- and Sudanic-speaking groups of the more sparsely populated north and northeast. Among the Western Nilotics are the martial Lango and Acholi—Uganda's sixth- and eighth-largest ethnic groups, respectively.[5] They are primarily stockbreeders; livestock, which plays a very minor role among the Bantu groups to their south, is their major means of exchange, their indicator of social status, and their economic mainstay and occupation. The Nilotic lifestyle, which includes the practice of shifting cultivation, has prevented the emergence of protostates and of powerful centralized authorities; instead, the Acholi and Lango have been organized into a multitude of strong clans. Both groups, which are hereditary enemies, strongly resisted the encroachments of colonial authority. After being vanquished, they resented the imposition of a virtual Bugandan overlordship, remaining suspicious of all southern groups. Forged into an anti-Buganda political alliance by Milton Obote, the Acholi and Lango became the cornerstone of political power in Uganda before the Amin interregnum.

East of the Lango and Acholi are found the Karamojong cluster of ethnic groups, also referred to as the Eastern Nilotics.[6] Closely related to groups across the border in Kenya (e.g., to the Turkana), the Karamojong are eminently well adjusted to the harsh, waterless environment of northeastern Uganda. Geographically and culturally isolated in an area that did not fall under government control until the 1920s, and was not allocated any development funds until the 1950s, the Karamojong are socially and politically highly decentralized and quasi-nomadic. Their main occupation is cattle raising, and they frequently conduct cattle-raiding sorties against each other and across the international border. Contingents of both the Ugandan and Kenyan armies have traditionally been posted along the mutual border of these two countries in order to patrol this endemically unruly and restless area.

Uganda's second-largest ethnic group, the Teso, are centrally located between the Karamojong, the Lango/Acholi, and the Ganda/Soga. In many respects a socioeconomic "bridge" between the more advanced Bantu-speaking groups of the south and the more backward Nilotic and Sudanic groups of the north, the Teso are fundamentally the modern sedentary, agricultural (cotton-growing) segment of the Karamojong.[7] Finally, in the far north the Central Sudanic–language cluster of peoples includes a variety of ethnic groups, some artificially bisected by the Zaire and Sudan borders. Among these one can note the Lugbara,[8] Madi, Kakwa, and other, smaller ethnic slivers that are often more powerfully "pulled" toward their kinsmen across the border than toward the distant Kampala. At times collectively (but erroneously) referred to as "Nubians," these groups are largely outside the mainstream of Ugandan socioeconomic and political life. Culturally and geographically isolated, they practice a mix of sedentary agriculture and stockbreeding. The poor soil in the region periodically forces many to migrate south or north into Sudan in search of work.

The intrusion of British authority in the region encapsulated within the new colonial boundaries this array of completely different peoples, with their diverse lifestyles, forms of social hierarchy, world outlooks, religious beliefs, and histories of mutual conflict and rivalry. The society that was to emerge after sixty years of colonial rule was a malintegrated one, with some segments virtually untouched by modernity due to socioeconomic neglect, and the rest marked by a multiplicity of intense cleavages that would be politicized with the advent of competitive politics.[9] The fundamental cleavage in Uganda, as manifest in 1988 as in 1900, is the sharp separation between the socially centralized, monarchically inclined, sedentary, "advanced" Bantu-speaking groups of the south and the pastoral, semi-nomadic, decentralized, "backward" Nilotic and Sudanic groups of the north. Within each of these "camps" exist equally sharp webs of intra-ethnic rivalry, but all of the groups are in opposition to the haughty and upwardly mobile Ganda, thus complicating the formation of stable political alliances and the emergence of systemic legitimacy.

Decades of differential socioeconomic evolution of the various parts of the country—and, in particular, the modernization of the south and the stagnation of the north—have further sharpened these cleavages and reinforced historical grievances. By the 1960s, despite belated efforts to correct some of the resultant regional imbalances, statistics from Uganda's different districts resembled data culled from completely different countries. For example, the Baganda, who constituted 16.3 percent of the population at the time, staffed fully 47 percent of the senior civil service posts (but only 4 percent of the low-paying police jobs) and were likewise overrepresented by 300 percent among the student body of Makerere University. The Teso, Uganda's second-largest ethnic group (8 percent of the population), had a minimal role in the civil service (2 percent) but constituted an important force in the police (15 percent); the Acholi and Lango, seriously underrepresented in the civil service, were overrepresented by 300 percent in the armed forces; and the Lugbara of the north were virtually absent from most modern structures of society, being underrepresented, for example, more than 900 percent at Makerere University.[10]

One further, and most important, polarizing factor has to be noted at this juncture—religion. The arrival in Buganda (and, eventually, in other parts of the country) of Christian missionaries of various denominations very rapidly polarized the country. Religious clashes and bloody miniwars periodically erupted in Buganda specifically, where the different Christian sects were politicized by "affiliation" with competing branches of the Buganda royalty, nobility, or clan chiefs. Religious affiliation became the criterion for upward mobility in the kabaka's court and in the administration of Buganda, with patronage also flowing along denominational lines. When the British threw their weight behind the Protestant factions in Buganda, they affected the Catholic-Protestant balance of power in the court, but not the population's greater Catholic predisposition. The kabaka's cabinet came to be a Protestant body (encompassing four Protestants, one Catholic, and one Muslim), with all key court officials and the prime minister (katikiro) traditionally always Protestant—this despite the fact that, throughout Buganda, Catholicism was the majority (49 percent) denominational affiliation. (Some 28 percent professed allegiance to Protestant sects, and 6 percent were Muslim.) Only the country's twenty county (*saza*) chiefs better reflected society's actual religious breakdown, by including ten Protestants and eight Catholics.

Indeed, religion and factional politics were so deeply intertwined in Buganda that, for all practical purposes, the different Christian denominations operated as political factions. These factions were intermittently threatened by Islam, which was seeping in from the coast and, at one time, was briefly considered the possible religion of the court.[11] Against this background of religious-political interpenetration, modern political parties in Uganda tended to be assessed by the electorate (both within and outside Buganda) primarily in terms of their secterian affiliation, and only secondarily in terms of the nature of their ethnic leadership or political programs. Further complicating the political picture was the fact that Catholicism was the majority denomination among the Ganda, but not of the *kabaka* or his court, whereas the Protestant faith had made greater inroads among the northern peoples (most of whom, however, retained greater allegiance to traditional religions). The cleavage between the Bugandan court religion and that of the masses meant that most Catholic Baganda found themselves unable to support a Catholic party politically, even one predominantly led by Ganda (e.g., Benedicto Kiwanuka's Democratic party), for by so acting they would be directly affronting their revered *kabaka*. Since on religious grounds they could not bring themselves to support a Protestant party either (e.g., Obote's Uganda People's Congress, or UPC, which was viewed also as the political vehicle of the despised northern Nilotics), the most advanced group in Uganda tended to be politically neutralized. *Outside* Buganda, however, many Bantu-speaking Protestant groups crossed the religious line to support the "Catholic" Democratic party (DP) because a vote for the "commoner" Ganda leadership at the helm was a resounding expression of anti-Buganda sentiments.

The Economic Context

Agriculture is the mainstay of Uganda's economy. Rich soils, a favorable climate, and plentiful rains have laid the foundation for a variegated and highly productive agricultural base. The country is self-sufficient in staple foodstuffs; up to 90 percent of its foreign earnings have traditionally come from the export of coffee, cotton, and tea. Together with limited quantities of mineral ores (copper), Uganda's exports have more than paid for its imports, producing positive balances of trade and giving the country the highest per capita income growth in East Africa during 1960–1965.[12] Even though imports quadrupled from 1961 to 1972 (due to heavy infrastructure costs), the doubling of exports during the same period maintained the favorable balance.

Despite its healthy agricultural base, the Ugandan economy has been both extremely resistant to efforts at crop-diversification and strongly affected by vacillations in global commodity market prices. Secondary industries have developed with great difficulty and levels of foreign investment have fluctuated widely—both a function of the much greater attraction of foreign investors to Kenya, with which Uganda was linked (together with Tanzania) in the East African community.[13] After independence, a host of other economic problems began to afflict the country. Profligate government spending, poor budgetary controls, the absence of strict fiscal accountability, and periodic revelations of gross fiscal mismanagement severely taxed the fiscal resources of the state. Large unbudgeted (and unauthorized) expenditures—especially, but not solely, relating to the armed forces—further complicated efforts at rational economic planning. Thus, despite a healthy balance of trade at the start, a major shrinkage in hard-currency reserves had developed by the time of Amin's coup, coupled with a severe liquidity and balance-of-payments crisis. The GDP growth rate declined to 2.1 percent in 1971, from its pre-1966 annual average of 5.2 percent. None of the country's Five-Year Plans attained projected investment targets, and a net outflow of private capital began to threaten the fiscal stability of the country.

This outflow of capital was directly related to Obote's 1969 "Veer to the Left" policies, which threatened the role of Asian entrepreneurs in the country. Until it was excised en masse by Amin's expulsions, Uganda's Asian community had played a dominant role in the country's commercial and industrial life. Tracing its origins to labor recruited for the construction of the Kampala-Nairobi railroad, and to the traders who followed to cater to the workers, this community rapidly acquired a stranglehold over Uganda's economy.

Despite discriminatory legislation, the booming economy generated major opportunities for individuals able to provide middleman services. Capitalizing on their modest funds, entrepreneurial proclivities, and willingness to work long hours for (initially) low profits, Asians formed much of the backbone of the economy. Thus, by 1910 a three-tiered division of labor had emerged in Uganda, and elsewhere in East Africa. As H.M. Morris has noted, "administration and agricultural development were thought to be European occupations; trade and craftmanship were relegated to Indians, and Africans were encouraged to work in the European agricultural system and to supply cheap labor in the towns. . . . The picture did not substantially change in the next forty years."[14] At independence, Asians possessed a quasi-monopoly over Uganda's retail trade (having gained dominance as early as 1903), controlled three-quarters of the country's wholesale trade, and owned the majority of the cotton gins and tea estates in the country. Moreover, as late as 1968, fully 80 percent of the positions in the free professions and 36 percent of the posts in the private sector of the economy (including the most senior posts) were held by non-nationals.[15]

African resentment over this economic stranglehold—felt most deeply in the countryside, where Asians were the most visible focal point of commerce—spilled out in the form of periodic riots and boycotts.[16] As the Obote regime began to legislate restrictive policies aimed at reducing the economic role of the Asian community, and began to promulgate "Socialist" goals, Indian traders rushed to repatriate their funds and investments. So monumental was this fiscal outflow that, immediately prior to the 1971 coup d'état, it became a major destabilizing factor in Uganda.[17] After the coup, of course, the ad hoc plunder of the treasury, economy, and society completely devastated the country. The infrastructural after-effects are visible to this day.

Prelude to Dictatorship: The Civilian Era

As some scholars have noted, it was the imminence of independence that gave birth to "nationalist" parties in Uganda, rather than the reverse.[18] Preoccupation with local, regional, ethnic, and parochial issues, the growth of subnationalism, and Buganda's strong sense of distinctive identity prevented the early development of a sense of nationhood, nationalist leaders, or even political parties.[19] At independence, the country emerged a "paper-nation,"[20] riddled with basic inconsistencies that were resolved in a series of bitter confrontations as late as 1964–1966. The after-effects of these confrontations also linger to this day.

The political history of Uganda has essentially been the story of a tug-of-war between Bugandan separatism and Ugandan nationalism, between traditional authority (the quasi-divine kabaka and other southern kings) and modern political authority, between center and periphery. Sectarian (Catholic-Protestant-Muslim), civil-military, ideological, and personality tensions further complicated the core political competitions.[21]

The colonial policy of indirect rule practiced in Uganda entrenched the country's basic ethnic and regional divisions, just as the growth of subnationalism later directed attention to regional and local political issues. Central government was seen as an alien authority; outside Buganda, it was also considered a vehicle for the political dominance of the Baganda. Local government and regional politics riveted the focus of the people, and the political parties that eventually sprang up were thus ethnically based. As narrow elitist formations (despite their claims to be mass parties), these weak, highly decentralized, regionally based parties were tied to parochial concerns and beholden to local power-wielders. The greater strength of the local district party organization over the national leadership was clearly visible in the 1961 elections: Fully 95 percent of the 185 African candidates had been born in the same district they were contesting. The parties were popularly identified in terms of their pro- or anti-Buganda stance and their Protestant or Catholic leadership; rent by personality clashes and highly elitist, they were poor mechanisms for social mobilization. Their influence often did not extend beyond the district capital, and as often as not they collapsed into their component parts through intense factional strife.[22]

The fact that most parties (including the "northern" UPC) had Ganda leadership worked against their chances of gaining wide popular support in non-Ganda areas outside their home region. For there they were viewed as modern vehicles for the perpetuation of Ganda supremacy—even when they were running on nationalist planks. At the same time, however, all political parties—irrespective of their ethnic composition or political hue—were shunned in Buganda itself. Frequently headed by Catholics (and thus unacceptable to the court), and commoners at that (in a Kingdom where status and privilege were paramount values), political parties were seen, even by Baganda intelligentsia and elites,[23] as an affront to the kabakaship. The principle of popular elections flouted the sacrosanct status of the monarchy, because it implied that power need not stem from either the kabaka or the Lukiiko (his council), and because it permitted the utterly unthinkable—the percolation of commoners to a social and political status above the kabaka himself.

Yet the devolution of colonial authority as independence approached was predicated on the elemental concept of "popular legitimacy." The fact that Buganda's contrary views on such a fundamental issue were totally ignored by Britain, and that its "special status" (as Protectorate) was not respected in the negotiations leading to independence, ultimately led to its attempted secession on January 1, 1961.[24] Although a constitutional formula was ultimately devised that ensured Buganda's acquiescence to independence as part of Uganda (entailing a quasi-federal system with the kabaka as president and no direct election to the central organs), the formula only temporarily papered over the country's internal irreconcilable differences.

The first major political party to claim nationalist credentials was the Democratic party. Established in 1956 by Ganda Catholics, the DP ("almost exclusively Roman Catholic in inspiration and membership")[25] sought political revenge for the historical discrimination of Catholics in Buganda.[26] Attempting to garner the vote of the disenfranchised Catholic Ganda majority, while appealing to anti-Buganda sentiments elsewhere (through its anti-establishment credentials), it was swept to power in March 1961. The elections, however, were totally ignored in Buganda; fully 98 percent of the electorate heeded the kabaka's appeal for an electoral boycott in protest of the objectionable principle of direct election of deputies. The few who did not heed the boycott gave Kiwanuka the vote necessary to capture 20 of Buganda's constituencies. Together with electoral victories elsewhere, the DP formed Uganda's first African government.

The Democratic party's main rival in 1961 was the Uganda People's Congress (UPC). Established in 1960 after a series of splits and mergers from the Uganda National Congress (the country's oldest party), the UPC was headed by Milton Obote, at the time the Langi representative (of chiefly descent) to the Legislative Council. The UPC, like the DP, was a decentralized hierarchy very much beholden to its district branches. Its core strength lay in the Nilotic districts—Lango and Acholi—although it capitalized upon anti-Buganda sentiments elsewhere and was strong in Busoga and Toro; later, by advocating a referendum on the Lost Counties, it gained important support in Bunyoro as well.[27] In the March 1961 elections, the UPC outpolled the DP, gaining 488,332 votes to the latter's 407,816; but Uganda's district representation electoral system gave the DP 43 seats to the UPC's 35.

The fact that Bugandan intransigence had resulted in the rise to power of a Catholic commoner, as well as a more realistic appraisal in the kabaka's court of the dangers implicit in an independent Uganda in which Buganda played no role, led to the creation of the King Alone (Kabaka Yekka, or KY) party. "Only in the broadest sense a party at all,"[28] the KY had only one platform: utter loyalty to the kabaka. Within months of its creation, and with hardly any political organization except the network of chiefs, the KY swept 65 of the 68 Lukiiko (local) seats, losing only the three Banyoro-populated Lost Counties, which were seething with anti-Buganda sentiment. The Lukiiko subsequently appointed the Buganda representatives to the National Assembly in accordance with the new Independence Constitution, which provided for indirect elections to Parliament. With neither the DP nor the UPC strong enough after the 1962 elections to govern alone, the KY was invited into a coalition with the UPC and received five of the fifteen cabinet portfolios.

The opportunistic alliance satisfied the immediate desires of both partners to oust the Democratic party and to assume power in its place. But the arrangement was otherwise an unstable marriage of convenience. Quite apart from the special constitutional provisions that had been granted Buganda (and the other kingdoms) in the pre-independence negotiations that rankled progressive elements in the country,[29] the coalition linked together ideologically incompatible partners. With the eventual eclipse of their common enemy (the DP), both the UPC and the KY began to disintegrate internally. The Kabaka slowly lost control over "his" deputies in Kampala, whereas factionalism in the UPC triggered a series of internal challenges to Obote's leadership of the UPC. The resurfacing of some of Uganda's basic inconsistencies finally shattered the coalition and caused a redefinition of the union.

The Kabaka Yekka, a loose association of traditionalists and secessionists unified only by distaste for the DP, slowly came apart. The KY's alliance with the UPC divided the party into polarized factions: a hard-line "Buganda-firsters" faction beholden to Mmengo Hill and a more outward-looking faction, the KY parliamentary wing. The latter—enticed by UPC blandishments of patronage and irritated by the Katikiro's precondition of ultraloyalty for nomination to the Assembly—increasingly began to cross the aisle to the UPC. To the Kabaka, the Buganda representatives were merely spokesmen to a quasi-confederal body; the weaning away of these delegates was seen not as a parliamentary tactic but as a fundamental violation of the conditions under which the kingdom had agreed to renounce its own claim to independence. Because similar crossovers had drained the parliamentary strength of the DP, a UPC majority emerged by 1964. It was capable of governing alone, if necessary, and anxious to amend the constitutional concessions granted to Buganda prior to independence.

Yet even as the UPC acquired a parliamentary majority, a similar decomposition of authority began to affect the party. Even more than other parties, the UPC was an opportunistic coalition of district power-wielders, ethnic leaders, and ideological viewpoints. Elitist to the extent of being virtually a structureless shell outside Lango and Acholi, the party began to come apart at the seams with the signing of the alliance with the Kabaka Yekka and the eclipse of the DP threat. Anti-Buganda factions were incensed by the coalition with Mmengo Hill inasmuch as the UPC had been specifically created to combat Bugandan influence; militants and the youth wing were alienated by the necessity to shelve cherished Socialist goals (due to the KY's opposition) and to accept what they believed to be anachronistic social and economic hierarchies as equal partners.

Obote's own role within this maelstrom of competitive factions was a balancing one; he attempted to avoid the alienation of the KY (until the 1964 referendum made this impossible) while buttressing his own power base against assaults to his leadership from the Left. His efforts were greatly complicated by the fact that the most explosive issue left pending from the colonial era—the status of the Lost Counties—required definitive resolution.

Simmering with popular discontent since its conquest at the end of the nineteenth century by Buganda, the largely Banyoro population of the "Lost Counties" was polled in November 1964 about its future status.[30] Obote's decision to proceed with the referendum brought about the immediate de facto demise of the KY-UPC alliance (in August 1964), and the verdict of the poll—reintegration with Bunyoro—unleashed KY efforts to overthrow him. When these failed, symbolizing the degree to which Buganda had lost control over events, the kingdom made its third attempt at secession in less than twelve years.

Buganda's parliamentary counterassault took the form of a motion by KY Secretary General David Ocheng[31] to have Obote dislodged. Capitalizing on Obote's prolonged absence from Kampala (in Lango and Acholi, consolidating his power base), Ocheng, who was also making overtures to the DP, called for the interim suspension of deputy Chief of Staff Idi Amin and an inquiry into the "gold and ivory affair." The affair stemmed from illicit dealings with Congolese elements during the Soumaliot rebellion in Congo/Kinshasa. Alleging various improprieties on the part of Obote, Amin, Minister of Planning (and cousin of Obote) Adoko Nekyon, and Minister of Defense Felix Onama, the motion passed with only four dissenting votes, signifying the degree to which Obote had become isolated in his own party.

When two weeks passed without any action by Obote, a second motion was introduced—with one dissenting vote—calling for Obote's resignation. The parliamentary motion did not take into account the true fount of power in Uganda, however. On February 22, 1966, security forces barged into the cabinet room and summarily dragged out the five key ministers involved in the intrigue against Obote, including Grace Ibingira, the ambitious secretary general of the UPC.[32] Seizing the initiative, Obote immediately assumed all executive powers and suspended the Constitution as well as (temporarily) the National Assembly. On April 15, the greatly intimidated Assembly convened to ratify a new unitary constitution, an executive president, vastly reduced powers for the country's traditional leaders and direct elections for all structures. Obote's "revolution" (as it was referred to) was upheld by the Supreme Court,[33] but it completed the alienation of Buganda.

On May 20, the kingdom ordered the "illegal" central government out of Kampala. The kabaka (still de facto president of Uganda) appealed for foreign military assistance while distributing arms in preparation for an insurrection. In the showdown that ensued, Obote declared martial law over the country and sent military units into Mmengo Hill to subdue the budding rebellion. The command of the force was in the hands of Colonel Idi Amin. His superior, Iteso Chief of Staff Brigadier General Shaban Opolot, who had married into Buganda nobility, had been overly equivocal throughout the constitutional crisis and was probably in the Buganda camp. He was subsequently purged from the army. In the sharp and unnecessarily brutal suppression of the revolt, more than 100 people lost their lives.[34] The kabaka, disguised as a commoner, fled into exile to London where he was to die in 1969 of alcohol poisoning. Following the confrontation, Uganda's four traditional monarchies were abolished and Buganda was carved up into three administrative districts. Though now faced with a rebellious and morose population in the south, Obote viewed the "Buganda problem" as finally resolved.

Consolidation and Collapse: 1966-1971

Unshackled from his unholy alliance with the KY and unburdened of the traditional-conservative veto-power restraints of the federal system, Obote moved to leave his personal imprint upon the East African political firmament. Not a "spellbinder, a martyr or a source of inspiration,"[35] nor for that matter either an intellectual or an innovator, Obote had always been dwarfed in East Africa by both Julius Nyerere, his mentor, and Jomo Kenyatta, the consumate political juggler. Even though Obote was now able to initiate new social, economic, and political policies, the reality of political power had not changed much in Uganda. The resistance of Buganda had been broken, but Ganda politicians and intellectuals had largely disassociated themselves from Kampala and the UPC. A belated policy of reconciliation was not very effective, especially as Ganda administrators—still in an absolute majority in the civil service—observed the greater developmental emphasis on the northern districts since the 1966 upheaval. Although Obote was meticulous in maintaining an equitable ethnic balance in his cabinet, this in itself won him little support from the segment of the country he had just physically subdued.

Obote emerged in 1966 as the victor in his tug-of-war for supremacy within the UPC, but the reality of power still eluded him. Factionalism and new centers of power continued to coalesce, all the while disputing Obote's leadership. These included the UPC secretary general and minister of defense, Felix Onama (who had grown rich and powerful through his transport empire), and Obote's own half-brother, A. A. Nekyon. Later, the rather lukewarm Socialist policies announced in 1969 triggered the derision—and desertion—of the UPC Left.

The "Move to the Left" initiatives in 1969 sent shockwaves through the country's economy, multiplying sources of opposition against Obote's leadership. Having alienated most southern ethnic groups by his uncompromising elimination of traditional kingship, Obote now appeared to be "moving along a broad front that would make for more enmity from those who were thriving on private enterprise."[36] Controversy still exists over the question of whether Obote's pronouncements were mostly rhetoric (aimed at the UPC radical wing) or whether they signified a definite commitment to a new order. For if carried to their logical conclusion, some of the reforms would have directly threatened the interests of societal groups supportive of the UPC and, indeed, a broad cross-section of the party's leadership itself. On the other hand, although the focus of the reforms was on the "common man," they left the bulk of society virtually untouched and only nibbled at the privileges of the establishment.

The *Common Man's Charter* was Obote's major catalog of Uganda's ills (capitalism, neocolonialism, income inequalities, expatriate economic exploitation) and their remedial prescriptions.[37] The latter included an emphasis upon collectives, state industry, government control of trade and commerce, the inculcation in Uganda of Socialist values, and a shift from the brokerage politics of the past to mass politics and the political mobilization of society. The first steps in implementing some of the objectives of the *Charter* were the nationalization in 1969–1970 of 85 mostly expatriate companies (although the services of expatriates were retained under very advantageous management contracts) and the closure of certain forms of enterprise to foreign capital.

The Move to the Left, and the nationalizations in particular, threw the economy into a tailspin from which it never recovered. A huge outflow of private capital commenced as Asians scrambled to repatriate their funds prior to further nationalizations or stiff currency controls. The capital outflow coincided with a bout of commodity production shortfalls and lower global commodity prices, which threw Uganda into a vicious fiscal squeeze and liquidity crisis. The Bank of Uganda minced no words in blaming the crisis on "uncertainties . . . about the role of the private sector . . . since the publication of the Common Man's Charter . . . and [on] indecisive policy in regard to . . . the Asian community."[38]

The socioeconomic and political malaise of groups disgruntled by Obote's 1969–1970 policies (and by the earlier 1966 "revolution") fueled growing levels of violent crime and civil unruliness (*kondoism*) throughout the country that the government appeared incapable of stemming. The still mystery-shrouded 1969 assassination attempt on Obote was symptomatic of the growing destabilization of Uganda. Following this event, the regime became more oppressive. Opposition parties were banned the very same evening Obote was shot in the cheek, and the armed forces, under Amin, were again sent on a rampage of intimidation in the "enemy" (Ganda) territory (Kampala). Specialized hierarchies of control—the Special Forces and the General Service Units[39]—were further built up and used as political counterweights to the regular army, which was itself too unruly and faction-ridden. Yet the more the regime relied upon the coercive instruments of the state to sustain itself, the more it was mortgaging itself to the security services, for some time now the most unreliable and unruly sectional group in Uganda.

Military Politics and Coup d'Etat

As Peter Willetts has noted, "Obote's greatest failure, and the one that made all his other achievements look somewhat hollow, was his unwillingness (or his inability) to tackle the privilege of unbridled power held by the Army."[40] Although the coup d'état that finally toppled Obote was largely a consequence of his estrangement from his chief of staff, Amin, the armed forces had long before become a destabilizing factor in their own right.

In 1964, a series of mutinies erupted in East Africa. They were sparked by various grievances and were regarded as essentially "pay-strikes." In Kenya and Tanzania, the mutinies were put down with varying degrees of firmness. But in Uganda the government equivocated, took little disciplinary action, and, indeed, virtually capitulated on the pay issue.[41] Subsequently, the armed forces were greatly augmented in strength; by 1967, they were the seventh largest on the continent, experiencing an average 48 percent annual increase and a 400 percent increase in defense allocations. Military salaries rapidly became the second highest in English-speaking Africa, and the military itself became a major venue for upward mobility.[42]

The vast expansion of armed forces provided opportunities for selective recruitment drives from favored ethnic groups. During the colonial era, the British tended to recruit from Acholi areas—allegedly because of the "martial" qualities and modest ambitions of the Acholi. Height criteria for new recruits also favored northern groups, including the Nubians. The policy of recruitment from Acholi areas was continued under Obote such that, by the late 1960s, the Ugandan armed forces included a large Nilotic component. Later, when Amin had risen to the top of the army command, he mounted recruitment drives in the far north of the country, especially among the Kakwa and, surreptitiously, also among Southern Sudanese refugees. Concentrating "his" recruits in certain key formations and juggling command appointments, Amin in effect strove to build up a force personally beholden to him. Between September 1970 and the 1971 coup, for example, twenty-two Nubian and Kakwa officers were appointed to the key Malire battalion; when the coup erupted in January, thirty-two of that battalion's forty-three officers either shared Amin's ethnicity or were personally loyal to him.

Fearing the potential threat posed by a unified army, Obote also practiced an array of "divide and rule" tactics. Operational commands were scrambled, different foreign military missions were appointed to train each battalion, competitions and jealousies among the army, navy, and air force were encouraged, and Obote's various protégés were played off against each other. In the long run, these tactics worked against the regime: Although they ensured that Amin would be able to move against Obote with only a small fraction of the highly divided army in 1971, the considerable pro-Obote support in the armed forces was internally much too divided to effectively ward off the power grab.[43]

Mutinous in 1964, heavily politicized during the UPC factional strife of 1964–1965, constantly used as a political prop by the regime, brutally unleashed on Kampala both in 1966 at the time of the clash with the Kabaka and in 1969 following the assassination attempt on Obote, the armed forces strutted around in the belief that they were above the law and co-equal with the government. (Amin had referred to himself as "part of the government" as far back as 1965.) Feared and disliked (particularly in Buganda), the army operated as an autonomous and highly unruly force, neither reprimanded by senior officers nor curbed by the political establishment. And at the head of the army stood Idi Amin, a totally unlettered Kakwa from the far north West Nile district, who had been promoted from auxiliary cook to chief of staff. One of only two indigenous officers at independence, Amin had become deputy chief of staff under Brigadier General Shaban Opolot. When the latter was purged during the 1966 Buganda crisis, Amin emerged in control of Uganda's military machine.

By 1970, however, a growing multifaceted rift had developed between Obote and his chief of staff. The two differed on a host of policies, especially Uganda's secret military support for the Anya Nya secessionist movement in southern Sudan and the necessity for autonomous security services such as the General Services Units. Amin was especially unable to get along with the force commander Akena Adoko, (who was responsible only to Obote) and (correctly) suspected him of being behind efforts to discredit him within the armed forces. The officer corps was seething with discontent at Amin's highly idiosyncratic manner of decisionmaking and frequent shuffles of operational commands. Moreover, in order to augment his personal following in the army, Amin had been conducting secret recruitment drives in his home-district, the West Nile—despite directives to increase the intake of Acholi-Langi conscripts—and was blocking the promotion of several of Obote's protégés (including Lieutenant Colonel David Oyite-Ojok), who were clearly being groomed to replace him.

The impetus for the 1971 coup d'état can be traced to the personal estrangement between Obote and Amin, and the looming threat to the latter's position at the head of the armed forces. "Promoted" away from direct operational control of troops to overall command of the armed forces, and surrounded and progressively forced to share authority with hand-picked northerner military officers, Amin was clearly being eased out of office. For aside from the various policy disagreements between the two men, Amin was under suspicion of a host of misdeeds, from embezzlement to murder. On January 25, 1970, Brigadier Pierino Yere Okaya—the army deputy Commander—was murdered outside his home, only days after publicly accusing Amin of cowardice at the time of the attempt on Obote's life.[44] The case was never satisfactorily resolved, although a number of officer suspects implicated Amin after torture. (One of these, Captain Guwedeko, was rapidly promoted to Brigadier after the 1971 coup.) Amin was also under pressure to account for the unauthorized expenditures (and/or embezzlement) of 35–40 million shillings of defense funds uncovered by the auditor-general's report. Leaving for the Singapore Commonwealth Conference, Obote had issued a strict ultimatum to Amin and Felix Onama (the Madi minister of defense) to account for the expenditures and to clear up Okaya's murder by the time of his return.

There are several versions of the events that occurred on January 25, 1971.[45] Amin's version is that, prior to his departure for Singapore, Obote left orders for a military takeover by Oyite-Ojok; that was nipped at the bud by personnel loyal to Amin, who then persuaded Amin to assume power. Obote's version refers to an Amin conspiracy to assassinate him upon his return from Singapore, which, when discovered by personnel loyal to Obote, precipitated a coup at an earlier date. Variations cited by others refer to the interception by staff loyal to Amin of a phone call from Singapore ordering Amin's arrest, resulting in the latter's preemptive coup. Whatever the precise causes of the upheaval, the coup was a purely personal power grab of an officer motivated by simple fear of eclipse, imprisonment, possibly even execution. Against such a background, it is not surprising that the regime that emerged in Kampala was a personal dictatorship, devoid of policy, guidelines, or consistency for the duration of the Amin interregnum.

Idi Dada Amin

"A latter-day Hitler or a simple soldier out of depth in international politics?" asked an early article in the *Sunday Times Magazine* as it surveyed some of Amin's post-coup behavior.[46] Less sanguine observers have suggested that Amin's bizarre actions, ravings, and cold-blooded brutalities stem from mental or physical disorders; representative choices include hypomania,[47] syphilis, manic-depressive attacks, and outright madness, although one journalist familiar with Amin regards it "neither true, nor adequate, to write him off as mad as many have done."[48] Still others have seen no anomaly in Amin's behavior, for if viewed as a "peasant-warrior" who is "not even semi-Westernized . . . at most sub-Westernized,"[49] he merely manifests the direct historical continuity of certain alleged African traditions.[50]

Amin was born in 1925 in Koboko county (the smallest in the West Nile District, itself the distant Sudanic fringe periphery of Uganda) to a Kakwa father (who had spent most of his life in Southern Sudan) and a Lugbara mother. His parents separated after Amin's birth, and his mother relocated with her son to the Nubian quarter of Lugazi, some 26 miles from Jinja (on Lake Victoria) near the Mehta family tea estates. There she consorted with military personnel, practicing witchcraft and traditional medicine, while young Amin peddled *mandazi* biscuits to assist the household income.

Amin joined the King's African Rifles in 1946 for want of a better career and served first as assistant cook. Unschooled, with a smattering of five languages but a total command of none, Amin nevertheless advanced in the army due to his physical prowess. He became Uganda's heavyweight boxing champion—retiring undefeated after holding the title for nine years—and endeared himself to his British officers by virtue of his athletic proclivities, including rugby. Muslim, uneducated, and with great physical strength and stamina, Amin was precisely the kind of material British officers seemed to prefer in the ranks of the colonial armies. In the infantry during the 1950s, Amin saw action in Kenya (against the Mau Mau);[51] in 1960–1962 (as lieutenant), he patrolled the Karamojong District in northeast Uganda. In both instances, charges of brutality nearly terminated his career, but he was treated leniently because of his other attributes. Attaining the highest rank an African could aspire to prior to independence (*effendi*) in 1960, Amin was one of two Ugandans to be commissioned—a fact that slated him to rapid promotion as the pace of Africanization in the armed forces quickened. Once he broke the NCO barrier, his routinized promotion could not be blocked. After each promotion, grudgingly given in light of his obvious limitations, he was regarded as definitely having reached his terminal rank; but he was promoted again and again in the absence of alternate local staff for senior office. Leapfrogging ranks, the unlettered NCO and former cook became colonel and chief of staff within six years.

Not surprisingly, the very same characteristics that had helped Amin move up the ranks in the armed forces were to become features of his military regime once he seized power. Specifically, force—the use or manipulation of brute force, at the personal level or in command positions—had always furthered Amin in his life and career. His strength, stamina, and willingness to use force compensated for attributes he did not possess—intelligence, insight, balanced judgment. His physique and stamina gained him entry into and later popularity within the colonial army. (According to his commanding officers, he was "a splendid chap, though a bit short on the grey matter.")[52] His sexual exploits (in the 1970s he had five wives and some thirty mistresses) won him barracks-room approbation. His zeal as an NCO (the tasks of which included the brutal "interrogation" of Mau Mau suspects) brought him promotion, and his unflinching use of force as Obote's "man" (in 1965, 1966, and 1969) led to further promotion to the summit of the military command. The values he had internalized and the "style" that had served him so well in the past—bulldozing opposition and the use of force to gain ascendancy—prompted him to order the liquidation of Okoya and to seize power. Once in control of Uganda, he institutionalized the use of murder, brutalization, and intimidation to "resolve" troublesome issues and societal problems; as a force-orientated dictator, he was prone to simplistic, unilateral, and "definitive" solutions.

In the past Amin had also been acutely deferential to his social superiors. British officers who served in East Africa have commented on the fawning docility he exhibited while under their command. Yet he internalized a host of resentments and grudges, remembered slights and degradations, and sought revenge against those unimpressed by him. As Martin put it, Amin was "a man with a big grudge—against all the real and imagined slights he feels he has suffered throughout his life"—a man who sought adulation and smiling approbation; "when it was not forthcoming he would bludgeon it out of them."[53] Once in power, he vented his pent-up wrath against all those toward whom he bore a grudge—the Asians, whom he expelled; the expatriates, whom he humiliated (by demanding that they carry him on a litter); and the staff college–trained officer corps, whose snickers had stung most and whom he hounded ferociously, liquidating all and sundry.

Truly "a man of the people" in a way that few African leaders have ever been, Amin brought into the policymaking domain all the simplistic notions, preconceptions, superstitions (guided by a Ghanaian soothsayer), parochialism, and prejudices of the "Common Man" that Obote could only talk about. Amin *was* the Common Man writ large, despite the high rank he had attained in the army, and he carried "cultural inputs into the political process in Uganda derived from his peasant origins. His entire style of diplomacy is striking for its lack of middle class refinements."[54] Few observers realized in 1971 that one of Uganda's most "marginal" men, heading a "lumpen-proletariat . . . class of semi-organized, rugged, and semi-literate soldiery,"[55] had actually seized power.

Despite his high rank and military authority, Amin always felt isolated and threatened within the military hierarchy. Never comfortable in the company of better-educated colleagues in the officer corps, and aware of their disdain over his deficiencies, Amin fraternized with junior personnel from the Sudanic and Nubian component of the armed forces. Nubian, Lugbara, and Kakwa NCOs; personal drivers and orderlies; illiterate Sudanese Anya Nya guerrillas surreptitiously recruited into the Ugandan army against Obote's orders—these were his true comrades. In any crisis, whenever his status was threatened, these were the friends and peers who sustained him in power.[56] And once he seized power, these were the individuals he promoted to top command positions.

In April 1971, for example, Amin promoted his personal orderly and driver, Private Ismail, directly to the rank of captain. Regimental Sergeant-Major Waris Ali became lieutenant colonel and commanding officer of the battalion stationed at Mbarara (where he was later implicated in the Stroh/Seidle murders); signals sergeant-major Beka became major and chief signals officer; and another signals sergeant-major, Musa, who played a key role in the coup was directly promoted to lieutenant colonel and commander of the Malire Mechanized Regiment. Indeed, the commanding general of the important Eastern Brigade in 1977, and a year later the chief of staff of the armed forces, had been a Southern Sudanese *tractor driver* in the prison service at the time of the 1971 coup d'état. Two other battalion commanders had been corporals, another a private, and a fourth an NCO in an army dance troupe before they were tapped for higher callings.

Officers who had proven their personal loyalty prior to the coup were similarly rewarded with high office and promotion. Captain Smuts Guwedeko (jailed for his role in the Okoya murder) was promoted within two years to brigadier general and commander of the air force; Lieutenant Hussein Malera, who spearheaded the extermination of all Acholi and Langi in the armed forces, was by 1974 brigadier general and acting chief of staff; Captain Charles Arube, a Kakwa, was by June 1972 brigadier general and chief of staff (but when he later ran afoul of Amin, he was murdered and dumped in the Nile). Scores of other examples can be cited as Amin restructured the ethnic and intellectual composition of the armed forces according to his own image. By 1977, of the top twenty-two officers in the army, seventeen were Muslim (in a country where only 10 percent profess Islam) and thirteen were from the West Nile District (the smallest in Uganda); among the latter, fully seven were Kakwa, four were Southern Sudanese, two were Nubians, and only three came from the rest of Uganda's ethnicities, which constituted 98 percent of the population.[57] The rank and file likewise reflected this highly skewed ethnic distribution. Indeed, by 1977, the vast majority of the troops were *non-nationals* (50 percent Sudanese and Nubians, 25 percent Zairiens), linked together by prospects of plunder and loot, power and mayhem.

Unfamiliar and impatient with the intricacies of government and administration, Amin ruled in the style of an oriental potentate. Cabinet ministers learned of policy decisions affecting their departments over the radio, as government by whim or gut-reaction became the norm. Those who tried to restrain Amin's impulses were physically abused; some were liquidated. The state treasury became an extension of his private coffers. Unbudgeted and unaccountable expenditures became common,[58] and the Bank of Uganda was routinely ordered to print more currency to "solve" the attendant problem of budgetary deficits. Although no accounts were kept, it is estimated that up to 50 pecent of available funds every year went toward the maintenance of the highly unruly armed forces, Amin's main prop and instrument of repression.

In the process, the Ugandan economy was thoroughly pulverized, pluntered, and looted. The cultivation of traditional cash-crops plummeted as farmers shifted to subsistence crops—now vital for their physical survival in an economy characterized by acute scarcity of both foodstuffs and consumer goods. Inflation soared by 1,000 percent and smuggling across the Kenya border reached monumental proportions as producers bypassed state hierarchies to barter their crops for commodities unobtainable locally. But even more important was the fact that entire societal strata—business people, professionals, Asians, civil servants, and educators—were either physically liquidated or driven into exile, producing a huge Ugandan diaspora abroad and acute manpower shortages at home. Estimates of the people brutally murdered during the Amin era (around 250,000) are a sad testimonial to the ravages under Amin of the former "pearl of East Africa." When in March 1976 Makerere University conferred upon Amin an honorary Ph.D., his eulogy included the phrase that "never in history has a leader done so much for his people in so short a time";[59] but the phrase "*to* his people" would be a more fitting epitaph of Amin's eight-year reign.

Personal Dictatorship and Societal Terror

Amin's 1971 coup was a personalist takeover spearheaded by a minority of the armed forces. Although Obote's ouster was greeted with a great deal of rejoicing in Buganda (and among Asians, who hoped for a rollback of Obote's socialist policies), neither the officer corps nor the bulk of the rank and file of the armed forces were truly supportive of the takeover. Yet Obote's divide-and-rule tactics had encouraged factionalism and division in the military, preventing the instant mobilization against Amin of pro-Obote loyalties in the armed forces. Resistance to Amin's coup was immediate and, at times, surprisingly fierce; but it was also highly disorganized and leaderless, and hence quite easily localized and crushed.

Aware of his own precarious position and of the fact that the ethnic composition of the armed forces was fundamentally inimical to his leadership, Amin was preoccupied, immediately after the coup, with consolidating his paramountcy within the military. The result was the brutal liquidation of most of the original officer corps and well over one-half of the rank and file of the armed forces, as well as the promotion to command positions of his old NCO cronies. By 1974, only three (13 percent) of the army's original twenty-three officers of the rank of lieutenant colonel and above (not counting Amin himself) were still in the service, and indeed, over one-half of the new officer corps was of pre-1971 NCO origin.

Despite the surplus of detailed documentation on Amin's brutalities, the horrors that transpired in Ugandan military camps and across the country were largely discounted at the time, even by diplomats residing in Kampala. All along, extermination squads composed of Nubian and Sudanese elements (e.g., the 3,000-man State Research Bureau, and the Public Safety units headed by the dreaded Nubi Ali Towelli) scoured Ugandan garrisons and purged entire ethnic groups, tracking and murdering key officers who had escaped the original dragnet. Lango and Acholi officers and troops were sought out in particular. According to one report, "From Mbarara to Moyo, Acholi and Lango servicemen were shot, hacked and clubbed to death by fellow soldiers."[60] The massacres rapidly spread to include elements of nearly every ethnic group in Uganda as unrest broke out in various garrisons. A rebellion was staged even by the elite Malire Mechanized Regiment, composed of Kakwa, Lugbara, and Madi personnel who were previously under the personal command of Amin and his prime power prop. After the revolt was crushed, its personnel were dispersed among the other battalions.

Simultaneous with the fratricide in the army, a massive bloodbath commenced, cutting a swath across Uganda as troops nominally under Amin's orders (although they often acted autonomously) initiated a reign of terror. Settling personal accounts, they arbitrarily arrested all and sundry, and executed real and imagined sources of opposition. An early decree in 1971 empowered the military to arrest anyone (including cabinet ministers) on the mere suspicion of sedition, setting the army above the law and holding it accountable to nobody. Many innocents were caught in these dragnets, becoming victims of the liquidation meatgrinder at the merest pretext or suspicion. In 1971, for example, sixty young Baganda volunteered for military service, having constituted the honor guard for Kabaka Mutesa's coffin, which was being repatriated from London; but they were casually murdered to keep the army "free" of Ganda personnel whose motivations for military service appeared suspect. Foreign (i.e., Kenyan and Tanzanian) personnel of the East African community services in Kampala and Entebbe were likewise swooped into the dragnets and murdered, triggering diplomatic complaints from Uganda's neighbors. In 1975, more than 600 civilians were killed in Moro (the capital of Karamojong) when a farmer killed a soldier for raping his wife and the army was called out to quell this "guerilla disturbance."[61]

By the end of Amin's first year in office, up to 10,000 people may have lost their lives; by the time Amin was ousted from power, as many as 250,000 were dead. Thousands of Uganda's most respected politicians, educators, administrators, entrepreneurs, and professionals had "disappeared" (a euphemism for liquidation), their bodies often dumped in the Nile to be consumed by crocodiles; Karume Falls Bridge, which spanned the Nile and was the preferred disposal site for Amin's victims, became popularly known as the Bridge of Blood. An early attempt by two Americans to confirm one massacre (in the Mbarara barracks) resulted in their own casual murder at the hands of the deputy commander, Major Juma, a taxi driver prior to 1971. As the United States would not allow such an incident to be brushed under the carpet, Amin finally had to appoint a Commission of Inquiry. The British presiding judge verified the atrocity and mailed the report from Nairobi, having fled Kampala in fear for his life.[62]

The reign of terror triggered internal population dislocations as well as emigrations to neighboring countries. Large numbers of Acholi/Lango soldiers fled the massacres into neighboring Tanzania (where they were integrated into a loyalist Obote force) or Kenya; they were later joined by thousands of civilians, including some of Amin's cabinet ministers and wives, who were also fleeing for their lives. "Political murder has become institutionalized in Uganda," commented *The Guardian*; "fear has become a weapon of government."[63] Within Uganda, urban dwellers fled to the greater sanctuary of their home villages, even as entire rural communities, exposed to the ravages of undisciplined troops and the vengeance of liquidation squads, relocated to more secure areas in the bush; away from roads, means of communication, and modernity. Some villages became virtually depopulated; others saw the decimation of large numbers of their male population. Patterns of cultivation and commerce shifted as the economy collapsed. The growing of subsistence crops became vital for survival, and the collapse of trade and commerce after the 1973 expulsion of Uganda's Asian community reintroduced barter as a substitute for commerce based upon money.

The huge gaps in the army caused by the ethnic massacres were rapidly filled by illiterate and ill-trained recruits, many of them nonnationals. It was this group that became the most powerful stratum in society. Four thousand new recruits joined the army in 1971 alone, enlisted from the Nubian, Sudanese, Zairien, Rwandese, Madi, and Lugbara communities,[64] and the proportion of the first four groups in the armed forces increased over the years as the others in due time began to be regarded as untrustworthy. At the outset, Nubi and Kakwa personnel alone had access to the garrison armories; but after Amin lost the confidence of his own kinsmen, the Nubi Muslims, "a very tiny priority of the population, [came to] hold every key position in the Defence Council, the Government and the Army."[65] A mercenary army came into being. By 1977, nearly three-quarters of its troops were non-Ugandan in origin.

Soon Amin's forces exceeded in strength the pre-1971 army, ongoing purges notwithstanding; by 1977, their numbers stood at 21,000, triple their original complement. Less than one-quarter of the original army was intact, and given its repressive duties and non-national composition, it was more of an alien occupation force than a defense force. Sharply differentiated from Ugandan society on practically every dimension—social, ethnic, educational, and religious—and only loosely controlled from Kampala, the armed forces were a coterie of unruly and autonomous occupation garrisons responsible for the control and repression of specific regions, living off the land by terrorizing farmers, and headed by illiterate petty warlords with the power of life and death over their fiefdoms. In all respects, Uganda had become "A Lawless State," as the International Commission of Jurists referred to it in a 1973 report.[66]

Although some observers have detected "phases" in Amin's brutalization of Uganda, any attempt to systematize (chronologically or ethnically) his killings and repression tends to be meaningless when viewed from the perspective of his eight years in power. At the outset the main groups to suffer were the Lango, Acholi, and (to a lesser extent) the Iteso (with a further pogrom of these groups in 1976); but by the time Amin was ousted, every ethnic group, including his own, had been ravaged and alienated.

The disaffection of a single officer, the discovery of a plot, an assassination attempt, or the voicing of the slightest criticism (even the rumour of any such occurrence) was more than sufficient grounds for a wave of indiscriminate killings of entire groups of people.[67] After the ill-fated September 1972 invasion from Tanzania, for example, the Ankole population in the Mbarara area felt Amin's wrath for joyfully welcoming Obote's advancing troops. A 1972 Lugbara conspiracy to overthrow Amin (due to grievances expressed over the ascendance of the Nubians in the army) resulted in the deaths of hundreds of Lugbara. The 1974 mutiny, spearheaded by the (Christian) Kakwa chief of staff, Brigadier Charles Arube (captain in 1971), led to a selective but thorough purge of the army's Kakwa ethnic component (concentrating upon Christian personnel) and the elite Malire Mechanized Regiment. More than 500 men of that unit were killed in the reprisals that followed the mutiny, as Amin pulverized the regiment that had helped him come to power and that he had viewed as the most reliable in the army. Punitive expeditions were subsequently dispatched to the West Nile District to teach the region "a lesson." Amin's own father, old and sick, joined the refugee stream to Sudan in fear for his life, as the army spread havoc and panic in Amin's home area.[68] Telling is the fact that in 1979 the West Nile greeted the advancing Tanzanian army as liberators, as did other areas of Uganda.

By 1975, Amin could not feel secure even with his own ethnic group. He had received warnings from tribal elders that a popular rebellion would follow if any more Alur, Madi, Lugbara, or Kakwa troops or farmers were victimized.[69] Partly because of these warnings, all except one of the Lugbara officers to rebel (Colonel Michael Ondogo) were "forgiven" their sins and gently shunted from sensitive posts; likewise, the Malire massacres (and Arube's execution) were the only ones affecting Kakwa personnel. The only elements to remain loyal to Amin to the bitter end—and who fought for the regime in 1979—were the "foreigners" and assorted social outcasts in the army. To them, Amin's reign had been their only opportunity for social advancement, employment (as soldiers), status, and pecuniary gain. And, having fled into exile in 1979, they continued to harass northern Uganda after liberation with their armed banditry assaults from across the border.

Thus, starting with a measure of popular acclaim (if only among groups that bore grievances against Obote), Amin turned out to be his own greatest enemy, alienating every stratum in society—quite apart from the fact that Uganda's army, "with a record of mutiny, of slaughtering each other, of bullying private citizens, and of building up among themselves tribal cliques,"[70] could hardly have been considered capable of providing stable government.

Every societal group was affected by the brutality emanating from Kampala and the garrison towns; no one was immune. The countryside simmered with discontent as military units plundered it. The cities felt the full brunt of the shattered economy as tens of thousands lost their jobs or prospects of employed labor with the departure of the Asian community. Entire economic sectors—including tourism, Uganda's second-largest cash earner in 1971—simply disappeared.

Intellectuals, civil servants, and teachers felt the brunt of Amin's anti-education bias. Many were fired in order to provide employment opportunities for less qualified or totally incompetent Nubians and Muslims in general; others, rejecting the intellectual aridity of the Amin administration, fled to safety abroad. Christians, always resentful of the powerful pro-Muslim bias that accompanied Amin's rise to power, were traumatized by the 1977 murder of Archbishop Janani Luwum and by Amin's attempt to pass off the murder as a highway accident.

At least twenty-two known and identifiable plots, conspiracies, mutinies, or attempted assassinations punctuated Amin's eight years in office. Virtually every group in the army and every key military leader of yesteryear was involved in a plot against Amin, including (in 1978) his most trusted Kakwa-Nubian lieutenants. His motorcar convoys were ambushed numerous times; his residence was invaded by vengeance-seeking troops; officers turned up to "arrest" him as well as to beg him to step down for the good of the nation; his wives and mistresses betrayed him to his enemies; and there were even attempts (in 1974) to shoot down his plane during state flights to and from Nairobi and Mogadishu.

In every instance, Amin's "paranoic makeup,"[71] suspicious nature, and attention to security saved him. He constantly switched the routes of his motorcades and flight plans; he rotated conjugal visits to his wives and mistresses so that no one could guess his whereabouts; and he often drove around in modest nonescorted vehicles while his official limousines (at times with a "double" in it) attracted ambushes and grenade attacks. He never attempted compromise, however, and his crude humor did not know mercy; nor was he ever afraid of world disapprobation as he pursued his bloody path through Ugandan history.

Administrative and Economic Decay

Amin's Uganda was not a *military* dictatorship but a *personal* dictatorship headed by the chief of staff. Uganda became the personal fiefdom of a brutal despot, within which there was no semblance of law and order, established administration, or set policy guidelines. This was a tyranny where personal whims dictated policy, expertise played no role in government and administration, the economy was but a source of plunder for the ruling elite, and foreign policy was rooted in the whims and biases of the paramount leader.

None of this was obvious at the outset. Amin commenced his reign with the typical pledges of a brief military interregnum aimed at correcting Obote's "ill-conceived" ideas and "politically motivated" Move to the Left programs. Following this interim administration, competitive politics were to be reintroduced and Obote himself was to be given a chance to seek another term in office. Most political prisoners were released; the General Service Unit was dismantled, the state of emergency in Buganda was lifted, and Obote's recent economic decrees were rescinded. Specifically, commodities previously centralized under the commercial monopoly of parastatal agencies were decontrolled, and (much to the satisfaction of Asian and foreign elements) the state share in foreign companies was reduced from 60 percent to 49 percent. Moreover, Amin's first cabinet, though not especially distinguished, did include an ethnically balanced group of technocrats and only one military officer. Abu Mayanja, the veteran KY leader, was also included in an effort to garner support from Buganda.

It rapidly became clear, however, that Amin was not an administrator; he was not capable of relegating authority or reaching balanced decisions, nor was he ever really concerned about providing Uganda with good government. Rational planning, the weighing of alternatives, and fiscal restraint were quite beyond this man of impulses and whims. Martin has noted that "Amin finds it well-nigh impossible to sit in an office for a day. He cannot concentrate on any serious topic for half a morning. He does not read. He cannot write. The sum total of all these disabilities makes it impossible for him either to sit in the regular cabinet meeting, to follow up cabinet minutes, or to comprehend the briefs written to him by his ministers."[72]

Amin's poor and broken English put him at a disadvantage in sessions with his ministers—and his Luganda was little better. Addressing various audiences throughout the country (in several dialects and in gutter language), debating parochial issues (venereal disease, wigs, the propriety of trousers for women, crop planting, and monogamy), Amin, with his extroverted personality and his penchant for "meeting the masses," has been likened to "an American candidate in a Presidential election campaign."[73]

Intimidated by his more competent and better-educated ministers, Amin delighted in undermining their authority and mocking their helplessness. Cabinet meetings rapidly became meaningless as Amin, in his boredom, stopped attending them. By 1972, all pretense that the cabinet was playing a role in decisionmaking had disappeared. Major policy announcements (often contradictory or unimplementable) were personally proclaimed by Amin without consultation with his ministers—indeed, often while the cabinet itself was grappling with the issues involved. As the defecting Minister of Finance Andrew Wakhweya summed it up in 1975, "The government is a one-man show. Impossible decisions are taken by General Amin which ministers are expected to implement. The decisions bear no relationship to the country's available resources."[74] Ministers who dared either to contradict Amin or to restrain some of his more extravagant impulses were at times physically brutalized or handwhipped by him. In fact, the entire cabinet was symbolically "recruited" into the army, making ministers liable to summary military discipline: The more educated were eventually "replaced by less literate people so that [Amin] could communicate with them."[75] In due time, many ministers (including his own brother-in-law and foreign minister) joined the flight of Ugandan intellectuals to sanctuary in Kenya or Tanzania.

Totally frustrated by what he perceived as petty debates and absurd technicalities during cabinet meetings, and intimidated by the mere presence of his ministers, Amin in 1973 ordered his cabinet on a nine-month "vacation," following which he integrated into its membership some of his military cronies. By 1975, the body had become largely military in composition (most of its members were NCOs prior to 1971) and overwhelmingly Muslim and Nubi as well. Indeed, by 1977, only two of the twenty-two ministers were Christian, although only 20 percent of the twenty-two (skilled) permanent secretaries were Muslim. At all times the Defense Council (the supreme military body that, on paper, "collegially" ruled Uganda, and to which Amin was "accountable") was of much greater importance than the cabinet—but not because of the military personalities within that body (as noted, most had been NCOs and orderlies before the 1971 coup and were even less sophisticated than Amin). Rather, this was the only grouping of his *true* social and cultural peers, within which Amin could deliberate state "policy" in the vernacular—often in all-night semidrunken beerhall sessions the "conclusions" of which were forgotten the next day, unrecorded and irrelevant.

Rarely consulting his ministers or senior civil servants, Amin based his state policy on gut reactions and personal whims. At times, even dreams, "divine guidance," and inspiration from his soothsayers were the source of his decrees, as was allegedly the case in his decision to expel Uganda's Asian community. But since policy emanated from neither structures nor hierarchies, nor was it entrusted for implementation (where feasible) to the bureaucracy, the gap between rhetoric and reality was always immense in Amin's Uganda. Policies were announced and edicts were published, but (except for matters of particular concern to Amin) few were implemented or followed up. Consequently, the extreme centralization of decisionmaking power in Amin's hands went hand in hand with acute administrative chaos; dictatorial power coupled with bureaucratic anarchy best described the situation in Kampala. As one correspondent put it, "it is not that the right hand does not know what the left hand is doing: the right thumb does not know what the right index finger has done."[76] Or as Colin Legum summed it up, "the General has singularly failed to produce an effective or stable military or political group at the center of power."[77]

Amin's impulsive, crude, and aggressive style also manifested itself in the domain of international relations, into which he constantly intruded. After early attempts on the part of ministers and diplomats to restrain Amin's crude, inchoate outbursts (or at least to rephrase his intemperate tantrums into more grammatically correct English), Amin's highly personal, uninhibited, and offensive messages and international pronouncements to world leaders became an embarrassing fixture on the international scene.

Commenting on Amin's curious popularity *outside* his own country, his clown-like image notwithstanding, an African diplomat in Nairobi noted that "the common men in Africa look up to him as fearless, as a great man, because he goes around saying what he thinks."[78]

Certainly Amin's surgical "solution" to the "Asian problem"—in the process standing up to and defying Great Britain—brought him instant adulation in many parts of Africa. His adding insult to injury by commencing a banana and vegetables "Save Britain Fund" (to assist that country in its economic woes), and other pronouncements (such as "offering [himself] to be appointed Head of the Commonwealth" in 1975), were likewise diplomatically crude but popular acts of thumbing the nose at the ex-imperial power. Nor did he hesitate to retaliate against Britain's suspension of aid after his Asian expulsions: Thirty-six British enterprises were nationalized in January 1973, and some eighty-seven more shortly were to close down as a mini-exodus of Britons developed. He humiliated the British foreign minister by forcing him to visit Kampala as part of the deal to release the hapless Dennis Hills and, in a much-publicized event, had himself regally carried in a litter by British expatriates. Yet, when in 1977 his various antics and taunts finally led to a rupture of relations with Britain (a step Britain rarely takes, no matter what the provocation), Amin reportedly could not grasp the reason for this "unfriendly" action.

In similar manner, Amin's original admiration for Israel (where he had earned his paratroopers wings)[79] rapidly turned into antagonism when his ambitions were frustrated by Jerusalem. Only months after coming to power, he shocked the Israeli government (then still his ally consequent to treaties signed under Obote) by requesting war materiel for the conquest of the Tanzanian port of Tanga, aimed at giving Uganda a sea outlet. A year later, enticed by promises of vast state aid from Libya's Qadaffi, he terminated all treaties with Israel and ordered Israeli personnel to vacate the country within a week. (The Israelis had anticipated this move and had transferred some of their costly construction machinery to Kenya, but debts totaling $50 million were left outstanding.)[80]

Continuing his anti-Israel vendetta, which earned him Libya's gratitude and military support right through the final phase of the 1979 Tanzanian invasion, Amin intimidated neighboring Rwanda into breaking relations with Israel by threatening to cut all transit trade through Uganda and to bomb Kigali into oblivion. Amin offered the Arab world a "masterplan" to destroy Israel in 24 hours, but in a three-day military exercise simulating the capture of the Golan Heights, 199 of the participating Ugandan troops were injured. He applauded the 1972 Munich Olympics murder of Israeli athletes, lauded Hitler's genocidal policies (even proposing to erect a monument to Hitler),[81] and deluged Jerusalem with a series of offensive telegrams. Though there is some question as to whether he had foreknowledge of the 1976 PLO hijacking of the Air France flight to Kampala (of Entebbe Operation fame), once it landed he certainly gave the terrorists his full support.[82]

Amin alternated between criticizing (alleged) Chinese aid for the Obote attempted comeback in 1972 and then inviting Mao for a state visit to Kampala; he likewise alternated between supporting a "dialogue" with Pretoria and, when rebuffed, offering "master-plans" for the liberation of South Africa. After warmly welcoming a French company that had come to make a film on him (a film that he prescreened upon its completion and heartily approved, entitled "Idi Amin Dada: No One Can Run Faster than a Bullet"), he threatened the arrest of all French people in Uganda unless the film was withdrawn from circulation in

France when it started to draw the laughter of huge audiences. He caused jitters in Rwanda by hosting the exiled and dethroned ex-Mwami, and he laid territorial claims against portions of neighboring states, including Rwanda, Kenya, Sudan, and Tanzania. Enraged over the withdrawal of U.S. aid after the Stroh/Seidl murders, he sent a highly undiplomatic cable to Nixon alluding to the latter's Watergate troubles and appointed an army private as permanent representative to Washington until such time as the United States had a "new president and government." When some of his more aggressive postures were vigorously countered, however, Amin backed down. An effort to foment Luo irredentism in Kenya was hastily terminated when Nairobi imposed an economic blockade on landlocked Uganda; and the appearance of U.S. naval units off the Kenya coast likewise terminated a plan to expel or arrest all U.S. residents following American criticism of Bishop Luwum's murder.

Following Amin's rise to power, Uganda's relations with most states deteriorated (Libya, Saudi Arabia, and Eastern Europe were the exceptions). Its relations with Tanzania were by far the most tense. President Julius Nyerere categorically refused to recognize Amin's rise to power, declared he would never sit at a conference table with a murderer, and granted Obote political refuge in Dar-es-Salaam. Reports of the ethnic massacres and civil unease in Uganda hardened Tanzania's posture even further, paving the road for the ill-fated invasion of Uganda by Obote's 1,000-odd troops from Tanzania on September 17, 1972. The operation was a disaster. Headed by Colonel David Oyite-Ojok and Lieutenant Colonel Tito Okello (both of whom later led the successful 1979 invasion), the sloppy land-air assault was greeted enthusiastically by the Ankole, through whose territory the force passed; but it did not produce the anticipated popular uprising in Kampala. Few bastions of pro-Obote sentiment remained in the army after eighteen months of massacres and purges, and the Baganda—the main ethnic group of the capital—certainly had no desire to bring their former tormentor back to power. Indeed, as he basked in the popularity of his anti-Asian decrees (and not the reverse, as was assumed in Dar-es-Salaam!), Amin easily repulsed the invading force with only limited Libyan/Palestinian assistance. (Some 399 Palestinian troops, whose efficiency in combat had never been tested, were flown in by Libya.) After this humiliating debacle, Nyerere—without letting up on either his opposition to Amin or his commitment to the liberation of Uganda—shackled Obote's army. The soldiers were demobilized and channeled into agricultural activities until 1979, when they were hastily forged again into a fighting force and sent into Uganda alongside the Tanzanian Army.

The "Solution" to the "Asian Problem"

Possibly no action of Amin was so domestically popular as his August 9, 1972, expulsion of noncitizens from Uganda, which exorcised the Asian economic stranglehold in Uganda. Popular though it was, the decree stemmed from Amin's personal bias against Asians; and, apart from its cruel inequity to a hitherto highly productive community, it hammered the last nail on the coffin of the Ugandan economy. The decision to expel the Asian community[83] was, according to Amin, inspired by divine guidance in the form of a dream, part of his oft-stated communion with the Heavens. (He had also claimed that the date, and manner, of his own death had been revealed to him.) At the same time, however, the decree constituted a very shrewd policy calculated to shore up support for Amin's regime by tapping deep-rooted anti-Indian prejudices in the country, even as the confiscation of the vast tangible assets of the community (shops, restaurants, estates, houses, etc.) promised to provide a flood of loot for his followers.

The August decree came after a number of harangues against the Asians' lack of assimilation into Ugandan society, their alleged monopolistic practices, and their basic disloyalty to Uganda.[84] In December 1971, some 12,000 pending Asian applications for Ugandan citizenship were rejected, sparking an early exodus of traders who could see the handwriting on the wall. Finally, in August 1972, the entire 70,000-strong community was ordered out of Uganda (with a minimum of possessions and funds) within three months. Diplomatic entreaties by England and other international organizations failed to sway Amin's decision, and the widely reported details of the crude manner in which he carried out the actual expulsion brought Amin world notoriety.[85]

The immediate repercussions of the expulsions were devastating, even if some advantages (e.g., the irrevocable transfer to national hands of most economic activity, the termination of capital outflow, and the foreign exchange drain on luxury consumer imports) also ensued. Trade and commerce collapsed, especially in the countryside, and never truly revived. The 4,000 of so vacated shops and enterprises, depleted of stock and plundered by the military, were re-allocated to the nationals by a committee composed of civilian and military officials, with the choice properties ending up in the hands of either army officers or highly connected civilians. A class of military shopkeepers briefly emerged in Uganda as officers and NCOs competed for larger shares of the spoils of military rule. Rapidly milked dry of their existing merchandise, most shops were abandoned after a very short time. Scarcity of local consumer goods and foreign exchange prevented the replenishment of stocks, and utter mismanagement and undercapitalization by the new owners rapidly eliminated from the productive commercial sector as many as 80 percent of Uganda's private enterprises. Milk, sugar, matches, salt, soap, bread, and other staples, became scarce commodities overnight, traded (when available) at about ten times the official price. Domestic cash crops started bypassing state purchasing agencies as vast smuggling rings developed—and the resultant *magendo* economic system survives to this day in Uganda.[86]

The Asians, moreover, were not only an economic and trading elite but also a major reservoir of professional skills and a source of employment. As many Ugandan families had employed 2-3 domestic servants each, as well as numerous other employees in the shops and enterprises, the Asian expulsion caused up to 50,000 servants to lose their jobs and brought about massive dismissals in the commercial and industrial sectors. These jobs were never filled, and many of the unemployed drifted into crime and brigandage.

The expulsion also swept out of the country thousands of skilled administrators and irreplaceable doctors, dentists, veterinarians, professors, and technicians. With their manpower cut by 50 to 75 percent, hospitals, schools, garages, and repair shops were forced to eliminate vital services; efficiency plummeted and entire sectors of enterprise collapsed. Indeed, the professional role of the Asians in Uganda had been so critical, and the post-expulsion dislocation in the country was so serious, that in due time large numbers of Indians, Pakistanis, and Arab professionals had to be recruited at very heavy cost to replace the Asians who had been expelled.

Government revenues likewise plummeted, because the Asian community, despite its modest size, had carried a very high percentage of the country's tax burden. At one stroke, Uganda forfeited 38 percent of its normal recurrent revenues[87]—a loss that occurred on a regular basis since none of the new economic landlords who replaced the Asians paid any taxes. The revenue shortfalls and higher import costs merged with the general post-1971 mismanagement of the economy to produce a perennially acute economic morass. The cost of living zoomed up by 152 percent between 1971 and 1974, and rose by a further estimated 239 percent between 1974 and 1979. (In 1978 petrol cost US$24 a gallon; a bar of soap cost $7.) In the late 1970s, inflation was running at the rate of 70 percent a year. Smuggling, which had reached monumental proportions (with 6 million shillings worth of coffee leaving the country illegally daily), was decreed a capital offence, and an economic police squad headed by a naturalized Briton (Bob Astles) was set up to stem the commodity outflow. All economic indicators (in both absolute and per capita terms) had declined significantly, including gross domestic product. Tax receipts, especially after 1975, were at a fraction of pre-1971 levels. Crop production was at an all-time low: In 1976, for example, cotton production was below 1948 levels, coffee exports were 40 percent below those of 1971, and copper exports were virtually nil. Vast unbudgeted expenditures for Amin's pet projects, and weekly cargo shipments from London of liquor, electronic and luxury goods, and gourmet food for Amin and the officer corps made a mockery of any pretense at fiscal management of the economy. When local funds were needed, new currency was printed—contributing to the 1,000 percent debasement of the Uganda shilling. And when foreign exchange was in short supply, debts were left outstanding, totally eroding the creditworthiness of Uganda. By 1976, most international suppliers (especially of oil and machinery) were demanding cash prepayment for any shipments destined for Uganda—the first time in the postwar era that any country had been regarded as intrinsically unreliable in its international financial dealings.[88]

The Collapse of a Dictator

In 1978, the core of Amin's power base crumbled. Until then, "Amin's sensitive understanding of the interlocking family and clan interests of the West Nile," as reflected in the composition of the Defense Council, which constituted the inner circle of Amin's family and cronies, "[explained] why the dissatisfaction characteristic of all the other provinces . . . did not materialize in the Far North except sporadically."[89] When Amin's Nubi-Kakwa alliance collapsed, the regime became ripe for overthrow. Yet long before the Tanzanian invasion, the Ugandan military had become an empty shell. Constant purges of the officer corps, the ossification of all training programs, the total absence of military discipline, the dozens of mutinies in every garrison and their bloody repression all attested to the fact that the Ugandan armed forces could hardly be relied upon to provide an effective military bulwark in the event of an external threat.

The Ugandan Defense Council was chaired by Amin, with General Mustafa Adrisi (an uncle, and minister of defense and interior) as vice-chairman. Other members included Major-General Isaac Lumago (a cousin, and chief of staff); Colonel Hassan Taban (a nephew, and the particularly nasty and rowdy commander of the Libyan-trained "elite" Marines), and Brigadier General Isaac Maliyamunya (also a nephew and a notoriously sadistic killer). By 1978, both a blood feud and the disintegration of the core clique had triggered the "disappearance" or demotion of Amin's hitherto most loyal companions.

The core clique fell apart as the result of some very fundamental divisions over precisely the question of whether a regime buttressed by such an unreliable and coercive force as the Ugandan army could remain in power. Much more aware of the long-run implications of Uganda's isolation and bankruptcy, the Lugbara Adrisi wished to improve the cost-benefits of the Amin dictatorship by transforming the army into a *national* force of (northern) groups with a stake in the continuation of th regime—a commitment its then non-national members (who could always flee home to Zaire or Sudan) did not necessarily possess. Amin's contrary preference for a largely Nubi force—virtually a mercenary army—was a function of his having already thoroughly alienated his own Kakwa ethnic group; it was possibly also due to his own suspected clandestine Nubi origins.[90]

This highly polarizing issue (complicated by a shootout between Adrisi and Taban) was resolved in typical Amin style with the 1978 demotion or "disappearance" of several of the dictator's former close collaborators. Adrisi, crippled in a car "accident," returned chastised and powerless from his hospital stay in Cairo to a Supreme Defense Council purged of three key ministers, two formerly omnipotent security heads, and certain others—most of whom were part of the Adrisi faction. These included General Ali Towelli, the former dreaded head of the Public Security Unit and chief executioner of the regime; the ruthless Lieutenant Colonel Juma Oris (Minister of Foreign Affairs) and Brigadier Moses Ali (Minister of Finance), both of whom were involved in the extremely embarrassing embezzlement of Saudi and Libyan funds for cultural-religious institutions that threatened to dry up Uganda's sole remaining source of foreign aid; and Major General Isaac Lumago, the then Nubi Christian chief of staff (who was replaced by a Muslim Nubi, Major General Yufu Gowon).

The factional in-fighting at the summit of power merged with another bout of mutinies across the country over the perennial delays in the payment of salaries; demands were made for more free beer and an end to the preferential treatment granted to Nubians in the army. In order to divert attention from the revolt (which spread like wildfire from garrison to garrison), and in order to create conditions that might allow Saudi/Libyan "forgiveness" of the embezzled funds that, contrary to the two states' demands, could not be refunded in view of Uganda's bankruptcy, Amin once again evoked the Tanzanian bogeyman, claiming that fighting had erupted on the Tanzanian border; he also appealed for vigilance and national unity. The most rebellious troops were shipped south to repel the "invasion," and Arab military and financial aid was urgently solicited. (Libya responded generously, shelving the embezzlement dispute.) Then, in a typical flight of fancy, and "having fought an entirely imaginary war with Tanzania, . . . Amin announced on November 1, 1978, that in reprisal for 'Tanzania's invasion' he had annexed the Kagera Salient"[91] of Tanzania. Ugandan troops promptly moved into the Tanzanian territory, plundering it of all it possessed.

Though taken by surprise by the Ugandan incursion, Tanzania rebuffed the invasion and, after some hesitation and a military buildup, sent across the border into Uganda a force of 40,000 troops. Earlier, Nyerere, who had not allowed his country to be used as a base for subversion against Amin, permitted Obote to call for a general upheaval in Kampala. Obote's long-dormant army was mobilized and sent into action alongside the Tanzanian Army. The combined force—and a motley of other Ugandan units fighting under separate commands and ethnic flags—slowly advanced on Kampala. Despite Libyan military support (air deliveries of war materiel, a fighting force of 2,700 troops, strafing runs on Tanzanian villages, and a harsh ultimatum issued to Tanzania), the advance on Kampala was clearly irreversible. As Amin's hold over Uganda continued to crumble, entire garrisons mutinied or deserted. Without diminishing the magnitude of the Tanzanian feat (at a cost of $500 million), the four-month war that pitched 70,000 troops against each other resulted in only 373 Tanzanian casualties—and only 86 of these were directly consequent to enemy action![92]

Amin's Palestinian mercenaries and the airlifted Libyan troops and armor were torn to shreds by the unseasoned Tanzanian force. Indeed, 600 Libyans died (many at Lukaya, where they made a tactically disastrous stand), as compared to 1,000 of Amin's soldiers. With half the country liberated, Amin continued to exhort his troops to resist even as he secretly boarded a jet to Tripoli (together with several wives, concubines, and twenty children) and went from there to exile in Riyadh, Saudi Arabia. Kampala fell with hardly a fight on April 10, 1979, and on June 3, Tanzanian troops reached the Sudanese border. Behind that border—and in Zaire—some 8,000 ex-Amin soldiers had retreated, many to seek their fortunes in Uganda in subsequent years as brigands and bandits.

Rebirth and Decay

The political evolution of Uganda since liberation provides a striking testimonial to the durability of basic societal cleavages. The Uganda Amin finally relinquished was "a country in ruins,"[93] a society in total cultural, moral, administrative, and socioeconomic shambles that had reached the "pits of economic disaster and chaos . . . [in which] services . . . were negligible, . . . respect for law was virtually non-existent [and] each man had learned to look after his own survival."[94] Yet, notwithstanding the social devastation that ultimately affected all groups in Uganda, ethnicity, regionalism, historical rivalries, and religious strife continued to polarize society. Buganda's continued resistance to being harnessed to "Nilotic" rule resulted in multiple assaults against central authority. And Obote (who eventually bounced back to power), having "learned" a lesson from his former "leniency" vis-à-vis Buganda, retaliated with repressive policies that, executed by his unruly army, verged on being genocidal.

Following liberation, a coterie of self-seeking factions moved into the political vacuum, united primarily by a desire to keep Obote from regaining his old throne. During the slow Tanzanian advance against Amin, a conference had been organized at Moshi on the future shape of post-liberation Uganda—a conference to which every aspiring politician flocked, seeking recognition and representation. Twenty-eight political formations gained access into what shortly became the Uganda National Liberation Front (UNLF) and the National Consultative Council (NCC). Both were dominated by southerners, including a number of Marxist intellectual pace-setters. Heeding Nyerere's wise counsel, Obote did not seek membership in either group out of the concern that his presence might immediately polarize the conference into violently antagonistic factions. The UPC was represented by loyal Obote political and military surrogates—Paulo Muwanga and David Oyite-Ojok, respectively. A conservative Muganda intellectual, Yusuf Lule, was elected the compromise head of the NCC; with the unanticipated early fall of Kampala, he found himself installed as the new president of Uganda.

Lule's presidency lasted barely seventy-two days. His parliamentary ouster came about as a result of his increasing promotion of narrow Bugandan interests and because of his rejection of the minimalist role granted him by the NCC, which, under the sway of radicals, wished to tightly control the executive. With the NCC subsequently deadlocked between alternate radical and UPC (Muwanga) candidates, Godfrey Binaisa (Obote's former Muganda attorney-general and a political lightweight who had not been admitted into the Moshi conference as a representative of a legitimate group) was brought in out of the wilderness as the next compromise president.

Binaisa, who had resigned over human rights violations during the latter's first presidency, also proved to be an inept leader—but not so much because of his similar problems with the NCC (which had transformed itself into a 127-member National Assembly). Rather, Binaisa proved to be uniquely incapable of arresting the frightful derailment of socioeconomic life in Uganda. He was never in control of the rampantly corrupt cabinet and administration; nor did he place national interests above his own overriding preoccupation with neutralizing political competitors, entrenching his presidency, and retaining political preeminence in Uganda. For as Reginald Green aptly points out, all the post-liberation governments in Kampala were overwhelmingly "concerned with advancing first their personal economic interests, second their personal political bases, third perpetuating themselves and their allies in power and only fourth doing the work of a government."[95]

Socioeconomic conditions under Binaisa greatly deteriorated as a wave of utter lawlessness gripped the country. Criminals, uprooted farmers, starving unemployed urban-dwellers, ex-Amin soldiers, and even units of the new UNLF Army terrorized the countryside and downtown Kampala, killing and plundering with impunity. Unemployment, severe social dislocation, famine, the settling of old scores, the lack of legitimacy of central institutions, the ongoing administrative vacuum and the general unruliness in a society where life for long had been cheap—all lay beneath the epidemic of daily multiple killings, robbings, and massacres that the Binaisa regime could do nothing to stem. And the social malaise was greatly aggravated by the formation of several private armies in the south following Lule's eclipse. For although Lule was hardly popular even in Buganda, his ouster symbolized the rejection, "yet again," of Ganda leadership in Uganda's public life.

Binaisa ultimately committed the same error as Lule—confusing the image and reality of his own presidential powers. Under constant pressure from the role-expanding parliamentary radical Left (which had been overrepresented in the NCC since Moshi), aware that Obote was patiently lurking in the wings, and threatened by the voracious ambitions of political newcomers such as Defense Minister Yoweri Museveni,[96] Binaisa initially tried to disencumber himself of the latter's political menace; failing that, he attempted to neutralize the UPC threat. Relying on his presidential *de jure* powers and on the general anti-UPC sentiment in the NCC, Binaisa dismissed the only obviously "undismissable" deputy chief of staff and long-time Obote lieutenant, Colonel David Oyite-Ojok. The latter promptly overthrew Binaisa in the name of the NCC, citing in justification the regime's only obvious corruption.[97]

The twice-proven "ineptness" of the NCC presidential nominees constituted unassailable grounds for the "normalization" of Ugandan political leadership via the ballot-box. This normalization in turn spelled the end of the excessive influence of the radical intellectuals in the National Assembly (most with Ph.Ds), whose populist credos were anchored in highly elitist political formations. It also opened the door for Obote's electoral comeback, which could no longer be legitimately denied inasmuch as he had allowed the "new forces" in Uganda to take their crack at political leadership and nation-building. Moreover, Tanzania, reeling from the financial cost of the invasion and of the continued maintenance of peace-keeping troops and police in Uganda, wished to hand over all residual powers to a more stable and legitimate administration in Kampala.

The Second Overthrow of Obote and the Rise of the South

The December 1980 elections—the first in Uganda since 1962—underscored the fact that ethnic and religious affiliations continued to dictate voting behavior in Uganda. The main political protagonists were the same—a "Protestant" northern UPC with an electoral monopoly in the Langi-Acholi districts versus a southern "Catholic" DP entrenched (in the absence of a resurrected Kabaka Yekka) in Buganda. Neither Museveni's originally much-touted Banyankole (i.e., western) Union of Patriotic Masses nor the tiny Bugandan monarchist Conservative party affected the outcome. An organized UPC machine trounced the as-ever faction-ridden DP (led by ex–Syracuse University Ph.D. Paul Ssemogerere), gaining 74 of the 126 delegates at stake (the UPM elected one, the CP none), in what a Commonwealth watchdog team deemed "a valid electoral exercise" (despite some irregularities).[98]

Obote's electoral victory, disputed from the outset and fueled by the insular paronoia of southerners, triggered the emergence of guerrilla movements against his rule. The southern attempt to reverse by force of arms (as in 1966) what had been lost at the ballot box in turn stiffened Nilotic resolve not to lose control of the state "this time." The two vectors resulted in a bloody civil war that further devastated the prostrate country.

Obote inherited a bankrupt country in the throes of total anarchy following the cruel letdown of the initial euphoria of liberation. Hopes of rapid reconstruction following the ravages of the previous decade were dashed by the decadent self-seeking quest of politicians, long-starved of patronage and graft, to make up for lost time. Foreign suppliers refused credit (as they had done during the Amin era), aware that Uganda's precarious foreign reserves sufficed for less than two weeks of imports. All commodities remained in short supply; indeed, the capital had only three-days' reserves of petrol. The once-vibrant Asian sugar and tea estates remained derelict, and the level of cotton production was down to that of 1914! What was by then one of the world's highest inflation rates (3,000 percent since Amin's overthrow) made urban survival impossible inasmuch as basic wages were insufficient to purchase more than two bunches of plantains a week.[99] Daily criminal and political violence in a country awash with weapons, including sophisticated hardware, was so integral a part of life in Kampala that international relief agencies were threatening to pull out their staffs and to terminate humanitarian efforts in the country.

"All constraints that a State exerts on human behavior were absent"[100] in this country, where life had for long been cheap, where differences had been routinely settled by an exchange of bullets, and where any central government was increasingly viewed as inherently illegitimate, venal, or threatening. According to one observer at the time, "Living in Uganda is so precarious these days that people are killed for their watches or radios, and no one dares drive around in a luxury car."[101] Ugandan professionals who had returned home at the first flush of liberation were streaming out of the country in utter disgust. Exit curbs more stringent than those under Amin were soon imposed as many talked of the "good old days under Amin." As another observer put it, "utter panic" was the state of mind of urban dwellers in the last days of the Binaisa administration.[102]

In the north and east, large roving bands of brigands and ex-Amin troops swooped through entire districts plundering and massacring everything in their way, at times under the banner of the "National Rescue Front"! And in the south and west, Museveni (who had failed to carry his home town in the election) and disgruntled militant elements of the defeated DP were mobilizing private armies and raising the call to arms against Kampala. (At one time a bizarre wall-to-wall anti-Obote conclave assembled in Nairobi that included ex-Amin forces, including Brigadier Moses Ali, Uganda's two ousted presidents, Museveni, and others.) Straddling coffee-growing areas (coffee being Uganda's sole export crop), the spreading rebellion threatened to economically stifle the new regime in Kampala.

Like Lule and Binaisa before him, Obote proved incapable of arresting the endemic violence in Uganda (advances were attained in other domains, however). Moreover, the totally uncontrollable loot-hungry and trigger-happy army turned out to be the most destabilizing factor in Uganda. Having unleashed the full venom of his overwhelmingly Nilotic Army against the southern guerrilla movements, Obote ensured the multiplication of new sources of grievances against Kampala. In what became the major battle zone (i.e., the Luwero triangle northwest of Kampala), the army, fearful of combat and incapable of locating an enemy that melted into the bush, increasingly vent its vengeance on the "enemy" population. By 1984, the United States was publicly accusing the Ugandan Army of direct or indirect culpability (via induced famine) in as many as 300,000 civilian deaths.[103]

As Museveni's more disciplined troops slowly gained ascendance and began to converge on Kampala, the Nilotic (i.e., Acholi-Langi) alliance at the core of Obote's power base became unglued, thereby sealing Obote's fate and setting the stage for an Acholi coup. Two little-reported coup plots (in 1981 and 1982), stemming from disenchantment with the Acholi dominance in both army and society, had been quelled by Chief of Staff Oyite-Ojok but remained a testimonial to the quasi-anarchy reigning in the armed forces. Bloody factional fighting between Langi and Acholi troops erupted intermittently during 1982 and 1983 as rebellious Acholi units chafed over their perceived greater frequency of service in combat zones in the south compared to their Langi cousins. Obote's last chance to maintain control over his sole power-prop, the army, disappeared with the December 1983 death of Oyite-Ojok in a helicopter accident. (Oyite-Ojok had been the army's most competent officer and veritable ethnic bridge-builder.) The critical position was not filled for nine months, and only then by a junior Langi officer after a series of blatant command shuffles and preferential Langi promotions that heightened Acholi-Langi tensions to the breaking point. With Museveni's troops at the gates of Kampala, bitter Acholi-Langi fighting erupted in the capital as Obote was toppled from office by General Bosilio Okello.

Setting up an all-Acholi cabinet (which briefly included Mawanga and Ssemogerere), the new junta attempted to negotiate a power-sharing formula with Museveni and other insurgent groups. Although some ex-Amin officers rallied to Okello and joined the cabinet, Museveni rebuffed these advances and, on January 26, 1986, entered Kampala. Rejecting suggestions not to invade the heavily defended Acholi homeland, Museveni pressed on northward, encountering at the outset only minimal and ineffectual opposition. By mid-March, the entire country was again under central control, some areas having been "reconquered" for the fourth time since 1979.

The emergence of a southerner (Banyankole) in power in Kampala signified a major shift in the political center of gravity in Uganda. The tables were now completely turned, with the nationalist center in southern hands and the separatist center in northern hands. For notwithstanding the ease with which the northern regions had been brought under Kampala's control, by 1987 chaos was again threatening to engulf the country. In the always unsettled northeast, Karamojong cattle-raiders (now armed with machine guns and grenade launchers) devastated huge areas unchecked, forming a veritable wave of "human locusts."[104] In various countries bordering Uganda, although Obote had reportedly reclused himself in Lusaka, Zambia, several of his political and military lieutenants were recruiting troops, arms, and funds for a re-liberation of Kampala. Alcholi troops, regrouped by individual ex-UNLA officers, soon came to control the bulk of the countryside of their districts, fighting pitched battles with Kampala forces. A mystic priestess, Alice Lukwena, mobilized large numbers of unarmed northerners against Museveni's armies, offering potions of nut oil and magic rites as protection against bullets. During 1987, more than a thousand of her Holy Spirit Battalion cohorts were killed while clutching voodoo toys resembling anti-aircraft guns, helicopters made of wire, or rifles carved out of wood.[105] Other armed groups—composed of dispossessed farmers, school drop-outs, ex-Amin adventurers, and renegade military personnel—likewise formed to carve out their own anarchic zones of plunder and loot.

In Kampala, Museveni admitted that "we have not done much on the economic front." Indeed, the cost of doubling the National Resistance Army (NRA) to 50,000 and of sustaining the campaigns in the north drained Uganda's limited fiscal resources. Nor was Kampala itself very secure, what with sporadic gunfire and violent crime descending on the capital each evening and political plots and planned assassinations by a wide array of ex-UPC and other power aspirants continuing to threaten the stability of the new regime.

Thus, even though the Amin nightmare has ended, Uganda remains a society at war with itself. Despite a modicum of normality and economic activity in the south, the locus of political power in Kampala remains under siege from all directions. The initial euphoria generated by prospects of stability, national reunification, and reconstruction under Museveni's leadership have faded somewhat. Amin's brutal interregnum shattered the fragile ethnic and socioeconomic balance of power that had been inherited at independence and was already eroded by Obote's first presidency. The bits and pieces may yet be put together in Kampala. But as the country is "reconquered" again, new centripetal forces may be set loose to plague the country in the future. Ultimately, those forces may prove to be Amin's legacy to the much-tarnished Pearl of Africa.

Notes

1. For two recent surveys of Ugandan history, see T.V. Sathyamurthy, *The Political Development of Uganda 1900–1986* (London: Gower, 1986); and J.J. Jorgensen, *Uganda: A Modern History* (London: Croom Helm, 1981). See also the earlier study of Kenneth Ingham, *The Making of Modern Uganda* (London: Allen and Unwin, 1958).

2. See Lloyd A. Fallers, *Inequality: Social Stratification Reconsidered* (Chicago: University of Chicago Press, 1972), and *The King's Men: Leadership and Status in Buganda on the Eve of Independence* (London: Oxford University Press, 1964); Donald A. Low, *Buganda in Modern History* (Berkeley: University of California Press, 1971), and *The Mind of Buganda: Documents of the Modern History of an*

African Kingdom (Berkeley: University of California Press, 1971). See also Donald L. Low and R. Cranford Pratt, *Buganda and British Over-Rule 1900–1955* (London: Oxford University Press, 1960); A.D. Roberts, "The Sub-Imperialism of Buganda," *Journal of African History*, vol. 3, no. 3 (1962); and John Roscoe, *The Baganda* (London: Frank Cass, 1965).

3. See J.H.M. Beattie, *Bunyoro: An African Kingdom* (New York: Holt, Rinehart and Winston, 1960), *Understanding an African Kingdom: Bunyoro* (New York: Holt, Rinehart and Winston, 1965), and *The Nyoro State* (Oxford: Oxford University Press, 1971). See also A.R. Dunbar, *A History of Bunyoro-Kitara* (Nairobi: Oxford University Press, 1969).

4. See Edward I. Steinhart, *Conflict and Collaboration: The Kingdoms of Western Uganda 1890–1907* (Princeton, N.J.: Princeton University Press, 1977); H.F. Morris, *A History of Ankole* (Kampala: East African Literature Bureau, 1962); and Kenneth Ingham, *The Kingdom of Toro in Uganda* (London: Methuen, 1975). For a recent overview of Busoga history, see D.W. Cohen, "The Political Transformation of Northern Busoga 1600–1900," *Cahiers d'Etudes Africaines*, vol. 22, no. 2-3 (1982), pp. 465–488.

5. See Aidan W. Southall, *Alur Society* (Nairobi: Oxford University Press, 1970); John Middleton and D. Tait (eds.), *Tribes Without Rulers* (London: Routledge and Kegan Paul, 1958).

6. J.P. Barber, "The Karamajoa District of Uganda," *Journal of African History*, vol. 3, no. 1 (1962); and Neville Dyson-Hudson, *Karamajong Politics* (Oxford: Oxford University Press, 1960).

7. J.C.D. Lawrence, *The Iteso: Fifty Years of Change in a Nilo-Hamitic Tribe of Uganda* (London and Oxford: Oxford University Press, 1957).

8. See John Middleton, *The Lugbara of Uganda* (New York: Holt, Rinehart and Winston, 1965).

9. See E.A. Brett, *Colonialism and Underdevelopment in East Africa* (New York: NOK Publishers, 1973).

10. See the data in Nelson Kasfir's "Cultural Sub-Nationalism in Uganda," in Victor A. Olorunsola (ed.), *The Politics of Cultural Sub-Nationalism in Africa* (New York: Anchor Books, 1972).

11. H.B. Hansen, *Mission, Church and State in a Colonial Setting: Uganda 1890–1925* (London: Heinemann, 1984); F.B. Welbourn, *Religion and Politics in Uganda 1952-62* (Nairobi: East Africa Publishing House, 1967); and Arye Oded, *Islam in Uganda* (New York: John Wiley and Sons, 1974).

12. *Uganda Argus*, December 20, 1966.

13. For a survey of the Ugandan economy on the eve of independence, see David H. Davis, *The Economic Development of Uganda* (Baltimore: Johns Hopkins Press, 1962); Walter Elkan, *The Economic Development of Uganda* (London: Oxford University Press, 1961); and *Area Handbook for Uganda* (Washington, D.C.: Government Printing Office, 1969), pp. 221–378.

14. See H.M. Morris, *The Indians in Uganda: Caste and Sect in a Plural Society* (London: Weidenfeld and Nicolson, 1968), p. 11. See also Dharam P. Ghai and Yash Ghai (eds.), *Portrait of a Minority: Asians in East Africa* (Nairobi: Oxford University Press, 1970); and Michael Twaddle (ed.), *Expulsion of a Minority: Essays on Ugandan Asians* (London: Athlone Press, 1975).

15. Jack D. Parson, "Africanizing Trade in Uganda: The Final Solution," *Africa Today*, vol. 29, no. 1 (1973).

16. For one example, see Dharam P. Ghai, "The Bugandan Trade Boycott," in Robert Rotberg and Ali Mazrui (eds.), *Protest and Power in Black Africa* (New York: Oxford University Press, 1970).

17. See Selwyn Ryan, "Economic Nationalism and Socialism in Uganda," *Journal of Commonwealth Studies*, vol. 10, no. 2 (July 1973), p. 144; and Bruce A. Blomstrom, "Capital Flight in East Africa," in Tom J. Farar (ed.), *Financing African Development* (Cambridge, Mass.: MIT Press, 1965).

18. See Donald Rothchild and Michael Rogin, "Uganda," in G. Carter (ed.), *National Unity and Regionalism in Eight African States* (Ithaca, N.Y.: Cornell University Press, 1966), p. 351. For more details, see, inter alia, Donald A. Low, *Political Parties in Uganda 1946-1962* (London: Athlone Press, 1962).

19. See Lloyd A. Fallers, "Ideology and Culture in Ugandan Nationalism," *American Anthropologist*, vol. 63, no. 4 (1961); B.D. Bowles, "Nationalism in Uganda 1950-62" (Ph.D. thesis, Makerere University, 1971); R.C. Pratt, "Nationalism in Uganda," *Political Studies*, vol. 9, no. 2 (June 1961); and Aiden W. Southall, "The Concept of Elites and Their Formation in Uganda," in P.C. Lloyd (ed.), *The New Elites in Tropical Africa* (New York: Oxford University Press, 1966).

20. See Peter Gukiina, *Uganda: A Case Study in African Political Development* (Notre Dame, Ind.: University of Notre Dame Press, 1972), p. 109.

21. For an overview, see David Apter, *The Political Kingdom in Uganda* (Princeton, N.J.: Princeton University Press, 1961); M.S.M. Kiwanuka, "Nationality and Nationalism in Africa: The Uganda Case," *Canadian Journal of African Studies*, vol. 4, no. 2 (Spring 1970); and May Edel Mandelbaum, "African Tribalism: Some Reflections on Uganda," *Political Science Quarterly*, vol. 80, no. 3 (1965). For a radically different perspective, see Mahmood Mamdani, "Class Struggles in Uganda," *Review of African Political Economy*, no. 4 (1975), and *Politics and Class Formation in Uganda* (London: Heinemann, 1976).

22. See Fred G. Burke, *Local Government and Politics in Uganda* (Syracuse, N.Y.: Syracuse University Press, 1964); Cherry Gertzel, *Party and Locality in Northern Uganda 1945-62* (London: Athlone Press, 1974); Colin Leys, *Politicians and Policy: An Essay on Politics in Acholi 1962-65* (Nairobi: East Africa Publishing House, 1967); and Low, *Political Parties in Uganda*.

23. It is noteworthy that, in Buganda, modernization proceeded from the top downward so that few cleavages arose between chiefs and masses, and the kabakaship (as a symbol of the unity of the nation) remained popular and untarnished. See Allan Renwick, "Makerere and Uganda's Elite," *Africa Today* (December 1963); and Fallers, *Inequality and Social Stratification Reconsidered*, p. 159.

24. For a statement of Buganda's views, see "Buganda's Position" and "Buganda's Independence," both of which are pamphlets issued by the Information Department of the kabaka's government, Mmengo (Kampala), 1960. The declaration of independence had few repercussions and was of no practical import inasmuch as the kingdom had no intention (or ability) to defend its secession.

25. Low, *Political Parties in Uganda*, p. 22.

26. As a Bugandan minister, the DP leader, Benedicto Kiwanuka, had been denied the katikiroship in 1955 solely because of his religious affiliation; other Ganda politicians who joined the DP did so because they believed they had no future in the Protestant establishment of the Buganda court.

27. See T.V. Sathyamurthy, "The Social Bases of the Uganda People's Party," *African Affairs* (October 1975). See also Low, *Political Parties in Uganda*; and Gertzel, *Party and Locality in Northern Uganda*. For details on the early political era in Uganda, see especially Grace S.K. Ibingira, *The Forging of an African Nation* (New York: Viking Press, 1973); H.F. Morris and James S. Read, *Uganda: The Development of Its Laws and Constitution* (London: Stevens, 1966); and Gukiina, *Uganda: A Case Study in African Political Development*.

28. See Kasfir, "Cultural Sub-Nationalism in Uganda," pp. 85, 89–94. See also Cherry Gertzel, "How the Kabaka Yekka Came to Be," *Africa Report*, vol. 9, no. 9 (1964); and I.R. Hancock, "Patriotism and Neo-Traditionalism in Uganda: The Kabaka Yekka," *Journal of African History*, vol. 11, no. 3 (1970).

29. These provisions included the elevation of the kabaka, Mutesa II, to the presidency and the kyabazinga of Busoga to the vice-presidency (so that no "commoner" would be politically "above" these traditional leaders), as well as a quasi-federal system under which the Lukiiko chose Buganda's deputies to the National Assembly (through indirect elections). See Ibingira, *Forging an African Nation;* Rothchild and Rogin, "Uganda," pp. 370–379; and G.F. Engholm, "The Westminster Model in Uganda," *International Journal* (Autumn 1963).

30. See Cherry Gertzel, "The Lost Counties," *Africa Report*, vol. 17, no. 5 (1962); Andrew R. Roberts, "The Lost Counties of Bunyoro," *Uganda Journal*, vol. 26, no. 2 (1962); and Terence Hopkins, "Politics in Uganda: The Buganda Question," in Jeffrey Butler and A.A. Castagno (eds.), *Boston University Papers on Africa* (New York: Praeger Publishers, 1967).

31. Ocheng was a northerner from Acholi who, having long resided in Buganda and with extensive landholdings there, was oft-touted as "proving" the KY's "national" credentials. Regarding the "gold and ivory affair," see A.B. Majuju, "The Gold Allegations in Uganda," *African Affairs* (October 1987), pp. 479–504.

32. The ministers languished in internal exile in Lango until the 1971 coup d'état. Subsequently, Ibingira was appointed by Idi Amin as ambassador to the United Nations. It is noteworthy that at no time during Obote's first reign did Uganda have more than sixty political prisoners.

33. See "Uganda v. Commissioner of Prisons *ex parte* Matovu," *East African Law Reports* (1966), pp. 514–546. See also Crawford M. Young, "The Obote Revolution," *Africa Report*, vol. 11, no. 6 (1966); Ali Picho, "The 1967 Republican Constitution of Uganda," *Transition* (Kampala, December 1967–January 1968); G.F. Engholm and Ali Mazrui, "Violent Constitutionalism in Uganda," *Government and Opposition* (July 1967); and Emory Bundy, "Uganda's New Constitution," *East African Journal* (June 1966).

34. For different versions of these events, see Mutesa II, *Desecration of My Kingdom* (London: Constable, 1967); Akena Adoko, *Uganda Crisis* (Kampala:

African Publishers Ltd., 1970); and Milton Obote, *Myths and Realities* (Kampala: African Publishers Ltd., 1970).

35. See G. Glentworth and I. Hancock, "Obote and Amin: Change and Continuity in Modern African Politics," *African Affairs* (July 1973). See also Ali Mazrui, "Leadership in Africa: Obote of Uganda," *International Journal* (Summer 1970); and John D. Chick, "Uganda: Quest for Control," *The World Today* (June 1984).

36. Legum (ed.), *Africa Contemporary Record 1970–71*, pp. C146–C152.

37. See Milton Obote, "The Common Man's Charter, with Appendices" (Entebbe: Government Printer, 1970). For analysis, see Tertit Aasland, "On the Move to the Left in Uganda 1969–71" (Uppsala: Scandinavian Institute of African Studies, Research Paper No. 26, 1974); A.G.G. Gingyera-Pinyewa, "On the Proposed Move to the Left in Uganda," *East African Journal* (February 1970); Selwyn Ryan, "Economic Nationalism and Socialism in Uganda," *Journal of Commonwealth Political Studies*, vol. 10, no. 2 (July 1973); and Irving Gershenberg, "Slouching Towards Socialism: Obote's Uganda," *African Studies Review* (April 1972).

38. *Bank of Uganda Quarterly Bulletin* (March 1971), p. 21, as cited in Ryan, "Economic Nationalism," p. 144.

39. The Special Forces, during the Obote years, consisted of a riot-control paramilitary force attached to the police. The General Service Units, a 1,000-man force headed by Obote's cousin (Akena Adoko), engaged in the gathering of intelligence and served as the Presidential Guard. With the rise to power of Idi Amin, both were transformed into assassination squads.

40. Peter Willetts, "The Politics of Uganda as a One Party State," *African Affairs*, vol. 74 (July 1975), p. 298.

41. For a discussion of the mutinies, see Henry Bienen, "Public Order and the Military in Africa," in his *The Military Intervenes* (New York: Russell Sage Foundation, 1968).

42. Morrison et al., *Black Africa*, pp. 116, 119, 194.

43. For a more detailed analysis of the Ugandan armed forces, see Decalo, *Coups and Army Rule in Africa*, pp. 201–211.

44. Following the attempt on Obote, Amin was conspicuously absent when state officials converged at the State House to assess the significance of the assault. A delegation rushed to Amin's house to see if he was safe and to invite him to the deliberations under way. For some reason Amin panicked when he saw the delegation at the gate and, half-dressed, climbed over his barbed-wire fence (wounding himself) and escaped to the sanctuary of a loyal Nubian unit. Only when he had been assured that there was no plot against him did he appear in Kampala, where Okoya accused him of cowardice and desertion. A few days later, Okoya was murdered. See Henry Kyemba, *State of Blood* (London: Corgi, 1977), pp. 29–32; David Martin, *General Amin* (London: Faber and Faber, 1974), pp. 70–74; and Ali Mazrui, *Soldiers and Kinsmen in Uganda: The Making of a Military Ethnocracy* (Beverly Hills, Calif.: Sage, 1975), pp. 151–152.

45. Judith Listowel, *Amin* (London: Irish University Press, 1974); Ruth First,

"Uganda: The Latest Coup d'Etat in Africa," *The World Today* (March 1971); and Martin, *General Amin*. See also Legum (ed.), *Africa Contemporary Record 1970–71*, pp. B188–B190; *The Observer* (London), January 31, 1971; *Sunday Nation* (Nairobi), February 14, 1971; *Uganda Argus* (Kampala), January 27, 1971; and Michael Twaddle, "The Amin Coup," *Journal of Commonwealth Studies* (July 1971).

46. Cited in Martin, *General Amin*, p. 13.

47. Hypomania is "a mental state in which thought processes are speeded up." See Legum (ed.), *Africa Contemporary Record 1972–73*, p. B270; see also *The Times* (London), October 25, 1972; and Colin Legum, "Behind the Clown's Mask," *Transition* (Accra, October 1975–March 1976). For a more recent and more detailed account of Amin's psychotic condition, see the prognosis of one of his former doctors, Professor John Kibuka-Mosoke, in *The Observer*, May 1, 1977.

48. Ibid., p. 14; Martin, *General Amin*, p. 14.

49. See Ali Mazrui, "Racial Self-Reliance and Cultural Dependence: Nyerere and Amin in Comparative Perspective," *Journal of International Affairs*, vol. 27, no. 1 (1973), p. 114. According to Kyemba, in *State of Blood*, Amin "cannot write. . . . No one has ever received a handwritten letter from him" (p. 46).

50. For a representative cross-section of some of the literature of this genre, see Ali Mazrui's writings, including "Resurrection of the Warrior Tradition in African Political Culture," *Journal of Modern African Studies* (March 1975), "Phallic Symbols in Politics and War: An African Perspective," *Journal of African Studies*, vol. 1, no. 1 (1974), and *Soldiers and Kinsmen in Uganda*.

51. "The Kikuya spoke in fear of 'Corporal Amin.' . . . They had experience of his practice in stuffing a handkerchief down the throats of Mau Mau suspects." See Colin Legum, "Behind the Clown's Mask," p. 88.

52. Martin, *General Amin*, p. 13.

53. Ibid., p. 249.

54. Mazrui, *Soldiers and Kinsmen in Uganda*, pp. 46, 47.

55. Ibid., p. 127.

56. When he panicked after the 1969 Obote assassination attempt, Amin called for help from his Nubian NCOs and ordered them not to obey the orders of their superior officers. In 1970, returning from a visit to Cairo during which his powers had been whittled down, and suspecting Obote's intentions to purge him, he secretly ordered a detachment of Nubian troops and NCOs to greet him at the airport. This group formed his security guard in the next few weeks. (Not one officer had been informed of the impending return of the chief of staff!) At the time of the coup, his major support in the army were the Nubi-Kakwa NCOs he had personally selected and the Malire Mechanized Regiment that he had commanded and packed with loyal Sudanic officers.

57. Legum (ed.), *Africa Contemporary Record 1977–78*, p. B442.

58. See some of the (admittedly not disinterested) accounts in Kyemba, *State of Blood*. Kyemba was Obote's personal secretary, and he served in Amin's cabinet before fleeing abroad several years later.

59. *Daily Telegraph*, March 20, 1976.

60. See "Uganda Under Military Rule," *Africa Today*, vol. 20, no. 2 (Spring 1973); *The Times* (London), September 28, 1971.

61. Legum (ed.), *Africa Contemporary Record 1975–76*, p. B354.
62. See "The Report of the Commission of Inquiry in the Case of the Two Missing Americans in Uganda," *Transition*, no. 42 (1972).
63. *The Guardian*, August 1, 1975.
64. See Legum (ed.), *Africa Contemporary Record 1971–72*, p. B270. For details on the Nubians, see Barri A. Wanji, "The Nubi Community: An Islamic Social Structure in East Africa" (Sociology Working Paper No. 115, Makerere University, n.d.); Dennis Pain, "The Nubians: Their Perceived Stratification System and Its Relation to the Asian Issue," in Michael Twaddle (ed.), *Expulsion of a Minority: Essays on Ugandan Asians* (London: Athlone Press, 1975); Nelson Kasfir, "Explaining Ethnic Political Participation," *World Politics* (April 1979), and "Uganda: Nubians and Southern Sudanese," *Africa Confidential*, May 3, 1974.
65. Legum (ed.), *Africa Contemporary Record 1977–78*, p. B434.
66. See the *Journal of the International Commission of Jurists* (June 1973). See also the detailed indictments in Michael H. Posner, *The Lawyers' Committee for International Human Rights* (New York: International Commission of Jurists, June 1978); and *Human Rights in Uganda* (London: Amnesty International, June 1978).
67. See S. Kiwanuka, *Amin and the Tragedy of Uganda* (Munich: Weltforum Verlag, 1979); Jeffrey J. Strate, "Post-Military Coup Strategy in Uganda: Amin's Early Attempts to Consolidate Political Support" (Athens, Ohio: Papers in International Studies, Africa Series No. 18, 1973).
68. See *The Observer*, November 3, 1974.
69. Legum (ed.), *Africa Contemporary Record 1972–73*, pp. B272–B273.
70. *The Times*, September 28, 1971.
71. Legum, "Behind the Clown's Mask."
72. Martin, *General Amin*, p. 223.
73. Legum (ed.), *Africa Contemporary Record 1971–72*, p. B235.
74. *The Observer*, January 19, 1975.
75. This statement was made by one of Amin's ministers. See Martin, *General Amin*, p. 224. In 1972, Amin retired twenty-two of Uganda's most senior and experienced civil servants, replacing them with totally uneducated West Nilers and Nubians. See Legum (ed.), *Africa Contemporary Record 1972–73*, p. B273.
76. Legum (ed.), *Africa Contemporary Record 1978–79*, p. B422.
77. Legum (ed.), *Africa Contemporary Record 1973–74*, p. B294.
78. *Washington Post*, May 5, 1974.
79. Unlike Bokassa, Amin was relatively unostentatious and wore only his paratroop wings and a few legitimately earned campaign ribbons.
80. See Samuel Decalo, "Libya's Qaddafi: Bedouin Product of the Space Age," *Present Tense* (New York, January 1974); "Israel's Year in Africa," in Legum (ed.), *African Contemporary Record 1972–73*, pp. B123–B136, ibid., pp. B285–B286 and C68–C85; *Uganda Argus*, March 27 and 31, 1972; and Israel, Ministry of Foreign Affairs, Information Division, "Israel and Uganda" (Jerusalem, 1972).
81. He withdrew the latter suggestion after "his friends, the Russians . . . told him the true facts about Hitler, which he had not known before." See Legum (ed.), *Africa Contemporary Record 1975–76*, p. B345.
82. The state of the Ugandan Army can be judged by the fact that most of the troops and officers were drunk on the night of the Israeli rescue raid, and that Amin himself did not learn about the raid until the next morning.

83. Earlier, in July 1970, some 19,000 Italian residents in the country were expelled, and their property—worth an estimated £40 million—was seized without compensation. Later, in 1972, some 500 Israeli technical assistants and their families were evacuated at Amin's request.

84. *Uganda Argus*, December 9, 1971.

85. Britain's subsequent termination of subsidy and technical assistance programs triggered Amin's retaliatory seizure (January 4, 1973) of a large number of the British firms in the country. See Timothy Shaw, "Uganda Under Amin: The Costs of Confronting Dependence," *Africa Today* (Spring 1973); Justin O'Brien, "General Amin and the Ugandan Asians," *Round Table* (January 1973); and H. Patel, "General Amin and the Indian Exodus from Uganda," *Issue* (Winter 1972). See also Legum (ed.), *Africa Contemporary Record 1972–73*, pp. C88–C96; Yash Tandon, "The Asians in Africa in 1972," ibid., pp. A3–A19; and John S. Saul, "The Unsteady State: Uganda, Obote and General Amin," *Review of African Political Economy*, no. 5 (January–April 1976).

86. Reginald H. Green, "Magendo in the Political Economy of Uganda" (Brighton: University of Sussex, Institute of Development Studies, 1981).

87. Jack Parson, "Africanizing Trade in Uganda: The Final Solution," *Africa Today*, vol. 29, no. 1 (1973).

88. Legum (ed.), *Africa Contemporary Record 1976–77*, p. B374.

89. Legum (ed.), *Africa Contemporary Record 1978–79*, p. B423.

90. Peter Woodward, "Ambiguous Amin," *Africa Affairs* (April 1978).

91. Legum (ed.), *Africa Contemporary Record 1978–79*, p. B426. Amin later challenged Nyerere to meet him in the boxing ring to resolve their dispute by personal combat, promising that he would fight with one arm and with weights on both legs.

92. Tony Avirgan and Martha Honey, *War in Uganda: The Legacy of Idi Amin* (London: Zed Press, 1982), p. 39.

93. *The Rehabilitation of the Economy of Uganda*, vol. 1 (London: Commonwealth Secretariat, 1979), p. 3.

94. Legum (ed.), *Africa Contemporary Record 1981–82*, p. B298.

95. See Green, "Magendo," p. 5. And for an excellent review of the early post-liberation period, see Cherry Gertzel, "Uganda After Amin: The Continuing Search for Leadership and Control," *African Affairs* (September 1980).

96. Locked in a tug-of-war for control of the UNLF Army with Obote's surrogate Oyite-Ojok, Museveni had been a UPC leftist, expelled when the party Youth League was disbanded. Blossoming as a Marxist during his studies at Dar-es-Salaam, and as a foreign volunteer in Mozambique's struggle for independence, Museveni participated in the attempted invasion of Uganda in 1972. Unable to deliver on his pledge of 3,000 fighting Banyankole for the attack on Mbarara, he was never again trusted by Obote. A teacher in Tanzania until 1978, he participated in the final invasion of Uganda; from the outset, he was secreting arms for his subsequent falling out with Obote.

97. See Legum (ed.), *Africa Contemporary Record 1980–81*, p. 360.

98. *The Times* (London), December 15, 1980; *Africa Research Bulletin*, Political Series (January 1981).

99. *Africa Research Bulletin,* Economic Series (September 1981).
100. Avirgan and Honey, *War in Uganda,* p. 208.
101. *Africa Research Bulletin,* Political Series (September 1979).
102. *Africa Research Bulletin,* Political Series (February 1980).
103. *Washington Post,* August 4, 1984; *The Guardian,* June 19, 1985; and *Africa Research Bulletin,* Political Series (July 1983).
104. *Africa Confidential,* March 18, 1987, July 8, 1987.
105. *Africa Research Bulletin,* Political Series (February 1987).

4 Jean-Bedel Bokassa
"Emperor" of the Central African Republic

With the fall of the highly idiosyncratic regime of Emperor Jean-Bedel Bokassa the First on September 20, 1979, the last of Africa's classical personal dictatorships disappeared. A volatile country beset by a multitude of socioeconomic tensions that (as one Western ambassador rather ungraciously put it), were it a private enterprise, "would have been wound up as a bad bet long before 1960,"[1] the Central African Republic (CAR) is one of Africa's most isolated and little-studied countries. It was virtually falling apart prior to the rise of personal dictatorship. After he seized power in Bangui, Bokassa ruled the CAR as his personal fiefdom. In some ways the most innocuous of the three dictators under analysis, neither as brutal as Amin nor as demented as Nguema, Bokassa nevertheless became increasingly idiosyncratic in his policies (which culminated with his being crowned emperor, Napoleon-style). Though these policies were a major embarrassment to Paris, France nevertheless continued to prop up the regime. The brutality with which the 1979 student demonstrations in Bangui were quelled, and revelations of Bokassa's personal role in some of the subsequent atrocities, finally propelled a reluctant France to engineer his ouster. In a bloodless military intervention not camouflaged even as an internal upheaval, Bokassa was deposed by French force of arms; and thus the stage was set for a return to normality.

The Central African Republic, known during the colonial era as Oubangui-Chari,[2] is a landlocked 2,000–3,000-foot plateau. Heavily dissected by streams and rivers, it is located near the geographical center of the continent. Forming the watershed between the Chad and Congo water basins, it is essentially a transitional zone; its 240,376 square miles stretch from the dense equatorial forests of the south to the treeless savannalands of the north.

Ravaged as few territories have been by slave raids, devastating epidemics, and exploitative colonial rule, the country to this day bears

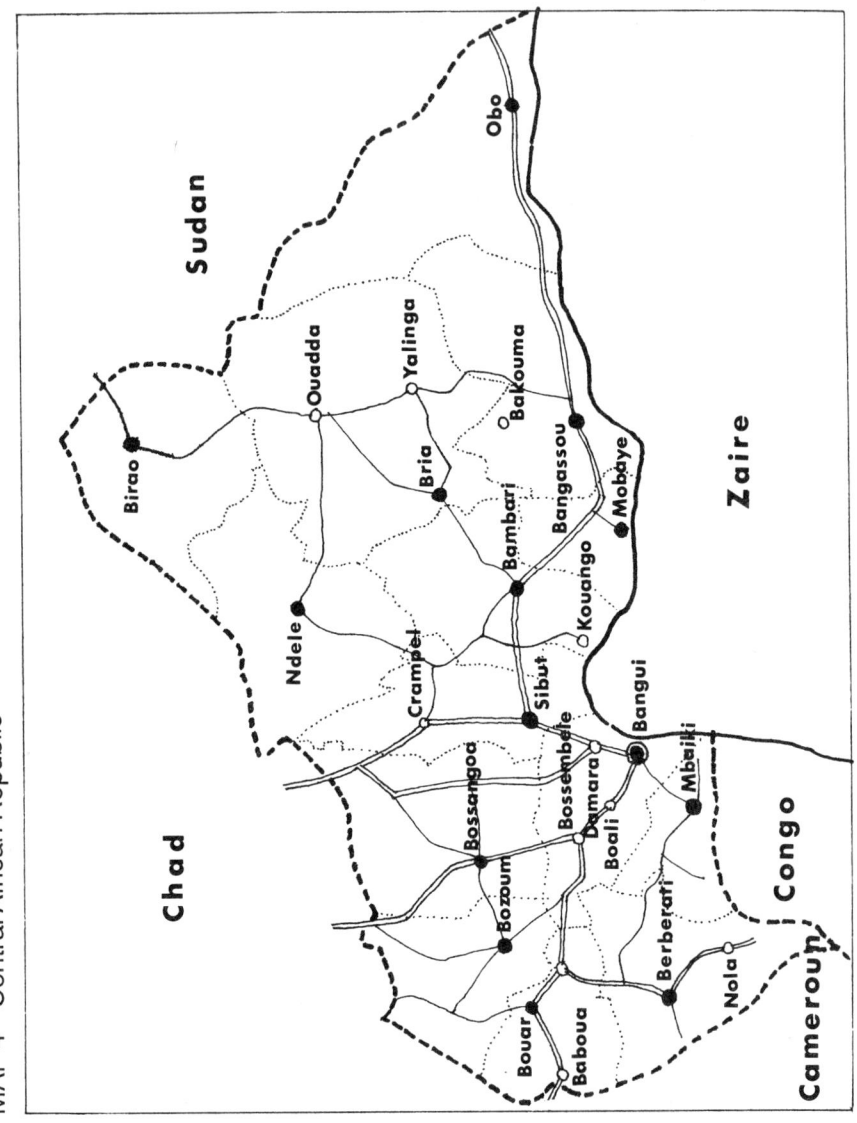

MAP 4 Central African Republic

the scars of its violent past: indeed, large areas are virtually depopulated. The entire east and northeast, which suffered the brunt of the slave raids from Ouadai, Baguirmi, and Darfur (currently in Chad and Sudan) as well as those of Central Africa's most dreaded Arab slave raider, Rabah,[3] have a population of only 71,000 in 87,200 square miles. The Nola forest regions in the extreme south, decimated by virulent sleeping sickness epidemics in 1910–1930, are likewise empty. The 1971 UN demographic estimate of 1.6 million gives the CAR an overall low population density of 6.6 per square mile, ranging unevenly from 0.6 in the east to more than 17 in the south.

The population is composed of some eighty ethnic groups, few of which are indigenous to the territory and most of which arrived at their current habitat in several waves during the eighteenth and nineteenth centuries. Harassed on all sides by enemies and slave-raiders alike, and hence prevented from establishing powerful protostates, these uprooted refugees in a country of refugees are among the least developed on the continent. It has been suggested that these historical factors have helped produce a Central African ethnic amalgam in which the similar experiences of the various populations far outweigh intrinsic ethnic differences.[4] But this contention appears to be grossly overstated and lacking in empirical validity in light of the constant politicization of ethnic cleavages and the prevalence of sharp interethnic competitions in Bangui. The country's centrifugal tendencies are powerful and have escalated with time. Its borders artificially divide many groups from their kinsmen in neighboring states. This external "pull," especially on the Sara, Zande, and Banda of the Central African Republic, has aggravated the domestic "obsession with tribal problems"[5] and resulted in the July 1966 law forbidding all mention in the republic of "race, tribe or ethnicity."[6]

The Ethnic Mosaic

The largest ethnic group in the country, the Banda, arrived between 1830 and 1890 from the Sudan and are located in the center and east of the country in the Bria–Bambari–Fort Sibut triangle.[7] Some clans set up the principalities of Dar Rounga and Dar Kouti (centered around Ndélé), which later fell to Rabah. In turn, Rabah delegated the principalities to his lieutenant, Mohammed es-Senoussi, the last great slave sultan in the region.[8] Raided for slaves from the north and east, the Banda were pulverized into myriads of subgroups which dispersed over a wide area of the country; they also went outside it, ranging from Sudan to Cameroun.

The Baya, or Gbaya, whose numbers are nearly equal to those of the Banda, are found in the north and west of the country in the areas of Bouar, Bossangoa, Boda, and Berbérati. They migrated to these areas between 1805 and 1830 from Cameroun (where many still remain) and Nigeria under Fulani military pressure, especially after the latter's victories in Adamaoua (Cameroun).[9] The Mandjia, an important subgroup, settled in the Fort Sibut area and in Haute-Sangha, Ouham, and Ouham-Pende. And in the southeast, the much studied Zande[10] (of complex Sudanese origin) migrated at the beginning of the nineteenth century to establish a number of powerful and highly stratified feudal principalities. They eventually allied with the Banda to their immediate west and resisted Rabah's slave encroachments from Dar Kouti.

The other ethnic groups in the country include the Sara in the north. The dominant group in neighboring Chad, and at one time administered in their entirety by Bangui, the Sara were ultimately detached from the CAR in order to counterbalance the Muslim populations of Chad.[11] And in the extreme southwest of the country, in the dense tropical forests, reside some 10,000 pygmies (the Babinga), who are remnants of a much larger community. The country continues to attract refugee groups as a result of local upheavals and population pressures in neighboring states—as in the 1920s, when some 20,000 Bororo (i.e., non-Muslim, nomadic Fulani) arrived in the Bouar-Bambari area.

Of all these ethnic groups, one has played (and still plays) a dominant social, economic, and political role. The "Riverines" or "Oubanguians" (a catch-all ethnic category embracing the various ethnic fragments residing along the different stretches of the Oubangui River)[12] were among the very first to come into direct contact with the French. Expert fishermen, and "a great trading people"[13] who monopolized all riverine trade for two centuries prior to the arrival of the French, the Yakhoma, Banziri, Sango, Bobangui, Buraka, and Mbaïka—like many other groups—are refugees from Sudan's Bahr el Ghazal. They escaped enslavement by taking refuge on the islands of the Oubangui, which they came to control. So important was their mercantile role and, later, their middleman and colonial-administrative function, that one of their dialects, Sango, became the *lingua franca* of the region and, since 1964, the sole national language of the CAR. Barely numbering 5 percent of the population, the Oubanguians utilized their upward mobility and educational proclivities to rapidly attain an undisputed stranglehold over the colonial and postcolonial civil service. Indeed, more than 60 percent of the positions in the administration are held by members of the Riverine clans—a fact that caused unrest during the colonial era and became a focus for deep resentments after independence.

Many of the ethnic groups in the region were organized in the precolonial era into small sultanates, but all were of minor geographical scope and little political weight. Although at times alliances and coalitions were formed, especially against the slave-princes of the north, intertribal warfare and competitions plagued the territory right through the first decades of colonial rule. Ethnic identity was not, however, significantly linked in the CAR with strong allegiances to *traditional* authority. The demise under French pressure of the last reigning sultans and the general antipathy of the other populations to strong chiefly authority have devalued the prestige of traditional rulers. Moreover, the authority and status of the chiefs were greatly tarnished by their association with the harsh concessionary system established in French Equatorial Africa— just as that system pulverized traditional values, proletarianized large masses of people, and caused population dislocations, all of which further detraditionalized society and weakened the hold of chiefs over their kinsmen. What developed in the CAR over the years was a poorly integrated amalgam of pockets of traditionalism within a highly proletarianized peasant society, seething with economic discontent and divided internally along ethnic, cultural, and religious lines.

The Colonial Heritage

Of all of France's colonial dominions, those in Equatorial Africa were by far the most brutally exploited and maladministered up to independence. And of the four territories of the French in this part of Africa, Oubangui-Chari was undoubtedly the one most rapaciously plundered. The scars of fifty-odd years of forced labor, pillage, atrocities, and wanton killings have left the countryside totally alienated, distrustful of all policies of the central government, and simmering with bitter hatred of Europeans.[14] This inter-racial tension is at times camouflaged by the overtly pro-French and open-door policies of all regimes to date in the CAR—France's most subservient client-state in Africa. But the resentment is there all the same, barely beneath the surface and focused at one of the most arrogant, patronizing, and exploitative *petite bourgeoisie* French expatriate communities on the continent. As one diplomatic observer has noted, "the local French community behaves as if 1960 [i.e., independence] has never arrived. Their incredible and undisguised contempt for, and arrogance towards, the locals is a reflection of their social and personal origins, for many are the children of those who so cruelly milked the country in the early 1900's."[15]

During much of the colonial era, the civil administration of Oubangui-Chari attracted few capable recruits. Among the least desired postings in the French empire, appointments to Equatorial Africa usually befell both novice colonial recruits and those due a major demotion. Both inexperienced individuals and misfits (shunted from more attractive posts due to their brutality, alcoholism, or other antisocial traits) found their way into the Oubangui-Chari administration.[16] Personnel turnover and staff vacancies were exceedingly high. In 1920, for example, fully 25 percent of the forty administrative subdivisions had no French personnel whatsoever; in Kouango, no fewer than twelve different *chefs de division* served less than a year each, and there were sixty-eight different heads of district in the sixty-three years between 1906 and 1969![17]

During Oubangui-Chari's first decades of colonial rule, the territory's human resources were harnessed to France's territorial expansion toward Chad and the Nile Valley, and a concessionary system was imposed that plundered the country and its population.[18] By far the most convenient overland route to Chad, the Oubangui allowed river transport from the coast to Bangui. As a result, "the straw huts of the administration post of Bangui became one of the most important strategic bases of the French African Empire."[19] Large numbers of porters were needed to forward to Chad the huge tonnage arriving up the Oubangui River at Bangui. Later, huge amounts of manpower were forcibly impressed into construction of the colony's tracks, including those of the Congo-Ocean railroad linking Brazzaville (the capital of French Equatorial Africa) with the Atlantic Ocean. (In the latter instance, so much labor was needed for the Congolese project hundreds of miles to the south that thousands of farmers were impressed from as far away as Chad.) Forced labor was used in all these projects, and the workers themselves were arbitrarily conscripted and callously treated. The result was high rates of mortality and anti-European sentiment. In 1902 alone, 10,000 Mandjia died while serving as porters for the French administration.[20] Concentration camps, maintained in subhuman conditions, kept the impressed labor from fleeing, while counterpart hostage camps (again with high mortality rates) imprisoned wives, children, and even chiefs as yet another deterrent to the avoidance of what was officially deemed voluntary corvée labor.

A poll tax in 1902, aimed at forcing the colony to pay for itself, further drained the strength and resources of the population. Chiefs who resisted the French demands were often summarily deposed, only to be replaced by the native cooks and guards of the colonial administration.[21] In the process, all traditional authority, chiefly prestige, and legitimacy were significantly eroded in the territory. The Baya, and especially the Mandjia, were most affected by the ever-escalating demands of Bangui for porters, labor, and taxes in kind. As a consequence, periodic population migrations (to avoid conscription labor), crop failures, famines, epidemics (due to the absence from the farmlands of large numbers of workers)—and ultimately violence and rebellion—were regular phenomena. Utterly alienated and driven to total despair, the Mandjia and the Baya staged a massive revolt in 1909–1911. A prolonged village-by-village reconquest of much of the country, which had submitted peacefully to French rule two decades before, became necessary. And by pitching traditional ethnic enemies upon the revolting regions, the French further exacerbated interethnic animosities. Moreover, the upheaval in 1909–1911 was not an isolated incident; localized or general rebellion flared in the colony with regularity, as in 1929–1930, during the 1930s, in 1944, and in the 1954 Berberati affair.[22] Large numbers of people died in the upheavals and during the natural calamities caused by the brutal colonial order. During the epidemics (which included sleeping sickness and smallpox), some Mandjia villages lost 80 percent of their inhabitants; the Nzakara population as a whole was decimated by 20 percent during the less virulent smallpox ravages.

The concessionary system that was imposed upon French Equatorial Africa divided Oubangui-Chari into twenty-seven unequal segments, each leased to a different company for exploitation. The companies, which were hastily set up and grossly underfinanced, entertained grandiose visions of instant enrichment. They were staffed at the local level by "adventurers of all nationalities,"[23] recruited at little or no pay, whose sole ambitions were to fulfill company (rubber) quotas and to enrich themselves. Only occasionally did their various atrocities reach the public eye; only the tip of the bloody iceberg was exposed, and the atrocities continued unabated. General Mangin, inspecting the colony in 1908, complained that "as a sample of our race the choice of agents could hardly have been worse. Unless the system is thoroughly changed, all kinds of abuse and vengeance will inevitably stain the history of this unfortunate colony."[24] Yet it was only in 1928, following André Gide's exposé, that French public opinion was shaken from its self-complacent torpor.[25] Indeed, when the scandals did break out, most striking was the fact that the mass floggings, killings, torture, sadistic orgies, and personal aggrandizement of company agents—all with the active and daily connivance of the French administration—had been so routine for decades.

Yet even when the concessionary companies were eventually reorganized and more carefully controlled, and their more sadistic agents purged, the rigid administrative authoritarianism of the past continued. Coupled with a strict and spiteful overapplication of the more severe and demeaning aspects of the *indegenat* penal code, the expatriate community's socioeconomic vise on Oubangui-Chari's development hardly seemed affected until the mid-1950s.

No ethnic segment or geographical district was immune from the abuses of the "role civilatrice" of France in Oubangui-Chari. And the population's fairly recent exposure to this wanton human destruction has left scars upon the current generation. For example, at least six members of the 1972 cabinet lost some immediate relatives to the ravages of the early colonial era.[26] The mother of Barthélemy Boganda—the country's first president—was beaten to death by the private militia of a concessionary company on a rubber-collection sweep, and Bokassa's own father (and the uncle of Boganda) was likewise beaten to death while in French detention for not "volunteering" to serve as corvée labor for the regional administration.

Later, when the rush for rubber, ivory, and gold petered out, the cultivation of cotton was forcibly imposed upon the population in an effort to draw it into the cash economy. Yet to many ethnic groups, agricultural activity was a demeaning female occupation: Males were meant to restrict themselves to hunting and fishing. Popularly referred to as the "white man's crop," cotton cultivation was highly unremunerative, even in regions where serious agrarian activity was common. Consequently, the mandatory cultivation of cotton had to be brutally enforced and periodically inspected, sparking off further bouts of colonial abuses that in turn fomented more alienation and revolt. Indeed, with the colonial reforms of 1945–1946 (which abolished forced labor, among other things), cotton cultivation plummetted as farmers abandoned the crop with a vengeance. Agricultural activity in general collapsed as a massive rural-urban exodus transformed the demographic map of Oubangui-Chari.

By 1949, even the mere provision of foodstuffs to the capital had become problematic.[27] By 1970, sprawling townships had replaced former major administrative centers. The CAR ranked second in Africa (of 32 states) in level of urbanization;[28] fully 27 percent of the population now lived in centers of more than 25,000 people. Bangui itself had experienced truly phenomenal growth: Its population rose from 39,000 in 1949 to 88,700 in 1962; to 152,000 in 1966; to 207,000 in 1974; and to more than 300,000 in 1981.

It was only in the 1950s that the colonial administration was forced under pressure from Paris to embark on the sociopolitical emancipation of the colony—a policy strenuously resisted by diehard conservatives in the resident expatriate community as too enlightened and far beyond the needs and capabilities of the indigenous populations. The emancipation drives led to major educational advances in what had been traditionally the least developed colony in the AEF. Starting from a scholarization rate lower than that of Chad (1.5 percent in 1936), the CAR stood at 34.5 percent by 1958. As a result of major education efforts after independence, it gained the distinction of being the third-ranking African state in terms of *rate of change* in literacy. Yet the CAR's education rates remain only average for Africa; the country's first-generation intellectual elite is extremely youthful and unsure of itself, and until the 1970s the country possessed only two indigenous M.D.s and no Ph.D.s in any field.

Economic Limitations

The Central African Republic boasts vast untapped mineral resources, immense prospects for timber exports and tourism,[29] and a potentially viable agricultural sector. Yet the country's economy is in a state of acute stagnation, subject to erratic gyrations in mineral and crop production. Agriculture is depressed due to the continuing rural-urban exodus, resistance to the cultivation of cash crops ("government crops"), and general animosity to all initiatives of the central government. The forestry and mining sectors, which could potentially impel the transformation of the country, are seriously constrained by prohibitive start-up costs and by the daunting distances between the deposits and Bangui, and between Bangui and the ocean. Gross mismanagement under Bokassa (whereby state coffers served the dictator's every whim), exploitative shady foreign consortia involved in quick in-out operations, and ecological ravages (e.g., the drying up of the country's sole transport artery, the Oubangui River)[30] have all played a role in humbling this potentially vibrant economy.

The bulk of the rural population is engaged in subsistence agriculture, which produces such crops as maize, manioc, rice, peanuts, bananas, and sorghum. Coffee and cotton—the two main cash crops—traditionally have made up 35–60 percent of the CAR's exports and provide the major source of income for the majority of the population.

Coffee, which is grown in the more humid areas of the extreme southwest of the country, is cultivated on both large European plantations and on small African farms. Production has increased erratically, reaching more than 13,000 tons in 1969–1970. Poor race relations and bitter memories of the abuses of the forced labor era have created acute difficulties for French farmers seeking to recruit workers for their fields. In addition, popular agitation has sought to exclude Europeans altogether from coffee cultivation in the CAR. African farms, by contrast, are small and inefficient: The intensive labor involved in growing the crop and the poor prices paid for undergrade beans have discouraged the expansion of the African share of coffee production.

Cotton, like coffee, is a crop indigenous to the Central African Republic, although its intense cultivation dates only from the 1920s. It is grown by some 25,000 African farmers north of the humid rain forests in the center and northeast of the country. The potential for major improvements in per-acre yields and overall crop tonnage is very bright, despite particularly sharp fluctuations in cotton production. At the root of these fluctuations is the fact that cotton is still associated in the minds of farmers as a compulsory crop. During the colonial era, and in the first years of independence, the various head taxes imposed on the traditional population could be satisfied only by payment in kind—originally in rubber, then in cotton.[31] To enforce the cultivation and delivery of cotton by the rural population, punitive expeditions were periodically dispatched by the regional administrations. Both the quantities exacted and the methods used to enforce compliance paid no attention to differential soil conditions and lifestyles in the country. Ethnic groups unaccustomed to agrarian activity, or residing in land unsuitable for cotton cultivation, were brutalized into planting it. Major abuses committed by local militias, marketing agents, or greedy chiefs were tolerated by the colonial administration so long as quotas were fulfilled. These quotas were in many cases impossibly high, leading to intermittent localized or general revolts. And where farmers did voluntarily cultivate the crop, low producer prices (a function of the high costs of collection and evacuation to the coast) discouraged the expansion of the acreage under cultivation, thereby keeping cotton production at depressed levels.

The massive disengagement of farmers from cotton cultivation following the liberalization of its forced cultivation caused production to plummet. Neither improvements in feeder roads and infrastructure nor boosts in producer prices (in 1974–1976) succeeded in making the crop of "last resort" significantly more popular; by 1969, however, production was back to its old peak.

Forestry and Mineral Resources

Some of the richest and least exploited forestry resources in Africa are found in the CAR. The country's dense, humid rainforest covers the extreme southern extremity of the country. Profusely covered with trees of up to 200 feet in height, the extremely valuable tropical hardwoods could make timber the CAR's leading export, if not for the costly evacuation to the riverways and the slow and wasteful route to the coast (a route that takes 2–7 months to cover). The country's forestry resources have thus remained virtually intact despite a tripling of tree-felling and the establishment of several expatriate companies. Even so, by 1976 timber was the second-highest export item after cotton.

The CAR is also known to have tremendous mineral wealth under its topsoil. Many deposits have been positively identified, and others are periodically discovered. For example, in 1971–1972, a Romanian team confirmed the existence of copper in Ngadé and a veritable mountain of iron (700,000 tons, with a 62.4 percent ore content) near Bogoin. Limestone exists near Bangui and at Fatouma, manganese at Bour-N'Gam, chalk at Bobossa, lignite, peat, and coal near M'Patou, mercury at Baboua, and other deposits elsewhere. Poor communications, the immense distances between deposits and the coast, and high start-up costs have thus far discouraged the exploitation of all but the low-bulk high-value minerals—gold, diamonds, and uranium.

Gold had its heyday in the 1930s and 1940s, when the territory exported between 1,000 and 2,000 pounds annually; current production is insignificant, however. In the 1950s, diamonds replaced gold as the CAR's prime mineral export, with peak production being recorded between 1950 and 1957 and new records set again in 1977–1978. The diamond industry is the largest in the country, employing over 50,000 people. The main deposits are found in the western extremity of the country and in the depopulated area in the center-east between Ndelé and Bakouma. By 1966, diamond exports accounted for 53 percent of the CAR's exports, although this percentage, too, has fluctuated erratically. Extracted mostly by private diggers and collected by non-nationals mostly from Sudan, Nigeria, and Sierra Leone, these high quality stones have been a major source of marketing friction between Bangui and the expatriate consortia set up for this purpose. Moreover, as a result of widescale smuggling to neighboring countries, thousands of carats of stones have been moved beyond Bangui's control; and under Bokassa's reign, large numbers went directly into his private coffers.

Many of Bangui's hopes for a more viable economy rest on the country's uranium deposits. Discovered in the vicinity of Bakouma between 1959 and 1961, 3 million tons of uranium phosphate reserves have been confirmed. Although a 1969 agreement set up a Franco-CAR company to produce 500 tons of enriched uranium per year, French interests withdrew their participation soon after, citing a global glut in uranium ore. French interest in the CAR's uranium was renewed, however, after the 1973 energy crisis and the grant of concessions in the country to non-French consortia. Yet new treaties signed in 1975—establishing a French-Swiss-CAR consortium—also failed to lead to active exploitation of the deposits, this time due to the emergence of various technical difficulties.

The CAR's principal imports are industrial goods and textiles, although virtually every modern commodity has to be imported up-river. High transport costs and custom duties, as well as the high cost of commerce in the CAR, have made Bangui one of the costliest capitals in Africa. Export coverage of imports, vacillating from the positive (116.1 percent) in 1972 to the negative (69.1 percent) in 1975, camouflages a seriously unbalanced economy whose extractive sector periodically rescues an intrinsically stagnant rural and agrarian sector. These fiscal shortfalls were greatly exacerbated by crass mismanagement during the Bokassa era, during which extravagant ad hoc expenditures and routine embezzlement of state funds by Bokassa's cabinet ministers highlighted the dictator's casual approach to fiscal management and accountability.

The visible wastage of scarce resources in Bangui—coupled with spiraling societal needs for jobs and services and fueled by the ongoing rural-urban drift and proletarianization—has reinforced the bitterness directed against all governments in Bangui—Bokassa's, Dacko's, and Kolingba's. These regimes have been fiscally, diplomatically, and financially sustained by France, which is unwilling to lose such a potentially rich client-state. But as the economy and society stagnate, pressures for a radical redistribution of political and economic power increase.

Decolonization and the Dacko Presidency

The abuses of the early concessionary system gave way to an equally oppressive colonial era notorious for its forced labor, compulsory cultivation of cotton, and poor race relations. Bangui's colonial administration was one of the last to conform to the spirit and letter of the post-1945 reforms and liberalizations of the French colonial empire. French mercantile interests and settlers, aware of the likely economic repercussions of liberalization on cotton and coffee cultivation (which overtly or covertly relied on forced labor), fought rearguard battles to protect the colony from the winds of change emanating from Paris. René Malbrant, the Chad-Oubangui-Chari deputy to the French National Assembly, argued passionately in 1946 against territorial elections for African representatives on the grounds that "among the natives of Oubangui-Chari it is impossible to find thirty-five General Councillors capable of assuming these functions."[32] A similar motion in Bangui rejected the envisaged liberalization on the grounds that it was "suited only to peoples more advanced than the inhabitants of French Equatorial Africa."[33] So incensed was the local French community at the very idea of Arican representation that seven French delegates resigned in disgust when the newly elected Oubanguians "dared" to criticize France's *rôle civilatrice* in the colony. Forced labor continued in one guise or another through the mid-1950s. Heavy-handed administrative authoritarianism sparked riots and rebellions, as in the prewar era.[34] And the racist petite-bourgeoisie mentality of the expatriate community continued to poison communal relations right through independence. The political evolution of Oubangui-Chari quickened with the emergence of Barthélemy Boganda as the territory's prime political leader. Elected in 1946 to the French National Assembly and in 1952 to the Territorial Assembly and to the AEF Grand Council, Boganda and his party (Mouvement d'Evolution Sociale en Afrique, or MESAN) immediately became the undisputed political force in the country. Unlike neighboring territories, pre-independence Oubangui-Chari was marked neither by a tug-of-war among competing African parties nor by the immediate politicization of ethnic cleavages. The general inertia of the traditional population and the minuteness of the modern African elite, coupled with Boganda's magnetic personality and crucial early support from the Church,[35] firmly established the defrocked priest[36] in the Oubanguian political center stage.

Impressed during his stay in France by the difference between the liberalism of Paris and the authoritarian racism of the French in Oubangui-Chari, Boganda lashed out against the colonial administration, which was dragging its heels in implementing reforms decreed in Paris. This action in turn transformed him in the eyes of the administration into a dangerous and radical demagogue; and despite his parliamentary immunity, he was harassed and even briefly imprisoned. As was precisely the case with the other defrocked priest in Equatorial Africa (Fulbert Youlou in Brazzaville), the more Bangui tried to discredit Boganda's reputation, the more his power base expanded—especially given the doubling of the electorate between 1952 and 1956. Boganda was reelected to the National Assembly in 1956 with 155,952 votes (compared with 20,230 for his nearest rival); the next year MESAN (which was not affiliated with any metropolitan grouping) won all the seats in the Territorial Assembly, while Boganda was elected president of the AEF Grand Council.

A strong charismatic leader,[37] Boganda was deeply concerned with core moral issues, the transformation of societal values, the regional unification of Equatorial Africa, cooperative economic activity, and a new work ethic. Assuming power in the first Autonomous Republic, Boganda relegated much of the day-to-day administration to his vice-president, Abel Goumba, in order to concentrate on his other concerns. Soon after, he died in a mystery-shrouded plane crash on March 28, 1959.[38]

The elimination from the Oubanguian scene of the stabilizing force of Boganda precipitated an intense bout of factionalism that was not resolved for the duration of Dacko's presidency. Abel Goumba, the country's first African doctor,[39] temporarily filled the vacuum but was forced to cede primacy to David Dacko, Boganda's second lieutenant and the minister of the interior.[40] The succession was hardly smooth, however, for with independence on the horizon a number of other political leaders were challenging Dacko's none-too-solid leadership credentials. Among these other leaders, in particular, were Etienne Ngounio (who at Boganda's death became mayor of Bangui, president of MESAN, and senator of Oubangui to the French Community), and Pierre Maleombho, president of the National Assembly.

The challenge surfaced in the form of a no-confidence motion in the National Assembly. Lodged by Goumba and backed by Maleombho, the motion appeared to have garnered the support of two-thirds of the delegates, thus presaging Dacko's constitutional ouster. However, Dacko promptly mobilized ethnic support from his home region, Lobaye. His ethnic kinsmen were brought to Bangui in trucks loaned by French expatriates supportive of his candidacy. Utilizing bribes and intimidation, Dacko cajoled sufficient deputies to beat back the challenge of the rebellious Assembly. The defeated Goumba consequently announced the formation of a new party—Mouvement pour l'Evolution Démocratique de l'Afrique Central, or MEDAC—as the spiritual successor of MESAN, moribund since Boganda's death. Fourteen deputies promptly declared for the new party, including Ngounio, who was nominally president of MESAN.

In the partial elections held on Sesptember 20, 1960, despite widespread intimidation, the new party garnered around 20 percent of the vote. An ethnic polarization was patently developing since MEDAC scored its major inroads among the Mandjia, while MESAN's core support was in Baya country. (Paradoxically, fully 74 percent of the electorate did not go to the polls in the capital.) Traumatized by MEDAC's strong showing, and egged on by MESAN militants and expatriate leaders to adopt a firm line, Dacko passed a series of decrees centralizing most power in his own hands, banning all other parties in the country, and arresting seven of MEDAC's deputies, including Goumba. The purge of the Goumba faction stabilized the political in-fighting in Bangui but did little to fortify Dacko's leadership. Generally weak and indecisive, Dacko never emerged in control of the Central African Republic. He was unable either to impose himself on the progressively independent and corrupt post-independence civil service or to provide viable policy alternatives to a country that was slowly sinking into an economic quagmire. Despite a series of laws that erected a "more repressive regime than the colonial system" (as Dacko himself admitted, "You say the colonial regime was more lenient. Of course it was!"),[41] his presidency was marked by a *deflation* of power and authority and not by the reverse.

Neither charismatic nor capable of commanding much respect, and temperamentally not cut out to be either ruthless or even firm with his colleagues, Dacko pampered the cabinet, National Assembly, and civil service, which rapidly became cesspools of corruption and mediocrity.[42] As one observer put it, Dacko was "a decent guy at a time when ruthlessness and a whip were necessary."[43] Aware that he could not fill Boganda's shoes, Dacko strove to antagonize as few strata in society as possible and constantly appeared surprised that his lack of firmness led to gross abuses of power on the part of his subordinates. Massive corruption seeped into all levels of government during his tenure as the new indigenous bureaucracy rushed to benefit from the fruits of office. Collegial rule, which Dacko stressed in contrast to Boganda's autocratic style, resulted in a situation whereby ministers were carving up for themselves autonomous politico-economic fiefdoms with accountability to no one. Although Dacko was neither blind to what was happening nor corrupt himself, his regime was marked by inefficiency and lack of leadership.

When Dacko finally initiated a series of purges of hundreds of officials (including prefects, mayors, and heads of state organs) because of their "exaggerated taste for pleasure" and "mediocre ardour for work,"[44] the rot was too deeply entrenched. Even government investigators were dropping cases and prosecutions on the payment of hefty bribes. Most of the twenty prefects and subprefects dismissed or imprisoned for embezzlement or incompetence in their districts rapidly percolated back to positions of authority, protected by their "patrons" in the cabinet. Neither the screening of those allowed to remain on the party lists for the May 1964 elections (only fourteen incumbents were judged sufficiently meritorious to be fielded again!) nor the austerity drives that marked much of Dacko's reign could curb the civil service's frenetic bout of self-enrichment and unresponsiveness to directives from the center.

By 1964, moreover, the economic picture had become acutely grave. Cotton production had dropped disastrously and the opening of new diamond fields had syphoned labor from the agrarian sector. Real GDP per capita actually declined during the Dacko era. Budgetary allocations and fiscal accountability were increasingly fictitious concepts. For example, the 1962 civil service payroll was double that of 1961 and bore no resemblance to the figures actually authorized; and the official freeze on new appointments was totally ignored by most ministries. In order to meet this severe unbudgeted fiscal drain, taxes were ruthlessly increased by 200–300 percent. In 1963, an onerous head tax was imposed on traditional farmers not paying income tax, and the business and turnover tax was increased by 10 percent. Moreover, since the patriotic (and voluntary) National Development Loan attracted few subscribers, donations began to be forcibly collected, as were compulsory monthly payments meant to sustain the operations of MESAN. Most of the latter levies, in particular, were embezzled by the collectors themselves, who also forced farmers to purchse party insignia, flags, and ornaments at wildly inflated prices.

These abuses fanned massive resentment throughout the countryside. Farmers arriving with their produce at state purchasing centers were likely to be "taxed," in one fell swoop, of all their annual earnings. A call was even heard for the return of colonial rule, which was perceived to be less exploitative than the avaricious and corrupt post-independence regime in Bangui. Not surprisingly, Dacko's efforts to spur higher agricultural production and stem the rural-urban exodus fell on deaf and resentful ears; and when René Dumont was brought to Bangui to assess the reasons for the collapse of the country's agrarian sector, he squarely linked it with the mushrooming class of "profiteers" in the economy.[45]

The 1966 Coup d'Etat

The coup d'état that ushered in fourteen years of personal dictatorship had, as elsewhere, complex causes and motivations. In justifiying the midnight assault against his own cousin, Bokassa cited a host of factors, from the dangers implicit in Dacko's recent pro-East overtures (and a budding leftist plot to topple him) to the utter governmental anarchy and economic chaos prevailing at the time. Certainly among Bokassa's first actions in office was the closure of the Chinese Embassy in Bangui and the arrest of Dacko's cabinet director and head of Internal Security, both of whom were allegedly setting up a People's Liberation Army.[46] But the true motivations for the December 31, 1965, coup were primarily *personal and corporate*, and the ripeness of the regime to any assault merely ensured its smooth and unopposed execution.

Faced with a socioeconomic morass to which he saw no end, Dacko had offered to resign the presidency in 1965. Although the party sycophants "convinced" Dacko to remain in office, new loci of opposition to Dacko were developing among ambitious members of the Banguian elite. Among those aspiring to supplant him were several of his own appointees, including Michel Adama-Tamboux, the rather mediocre though ambitious president of the National Assembly (who had replaced Maleombho when the latter was purged). Adama-Tamboux had forged a small group of supporters from the upper echelons of the civil service and the party. Other aspiring politicians were likewise plotting behind

Dacko's back, and a few were actually conniving with a number of ambitious officers in the country's security services.

Dacko had long favored the gendarmerie over the regular army, both in fiscal allocations and in supplies of materiel—a fact that drove a wedge between the two arms of the security forces.[47] Yet, although this was one cause for the disaffection of Chief of Staff Colonel Jean-Bedel Bokassa, who in 1965 marched uninvited into a cabinet session to demand increased allocations and cabinet representation,[48] it did not secure Dacko the support, or even the neutrality, of the gendarmerie and its commander, Jean Izamo. Indeed, a second triggering cause for the 1966 coup d'état was the discovery, on the same evening as the coup, of an alleged plot by Izamo to assassinate Bokassa and seize power in Bangui. Nudged by his subordinate, Captain Alexandre Banza, Bokassa preempted Izamo and seized power himself.[49] Whatever precipitated the actual takeover, Bokassa, for more than a year, had been thoroughly disenchanted with Dacko's political style, indecisiveness, and weak leadership. It must also have rankled him to hear Dacko stressing his familial relationship to Boganda when in reality Bokassa had a much closer and legitimate connection.[50] And the constant proddings by ambitious politicians afraid to challenge Dacko directly and by his deputy, Banza, slowly convinced the flamboyant and self-centred Bokassa that the nation was awaiting a savior along the lines of de Gaulle. When the new year dawned, the Central African Republic had a new leader whose highly idiosyncratic style left an indelible imprint.

Military Dictatorship and Personalist Rule

Bokassa's initial cabinet included three military officers, three Dacko ministers, and three key civil servants. The officers were paratroop commander Captain Alexandre Banza (the acknowledged mastermind of the coup, who was soon promoted to lieutenant colonel and appointed minister of finance and veteran affairs), Police Lieutenant André Magalé, who became a permanent (and very venal) fixture in Bokassa's regime, and Lieutenant Timotheé Malendoma. The civilian component of the government included Jean Arthur Bandio (Dacko's ambitious minister of the interior), Ange Patasse, and Antoine Kezza (both young civil administrators). Although Banza soon conflicted with Bokassa and was executed, most of Bokassa's original appointees continued to revolve around the pinnacle of political power for the duration of the military regime.

The initial policies emanating from Bangui were quite popular. Despite a brutal settling of accounts that accompanied the coup d'état,[51] Bokassa's decrees lashed out against the worst abuses of the civil administration. The dissolution of the National Assembly and the dispersal of its arrogant deputies and harangues against both the "thieves . . . of MESAN" and "the complacency of the self-seeking civil service" triggered waves of support for the regime that, in due time, virtually dismantled MESAN, outlawed forced party contributions, and eliminated several rural taxes on farmers.[52] A series of puritanical edicts later forbade both the entry of civil servants into night-clubs and the use of alcoholic beverages at official receptions (for economic reasons); one edict even specified the days and hours during which the playing of tom-toms was allowed in Bangui.[53]

The initial populist zeal notwithstanding, Bokassa was as sensitive to the interests of the urban elites as Dacko had been. None of the privileges of the ruling class were affected; indeed, Bokassa dismantled many of Dacko's austerity policies and denounced the rest as inequitable. He reassured the French expatriate community, which was dazed at the fall of their protégé, expressed an exaggerated filial piety vis-à-vis Paris, and expelled the Chinese Embassy, which Dacko had used as a counter-balance to the overly pro-French sentiments of his entourage.

Most army officers were promoted in the aftermath of the coup, and both military budget and salaries were sharply increased. Indeed, the coup d'état has been viewed as no more than a "hold-up of the Treasury,"[54] inasmuch as the prime beneficiaries in the CAR were the armed forces. Captain Banza, handsomely promoted for his pivotal role in the coup, became the first Baya ever to attain major national prominence (a fact that gained Bokassa considerable popularity in Baya areas); in ethnic terms, however, Bokassa's Mbaïka group were strongly promoted in both cabinet and administration (see Table 5).

Thus, initial assessments of Bokassa's administration were not unfavorable. He filled a power vacuum and provided the firm leadership that the CAR so badly needed. Reports of Bokassa's brutality and authoritarian inclinations were brushed aside as unfortunate excesses in a country always difficult to rule. Yet, as with Uganda's Idi Amin and Equatorial Guinea's Macias Nguema, the true dimensions of Bokassa's personality soon came into sharper focus.

Jean-Bedel Bokassa

Bokassa was born in Bobangui (50 miles from Bangui) on February 22, 1921, to a petty village chief who was later beaten to death at the local French prefect's office for committing a minor infraction. His mother subsequently committed suicide, leaving a family of twelve children

Table 5
Ethnic Membership of the CAR Cabinet

Ethnicity	% Pop.	Independence Cabinet (%)	Pre-coup Cabinet (%)	Post-coup Cabinet (%)
Banda	31	0	11	0
Baya	29	14	11	15
Mandjia	8.5	0	11	8.5
Riverine	8	43	44	15
Mboum	7	0	0	8
Mbaïka	6.5	0	0	23
Other	10	43	22	31
N =		8	11	15

Source: Morrison et al., Black Africa: A Contemporary Handbook (New York: Free Press, 1972), p. 202.

including the six-year-old Jean-Bedel. Raised by a grandfather, Bokassa was educated at mission schools, including one in Brazzaville, where he felt compelled to excel in physical activities in response to taunts referring to his unfortunate family history. After completing secondary school, Bokassa joined the French Army and saw action in Indochina. According to all accounts, he was a courageous soldier, fully deserving the twelve medals and citations awarded him for bravery and wounds suffered in action.[55]

Commissioned in 1949, Bokassa was demobilized from the French Army in 1961 with the rank of captain and charged with setting up a national army for the young republic. Having attended staff courses in France, he was very rapidly promoted to colonel in 1964; and at one point he advanced in less than two years to a rank normally requiring a minimum of eight years of service.[56] After seizing power he awarded himself the rank of general (1967) and marshal (1974)—for "supreme services to the State"—and when he ran out of rungs on the military ladder, he crowned himself emperor.

Bokassa's vanity was not unknown in Paris. His penchant for always wearing his *earned* decorations was viewed as a mild idiosyncrasy during his term as chief of staff; when he became head of state, however, his habit of adorning himself as well with the various courtesy Orders of Honor routinely exchanged with other heads of state came to be seen as symptomatic of his megalomania. In 1966, a photograph in *Paris Match* caused a full-fledged diplomatic incident. Showing Bokassa in his full regalia, it triggered a wave of ridicule in France and a formal complaint by the CAR ambassador.[57] Ironically, Bokassa had chosen an identical photograph for the state portrait to be hung in all public offices. But its availability to the wide public—from whom there was quite a demand due to its curiosity value—was restricted.

Once Bokassa assumed power in Bangui, no one could restrain his excesses. Increasingly it became hazardous to contradict him. Until his brutal liquidation, Lieutenant Colonel Alexandre Banza (in many ways the true mentor of the 1966 coup) was the only restraining influence on Bokassa. Everyone else in Bokassa's entourage encouraged his flights of imagination, flattered his vanity, and even concocted projects to appeal to his pride.[58] State policy became an extension of Bokassa's ego as the distinctions among the state, the presidency, and Bokassa as an individual became blurred.

Less than a year after seizing power, Bokassa signified his inclination to remain in office permanently due to his unique talents, cryptically noting that "I am everywhere and nowhere. I see nothing yet I see all. I listen to nothing and hear everything."[59] Long before his grandiose coronation as emperor and founder of an imperial dynasty, a veritable court had emerged around Bokassa. His cabinet had become a coterie of self-seeking sycophants; Bokassa himself held twelve ministerial portfolios and interfered whimsically in all the others. Ministers were shuffled with monotonous regularity, as often as six times a year,[60] preventing both effective government and ministerial competence.

Though variously rationalized, frequent cabinet shuffles became Bokassa's peculiar style of keeping his ministers under control and his locus of power and patronage sacrosanct. The tendency this encouraged among his cabinet ministers (especially such cronies as General André Dieudonné Magalé, who moved in and out of the government with acute regularity) was to frantically exploit all the fiscal rewards of high office during one's limited tenure. One veteran U.S. diplomat in Bangui referred to Bokassa's style as "allowing each corrupt influential his day in the sun,"[61] noting that, in exchange for this opportunity, ministers were willing to debase themselves beyond belief—much to Bokassa's amusement. Caught in their misdeeds, officials meekly admitted guilt, begged for presidential pardon, and docilely accepted temporary exile or demotion, knowing full well that their chances of bouncing back to office were great.[62]

Civil crimes were differentially assessed, depending upon the status of the offender. Petty thieves stealing out of hunger could be condemned to twenty years' hard labor (and in prison, as in 1972, they could be beaten to death). Yet an overly greedy cabinet minister caught stealing millions of CFA francs needed only to plead poverty and abjectly prostrate himself (at times literally so) before his benefactor in order to be forgiven and, after a period of exile to less lucrative sinecures, find himself in favor again. Some ministers were even "promoted to better paid jobs, on the grounds that their higher salaries will help them pay back what they owe."[63]

Although Bokassa's personal dictatorship was less demented than Nguema's and much less brutal than Amin's, the fount of all power and decisionmaking was Bokassa himself. All favor or reprimand, reward or punishment, promotion or demotion, emanated from him. Ministers, ambassadors, administrators, and petty officials feared to make decisions or undertake action—even on the most trivial matters—unless they were specifically and personally endorsed by Bokassa. Inertia, immobilism, and acute paralysis were the natural outcomes as "political life in the C.A.R [unfolded] like a play in which only a few of the 4,000 officials and agents have a part."[64] With telephones largely inoperative in Bangui, all government offices were enjoined to keep their radios on in order to hear the intermittent instructions sent directly from the presidential office.

Bokassa's every fancy and idiosyncrasy—however irrational or infeasible—became state policy. His power was absolute, his involvement in domestic and foreign policy was wide-ranging, and his administration was highly erratic and unpredictable, as a reflection of his emotional vacillations and periodic whims. Pursuing neither short-term nor long-run national goals or policies, Bokassa governed the Central African Republic as if it were his personal fiefdom for thirteen years.

As early as 1968, Bokassa's picture adorned the front page of *every* school exercise book in the entire country. A host of schools, hospitals, clinics, roads, and projects as well as the new university and air academy were named after him. Returning from a state visit to Ndjamena in 1968, Bokassa had himself carried off the plane in a litter, much as Uganda's Idi Amin would later do. Political prisoners, as if to symbolize that they had sinned against Bokassa's persona, were interned in Bobangui, his home village, where they paid off "their debt to society" by working on the president's residence and gardens.[65] Magnanimous amnesties (e.g., the release from jail of all "mothers" on Mother's Day, 1971), coupled with arbitrary executions (e.g., the simultaneous execution of all prisoners guilty of killing their wives) strengthened his personal base of power in Bangui.[66] But ridiculed abroad, and by expatriates at home, Bokassa was never fazed. Increasingly reluctant to meet foreign journalists and scholars because of his bad press overseas, he constantly reiterated his popularity among his subjects. After his ouster he persisted in this belief, risking the firing squad in 1986 as a test of his convictions.

Converted to Marxism late in 1969 after a brief visit to Brazzaville, Bokassa promptly initiated a pro-Eastern foreign policy in 1970. When it became clear that no tangible (i.e., material) benefits would be forthcoming, he relented and returned to the Western fold. Later, Bokassa was to announce his sudden conversion to Islam (following inducements by Libya) and his adoption of the Muslim name Salah-eh-Dinn (Saladin). Dozens of his sycophants also promptly "converted"—this in a country where Muslims were in the minority and deep anti-Arab sentiments dated back to the slave era. When disillusioned by Qadaffi's lack of generosity, Bokassa and his "court" casually reverted to their original faith. Adoring the pomp of state visits, he toured the world a number of times, taking with him large retinues of assistants and distributing gifts of diamonds. (Several such gifts to high French officials, including the French head of state, and lavish big-game hunting expeditions resulted in ugly political charges during subsequent French presidential elections.)

Bokassa's personal style of leadership manifested itself in a myriad of ways, even though formal government structures did not shrivel (as they had done in Uganda and Equatorial Guinea). In 1970, for example, he ordered all buildings along one of Bangui's main streets to be renovated immediately at the pain of prompt state confiscation; later, he required all banks to form a consortium to subsidize the construction of a luxury hotel. In February 1971, he temporarily closed down the CAR Foreign Ministry on the grounds that it was "inefficient"; a few months later, a national airline—Air Centrafrique—was set up by edict. The airline, denied routings or credit, and erected without support services or administration, collapsed at great financial cost, its sole jet flying only twice and then languishing at Bangui airport until it was resold to creditors.[67] The same year, in his effort to increase export revenues, he arbitrarily imposed unrealistically high cotton quotas to all regions. His threatening admonitions to those who did not perform their "duties" intimidated fearful local officials who mixed prime with yellow cotton, in order to meet their quotas—thus leading to the eventual downgrading of the entire country's crop in world markets and a severe loss of state revenue.

Combative and spiteful when ridiculed or scorned, Bokassa was both brutal and vengeful. At the time of the 1966 coup d'état, one of Dacko's ministers was beaten to death because in the past he "had not manifested all the outward signs of respect to the Army."[68] In February 1966, Dacko's chief of internal state security, the architect of the alleged pro-Chinese conspiracy, was "executed in brutal circumstances,"[69] as was Colonel Alexandre Banza three years later. Political prisoners and inmates of Bangui prison were routinely tortured or beaten at Bokassa's orders. (Their cries could easily be heard by nearby residents.) The public brutalization of prisoners in 1972 and the violent rampage against Bangui's schoolchildren in 1979—in both instances personally led by Bokassa—only underscored this well-known dimension of his character.

At the same time, his sentimental side was revealed by his quest for his illegitimate Vietnamese daughter, his magnanimity vis-à-vis the fraudulent first "Martine" who arrived, and his tearful outbursts at de Gaulle's funeral. A complex personality, who in 1986 risked the death squad by returning to the Bangui he had so brutalized, Bokassa ruled his country in an absolute manner for thirteen long years.

Thirteen Years of Personal Dictatorship

The first six months of Bokassa's regime provided a much-needed shake-up of the country's civil administration, which had become increasingly unruly under Dacko. A temporary upswing of the economy likewise bolstered the credentials of the military administration. Rapidly, however, conditions began to deteriorate, lethargy crept back into the administration, and Bokassa's tendency to dictate all aspects of public policy began to drive a wedge between him and his prime lieutenant, Alexandre Banza.

As urban unrest flared up in Bangui, the regime cracked down harshly on sources of protest and sealed off the country from outside scrutiny. Early in 1966, the Bangui Public Library was closed down and there commenced a selective ban on foreign newspapers entering the country. Issues of *Le Monde, Le Monde Diplomatique,* and *Afrique Nouvelle* were banned whenever they cast aspersions on Bokassa. The veteran Africanist Philippe Decraene gained the distinction of having all his past and future writings—on whatever topic and in whatever journal or newspaper—banned from the CAR indefinitely.[70] Foreign correspondents trying to fly into Bangui were generally denied visas. Information about domestic affairs increasingly reached the outside world from private sources rather than from news agencies or accredited resident reporters.

Aware of the mushrooming disillusionment with his regime, Bokassa moved to patch up his relations with France. In April 1968, Bangui dramatically resigned from the Customs Union of Central African States (UDEAC), formed shortly after independence, to join with Zaire and Chad in an ill-fated Union of Central African States (UEAC). The move, triggered by complaints that the richer coastal states were neglecting the insular ones within the UDEAC, had caused consternation in Paris, which regarded it as a U.S. conspiracy to displace France from Africa.[71] Putting the stillborn UEAC behind him, Bokassa made his peace with Paris, receiving in return a personal gift of a DC-4 plane and assurances of continued French military support for the regime. Detachments of the 11th French Division, elements of which were already in the country, were subsequently flown in to help stabilize conditions in Bangui; the official reason given, however, was to "acclimatize them to tropical conditions."[72]

The troops were invited into the CAR because of Bokassa's sense of acute insecurity, especially vis-à-vis Lieutenant Colonel Banza, his intellectual and tactical superior, the true architect of the 1966 coup, and commander of both the Infantry Battalion and the elite paracommando company. The only person who would stand up to Bokassa as an equal and dispute the effect on the country of the latter's flamboyant and unbudgeted extravagances, Banza was barely on speaking terms with Bokassa, even though both officers tried to avert an overt rift.

With the arrival of the French troops, Bokassa moved to downgrade his military competitor, shunting him from the important Ministry of Finance and Economic Affairs to the Ministry of Health and Social Affairs on January 13, 1968. In February 1969, after more friction, Banza's portfolio was downgraded to the subministerial level, and the Ministry of Health and Social Affairs was removed from his domain. A short time later, Banza mounted his anti-Bokassa plot, relying on his ethnic support in the armed forces. The plot was nipped in the bud when the Camp Kasai commander, Major Jean Claude Mandaba, refused to support Banza and arrested him instead.[73] In what was widely condemned as a "political assassination,"[74] Banza was tried by a military tribunal, condemned to death for treason, and executed—all within two days. (The chief of police, Kolotto, also "disappeared" forever around this time.) The loyal Mandaba was subsequently promoted to lieutenant colonel and, in 1971, to general and deputy chief of staff. In September 1969, the now "acclimatized" French troops flew out of Bangui, their mission completed. Sporadic unrest continued in the Baya areas for some time, with students in Bangui shouting "assassin" whenever the presidential vehicle was sighted.[75]

The swift and brutal liquidation of Banza did not eliminate all opposition to Bokassa, even though it removed his prime competitor for power. The harsh treatment meted to all those even remotely involved in the plot (including Banza's wife, who languished in jail for several years) severely cowed all those with pretensions to displace Bokassa and intimidated the officer corps and administration alike. The civil service in particular became increasingly fearful of acting on any matter in the absence of Bokassa's personal directives, especially after Bokassa began to pack the administration with Mbaïka, his ethnic kinsmen.

By 1969, the fiscal straits of the state had become intolerable. Impossible demands were being made on available fiscal reserves by unbudgeted ad hoc expenditures approved whimsically by Bokassa. The crass embezzlement of state funds by his lieutenants and favoritism in budgetary allocations to the army caused perennial budgetary crises. And the absence of even rudimentary fiscal accountability at any level brought chaos to the country. Neither statistical nor budgetary details were known or compiled, let alone published, by the ministries or the central administration. Always a problem in the CAR, fiscal restraint and accountability completely disappeared under Bokassa.

Bokassa never tolerated attempts to curb his ad hoc fiscal splurges, and his political style precluded the purge of colleagues caught in financial misadventures. Instead, periodic cabinet and civil service shuffles ensured that no individual could consistently plunder the resources at his disposal or acquire too powerful a base in any sector of the economy. Orderly planning was replaced by ad hoc allocations whenever a particular sector of the economy began to reel from the effects of mismanagement. Funds were routinely and casually transferred from one budgetary category to another, either when necessary or when Bokassa's whim so dictated; and development projects literally came to a halt as funds were syphoned off in midstream to accommodate new projects, which in turn ground to a halt at another date.

Largely because of these factors, the Bokassa regime, from its inception until its overthrow, was preoccupied with devising ways and means to generate more revenues from internal and external sources. Diplomatic relations, ideologies, and foreign postures were opportunistically adopted with the emergence of any prospect of capital infusion. Likewise, many of Bangui's periodic spats with Paris were in essence little more than gambits to attract greater fiscal infusions from the metropole.

In May 1968 Bangui reopened diplomatic relations with China, largely for pecuniary reasons; and in the next year it initiated the previously noted "Move to the East" policy. The proclamation that scientific socialism would henceforth be Bangui's state policy meant little more to Bokassa, however, than payment of lip-service to the ideology and awaiting financial rewards.[76] Although a spate of offers of technical assistance followed the new diplomatic initiatives, an alleged Romanian offer to link the CAR to the then-projected Trans-Gabonese railroad appeared to be the most valuable pledge.

Exact details of the origins of the misunderstanding with Bucharest are not clear, inasmuch as Romania claimed that no such offer had been made; but the "Romanian railroad" pledge was the *cassus belli* for an anti-French tirade by Bokassa over France's miserliness toward the CAR. In retaliation, the French ambassador publicly enumerated every item of assistance given Bangui since independence, rebutting Bokassa's contention that French aid could be "counted in drops."[77] In the ensuing diplomatic imbroglio, Bokassa downgraded the traditional status of the French ambassador as dean of the Diplomatic Corps and later expelled some sixty French agricultural technicians from the country.

Relations with France were mended in due course because both powers needed each other. Bokassa's emotional breakdown at de Gaulle's funeral was thus regarded by some observers as but a calculated move aimed at evoking sympathy and soothing the strained Franco-CAR relations. Regardless of whether Bokassa's outburst had been spontaneous, he was one of only two African leaders invited to meet with President Pompidou after the funeral, and a marked step-up of French aid to the CAR became evident in 1971. The anti-French tirades ended, the French ambassador returned to Bangui, and Kombot Naguemon (the architect of the pro-East tilt) was replaced in the cabinet. France's "most faithful ally" in Africa was back in the fold.

The France-CAR love-hate cycle resumed in 1971, with relations once again souring due to Bokassa's constant need for funds. A new clash developed over the continued control by Paris of the CAR's monetary policy through the joint Central Bank for French Equatorial Africa. Challenging the status quo, Bokassa called for the right of each state to issue its own currency, though still backed by the French franc (FF). In essence, he was demanding unlimited French treasury backing for, and subsidization of, the CAR economy and its present and future debts; but the implications of his demand—beyond its purely nationalist aspects—were neither clear to Bokassa nor understood in Bangui.[78] Whipping up a "spontaneous" demonstration of 30,000 people (many brandishing anti-French placards prepared weeks before), Bokassa inflamed the crowds with a comparison of the "value" of the CFAF and the french franc: Noting their lack of parity (i.e., the former was worth only .02 FF), he accusingly asked the crowds, "Where are the 98 centimes? That is the question."[79] However, the anti-French demonstrations that followed, amidst the chanting of Bokassa's demand that "our money should become our own property," were quelled by the police when, after pillorying the French Embassy, the crowds ominously shifted their march toward the Presidential Palace.

The violent anti-French sentiments expressed during the riots, as well as the roughing up of expatriates, spread panic among the foreign community in Bangui. Many people commenced the liquidation of their assets, stopped restocking, and curtailed credit facilities—all of which triggered massive economic dislocations and commodity shortages.[80] Bokassa's gambit did not pay off, either. Indeed, the only "concrete" benefit that resulted from his campaign was an agreement by France that the new 100,000 CFAF banknotes would carry Bokassa's picture. The campaign ended with the nationalization of one foreign bank and with rhetoric about the CAR's new fiscal autonomy.

The CFAF affair, in combination with the Air Centrafrique fiasco, further undermined the CAR's international prestige. Seizing upon legitimate grievances that Bangui was inadequately served by Air Afrique

(Francophone Africa's joint airline), Bokassa demanded that the regional headquarters of Air Afrique be relocated to Bangui. Rebuffed, he pulled the CAR out of the airline and established an independent Air Centrafrique.

The new airline, operating three planes, was largely inactive. It was granted neither landing rights in most airports nor credit for terminal and refuelling bills. One jet was even temporarily impounded abroad, due to nonpayment of accounts. Eventually all three planes were resold to Air Afrique (at a 50 percent loss) and the CAR rejoined that airline, with yet another of Bokassa's pet projects put to rest.

The CAR's extremely bad press overseas led Bokassa to attempt to stifle, at least in France, any articles critical of him. Although Paris did utilize certain legal statutes to prevent the publication of books critical of Bokassa, the latter's impetuous actions continued to attract critical reviews and resulted in a number of libel lawsuits that attracted even more attention. In July 1972, during what became his penultimate conflict with the press, Bokassa personally led into Bangui prison a squad of gendarmes who commenced the clubbing of its inmates. Citing their recidivist nature, Bokassa was in reality affronted by the burglary of the Presidential Palace a few days previously. The beatings resulted in three deaths.[81] Further beatings, personally ordered by Bokassa, could be witnessed and heard by residents adjoining the prison.[82] The brutality of these acts scandalized public opinion and triggered a massive bout of international criticism. Although Paris imposed fines on, and brought to trial, two reporters who wrote a sarcastic article on Bokassa entitled "Medals by the Kilo, Billions Down the Drain, More Laughable than a Clown, He Is Living Off Our Backs," the Franco-CAR alliance became increasingly burdensome, tarnishing France by association.[83]

As always, Bokassa rejected all criticism and retaliated with vilifications. He lampooned UN Secretary General Kurt Waldheim as "a pimp . . . colonialist . . . imperialist . . . dumb as a corpse," noting that civil servants daring to criticize foreign heads of state (as Waldheim and the corrections commissioner of New York City had done) would, in Bangui, be arrested and beaten up.[84] The international furor had hardly abated when the "Two Martines" affair broke into the spotlight, once again placing the Central African Republic and its leader in the worst possible light.[85]

The Final Years: Political Decay and Personal Empire

By the mid-1970s, the Bokassa regime had come under increasing pressure, domestic as well as external. All along, the stability of the dictatorship had rested on (1) France's direct and indirect support for the regime, (2) Bokassa's control of the security services and support from the civil service, and (3) the socioeconomic and political void in Bangui that retarded the formation of sources of opposition. All three were no longer supportive of the Bokassa dictatorship, even though it took the direct intervention of French force of arms to topple the regime in 1979.

From the outset, France had no illusions about Bokassa. Indeed, despite its acquiescence to Dacko's ouster, France retained faith in his leadership potential and ensured that he did not "disappear" as did other leaders who had crossed swords with Bokassa. In the aftermath of the French invasion in 1979, Dacko bounced back to power in Bangui. Without exhibiting any unusual political traits during his first presidency, and without revealing in his second bout as president that he had learned any new skills during his eclipse, Dacko nevertheless remained France's "preferred" ruler in Bangui.

In the interim, President Giscard d'Estaing tolerated Bokassa's bizzare antics and periodic anti-French vituperations as the unfortunate but necessary price of keeping the CAR firmly in the French orbit. Despite the CAR's spotty economy, some of the world's richest mineral deposits lay beneath its topsoil. Such a "prize" could not be allowed to fall under the sway of other foreign powers or domestic leaders who might turn out to be truly antagonistic to French interests. Bokassa was at least a reliable (and firm) surrogate ruler; in exchange for his continued fealty, France was quite content to "pander to his eccentricities."[86]

Of equal importance in propping up Bokassa's authoritarian regime was the warm personal relationship that developed between Bokassa and President Giscard d'Estaing. Bokassa always seemed to be feted with extra attention during his private or state visits to Paris, and these visits were much more frequent than those of many other Francophone leaders. The French president, an avid big-game hunter, was likewise regally treated during his periodic Central African safaris, when he stayed in Bokassa's lodges. In Bangui, Bokassa plied him with extravagant presents (which bordered on being bribes, as the French press alleged after Bokassa's overthrow), even as Giscard's family developed important financial interests in the country's hotelier and uranium sectors.

Bokassa's periodic anti-French outbursts thus threatened no one really; quite predictable, they could be assuaged by the granting of relatively small sums of "additional" financial aid and a brief chat with his "grand ami" in Paris. Even Bokassa's coronation as emperor, greeted with incredulity by much of the world, was deemed in Paris to be merely yet another price tag for the continued fealty of the Central African Republic. But the brutal suppression of the 1979 riots of Bangui's schoolchildren transcended the limits of French tolerance. For notwithstanding Bokassa's other attractions to Paris, his acts directly compromised France's own international reputation and the French presidency's own domestic sources of support. As the main prop of the Bokassa dictatorship, France had no alternative but to pull the rug from underneath its hitherto most loyal ally.

Despite his iron grip over the military, Bokassa faced increasing challenges from its officer corps in the 1970s. The CAR Army was no longer the puny, docile force it had been in 1966. Moreover, following its expansion and the localization of its officer corps, wild promotions both whetted ambitions for ultimate power on the part of some and created personal antagonisms among others. Although Bokassa was well served by some of his personal cronies (several of whom faced the firing squad after Bokassa's ouster), most of the conspiracies against him nevertheless arose from within the armed forces.

Despite his megalomania, Bokassa was well aware that his control of the armed forces kept him on the CAR throne. He thus pampered the army with large salaries and sophisticated materiel, turned a blind eye to the commercial activities of many of its officers, and even brought into the cabinet room some of his prime lieutenants. Defense allocations *doubled* between 1967 and 1969 alone, and remained the second largest allocation in the national budget. At the same time, however, Bokassa guarded against the presence of too many troops in the vicinity of the capital. Most of the units were stationed far away at Bouar (380 miles from Bangui) or at the virtually inaccessible Sudanese border, some 750 miles from the capital.[87] Except for his loyal Mbaïka Presidential Guard, which was heavily armed, regular troops were reportedly not issued live ammunition. Direct operational command was lodged in two trusted military cronies: Deputy Chief of Staff General Jean Claude Mandaba (who in 1971 was entrusted with the gendarmerie as well) and General André Dieudonné Magalé, a lieutenant in 1966. The latter was head of the National Police and a perennial revolving-door member of the cabinet; promoted into the cabinet for his unswerving loyalty to Bokassa, he was periodically dropped from it because of his outrageously corrupt fiscal misadventures.

The police force, too, was packed solid with Bokassa's ethnic kinsmen; by the 1970s, in fact, it had become an overwhelmingly Mbaïka force. The elite Presidential Guard (later the Imperial Guard) was likewise a Mbaïka force, with most of its personnel actually drawn from Bokassa's home village. Issued with the best uniforms and weapons, the formation was completely independent of both the police and the army, and it was commanded by the gargantuan General Josephat Mayomokila. The force was used not only as a Presidential Guard but also as a combat force that could be relied on to undertake the most gruesome tasks. It was the Presidential Guard personally led by Mayomokila, for example, that undertook the brutal dispersal of the student riots, and later the massacres, that preceded the collapse of the Bokassa regime.

Notwithstanding Bokassa's policy of keeping the army pampered and far away from the capital, promoting to command positions officers of proven loyalty to him, and building up powerful competitive power hierarchies, conspiracies, mutinies, and power grabs erupted with regularity in the mid-1970s. Several were barely reported in the press; others were highly publicized. On April 10, 1973, the second-ranking minister in the government, Minister of Public Works Major Auguste M'Bongo, was arrested for trying to enlist General Mandaba (much as Banza had done five years before) in an anti-Bokassa plot. (Later it was claimed that M'Bongo had been involved in the Banza conspiracy of 1969.)[88] Mandaba himself soon lost operational command when the armed forces fell under the nominal authority of Brigadier André Magalé, an officer who could constitute a threat to no one.

Foiled in December 1974 was a more serious coup attempt involving the top echelon of the gendarmerie, including its commander General Martin Lingopou. Unrest periodically swept the Bouar garrison during 1975–1976, and in 1976 two further conspiracies were foiled. In the first instance, in February, a grenade assault on Bokassa at Bangui airport led to a veritable witchhunt. Eight of the conspirators (including Bokassa's son-in-law, an air force commander) were executed hours after their court martial. All were also allegedly implicated in nine previous assassination plots against Bokassa, most of which were not announced at the time. In the second conspiracy some thirty officers and troops were arrested for plotting to kill Bokassa upon his return from festivities in Kinshasa; their motives, which were somewhat murky, revolved around a general desire for self-aggrandizement. Continued unrest in the armed forces attested to the fact that the military could no longer be regarded as intrinsically loyal to the regime.

The third factor originally supportive of the Bokassa dictatorship—the socioeconomic and political void in Bangui—was likewise rapidly changing in the 1970s. The relatively small, docile, unsophisticated elite of 1966 had become a large, voracious, upwardly mobile landed middle class, with increased demands. Corruption was endemic; everyone in the administration—from minister down—was deeply involved in syphoning into his own account as much state money as possible, with high rank simply allowing greater opportunities for embezzlement. In 1976, a Military Tribunal sent nine high officials (including two former foreign ministers and the former minister of posts) to prison for embezzlement, for periods ranging between two and eighteen years—and this was only the tip of the iceberg. Others, shunted aside by Bokassa's periodic purges (intended to redistribute patronage) saw their desire for self-enrichment thwarted. Still others, especially those from the non-riverine ethnic groups at the fringes of the privileged moneyed sector, seethed in anger (and envy) as they observed the crass corruption of the public administration.

The economy was in a total shambles. Trade, commerce, and banking activities had collapsed, especially in the countryside, and the country exhibited a general lack of confidence in prospects for the future. At the core of the CAR's economic malaise was Bokassa's irrational "overspending, overstaffing and overbuilding,"[89] and the extravagant way of life of the entire social elite.

The cost of living had mushroomed to insane heights, aggravated by soaring inflation, high transport costs from the coast, and constant shortages of all goods and commodities. Modern houses (many constructed with state funds by ministers who continued to live in slums) rented for $1,000 a month; the cost of an apple was 50 cents. Sugar trebled in price, meat quadrupled, and electrical appliances were rarely in stock. The Sahel drought in the distant north lowered the water level of the Oubangui River, cutting Bangui's communications with the outside world. Shortages of petrol (brought up-river on barges) triggered the collapse of internal commerce and brought hardship to the urban population.

The government's huge debts to the private (mostly expatriate) sector—and the refusal of the courts to schedule any commercial disputes in their calendars—reduced the willingness of companies to sell to the government on credit. Ministers received ordered goods only after advance payment had cleared the banks. No shipments were made to provincial centers except to established reputable clients. Not even the CAR's diplomatic missions abroad received their appropriations on time; in 1976, the Presidential Office even disclaimed responsibility (through an advertisement in the Swiss *Tribune de Geneve*) for debts piled up by CAR diplomats due to delays in the arrival of their salaries and budgetary allocations.[90]

Civil service paychecks were usually three or more months in arrears. The resistance of traders against extending credit to cashless civil servants and a delinquent government triggered official "retaliation" (i.e., petty harassments, confiscations, and, later, nationalizations), which became a regular part of life in Bangui. Discontent was thus high among the urban masses, in both the public and private sectors, and it was aggravated by Bokassa's imperial style of demeanor—long before he proclaimed himself emperor. Even the elite, which had preferential access to the spoils of office, was increasingly restless with Bokassa's wasteful policies, whimsical political and economic flights of fancy, and cult of sexual masculinity.[91] Thus, by the late 1970s an urban lumpen proletariat had developed in Bangui; allied with the civil service and elements in the army, it pressed for a fundamental rearray of power.

Bokassa's "solution" to the erosion of his popular legitimacy was a half-hearted attempt to create buffer structures to separate him from responsibility for the growing morass. In May 1974, the moribund MESAN was convened to reaffirm its support for Bokassa and to bestow upon him the rank of marshal (and a gold-and-diamond-studded "Marshal's" baton) for "exceptional services to the people." In January 1975, the trade union movement inscribed Bokassa in their rolls as the "Prime Worker of the Republic" and a "keen supporter of the people's interests."[92] And in Bokassa's further effort to project the image of an apolitical figure, the post of prime minister was created, charged with the day-to-day running of the government. Yet Bokassa was incapable of delegating power and taking a back seat, even as the premiership attracted upwardly mobile and not necessarily reform-minded personalities. None of Bokassa's premiers lasted very long in office. For instance, the (politically) astute appointment in 1975 of the veteran vice-president of MESAN, Elizabeth Domitien, was of short duration. Domitien, the acknowledged queen of Bangui's market-women and a figure of considerable influence and popularity who could have enhanced the regime's staying power, proved too threatening to the commercial interests of the president's female relatives and many mistresses.[93] Other prime ministers took their delegated powers too seriously, rapidly running afoul of Bokassa's intent to control all facets of life in the Central African Republic.

The Central African Empire

The idea of proclaiming himself emperor stemmed from Bokassa's adoration of pomp and splendor, and out of his desire to imitate Napoleon Bonaparte, an individual he particularly admired and identified with. His actual decision to set up an imperial dynasty was nevertheless reached quite impetuously, as the last in a series of wild policy gyrations that had seen the CAR shift from a "revolutionary" republic to an Islamic republic and finally to an empire. Nudged in that direction by cabinet ministers seeking to titilate his fancy, Bokassa was nevertheless not the only state leader in the region who was contemplating setting up a monarchy.[94]

Some $30 million was lavished on the coronation, which Bokassa referred to as "the greatest victory ever won by the Central African people." The cost was covered by special contributions from the French government and by "voluntary" assessments on local expatriate companies and civil servants. The event was roundly ridiculed abroad, and no head of state attended. Most African countries did not even send official delegations, and only 600 foreign guests (among the 2,000 or so invited) responded to the gold-embossed invitations. One of the few to defend the coronation was the French cabinet minister representing Giscard d'Estaing.[95]

Bokassa crowned himself with a $5 million crown (after the pope had refused a request to officiate), accompanied by the strains of Beethoven, Mozart, and tribal drums. He ascended a two-ton gold-encrusted throne and rode through Bangui's streets in a refurbished antique coach pulled by specially imported white horses flanked by resplendently uniformed lancers. Trailing a 20-foot-long red-velvet cloak trimmed with white fur, he received as a symbol of office a 6-foot diamond-encrusted sceptre and, while wearing a Napoleonic hat, later reviewed a parade that included both pygmy warriors and troops with Soviet weapons.

In the administrative "reorganization" that followed Bokassa's elevation to the throne, the emperor retreated to his "ancestral home" in Berengo (50 miles from Bangui), together with his retinue, which had now become the Imperial Court. The premier (at the outset, Ange Patasse) was given the task of administering the day-to-day affairs of the empire, and the crown prince (Prince George) was appointed secretary of defense. (The same son was eventually deported after a dispute with his father over his commercial activities involving exports of ivory from the CAR.)

Although it was assumed that Bokassa, after his coronation, would distance himself from the government to concentrate on the pomp and ritual of which he was so fond, this outcome never materialized. Berengo was no Versailles. Neither the artificiality of "court" life nor Bokassa's temperament freed the cabinet of interference from the emperor. Friction with Patasse over new extravagances suggested by Bokassa led on July 13, 1978, to the appointment of a more malleable premier, Henri Maidou. At the time regarded as the CAR's most competent administrator, Patasse had been a member of every Bokassa cabinet since 1966, having previously served under Dacko as well. Surviving every purge, though shuffled from ministry to ministry, he rarely opposed Bokassa and his impulsive policies. Indeed, Patasse was one of Bokassa's first cronies to convert to Islam in 1976 and had been one of those to encourage Bokassa's imperial inclinations. When elevated to the premiership, however, he mistook the myth of power at his disposal for reality. Bokassa had not been "kicked upstairs" but had simply reenacted another of his personal fancies. The falling out between the two leaders became inevitable after Patasse tried to rid his cabinet of Bokassa's cronies and to establish fiscal orthodoxy.

His replacement, Maidou, had the unfortunate task of steering the government during a turbulent era that was finally to lead to the collapse of the Bokassa regime.

The Fall of a Dictator

The spark that ignited the student demonstrations of January 19, 1979, was an imperial edict demanding that all pupils wear school uniforms bearing Bokassa's effigy. (The uniforms were manufactured by one of Bokassa's wives and sold exclusively in a store owned by another.) The edict epitomized both the greed of the regime and its insensitivity to the plight of a population heavily taxed and a civil service whose salaries were three or four months in arrears. Demonstrations against the edict got out of hand, and students, their ranks swollen by unemployed youth, attacked *Le Pacifique*—the center-city boutique owned by Empress Catherine. When the Imperial Guard opened fire, killing a number of students, the population of Bangui brought out its traditional weapons (bows and poisoned arrows). In the ensuing melee, some 100 soldiers were reportedly killed. As the Imperial Guard was a Mbaïka force and many of the demonstrators were northerners, the conflict had an ethnic dimension, aggravating even further the explosive situation.

The demoralized Imperial Guard was withdrawn and regrouped at its Kasai barracks. With a totally unreliable army in Bouar and along the Sudan border, Bokassa appealed for support from his friend Mobutu in Zaire. After some 300 Zairian troops were dispatched to Bangui, a ruthless counterassault commenced, employing mortars and machine guns. The brunt of the assault was aimed at the nonriverine ethnic quarters of the town and resulted in hundreds of deaths. Appealing for calm over the radio (in Sangho, a language Bokassa rarely used), thus signifying his awareness of the gravity of the situation, the emperor disclaimed all responsibility for the murderous rampage on the grounds that he had "not been President . . . for the past two years."[96]

On April 9, 1979, a new student disturbance developed at Bokassa University over perennial delays in the payment of subsidies. The disturbance then spread elsewhere and resulted in the stoning of a vehicle belonging to the Imperial Guard. The incident was the final affront to Bokassa's pride. On April 18, notwithstanding an earlier solemn pledge to protect the country's youth from harassment (in connection with the designation of 1979 as the Year of the Child), the Imperial Guard was unleashed on a savage rampage in which hundreds of children were undiscriminately bayoneted. Several hundreds more were arrested, only to be tortured and killed in prison—some by Bokassa himself. Again, the non-Mbaïka quarters of Bangui bore the brunt of the attacks.

The exact number of children who died in the infamous Ngaragbo prison or at the Kasai barracks (where witnesses saw students being machine-gunned to death) has never been established, although the number 500 frequently crops up in estimates. French reporters, invited by Bokassa to vindicate his version of the incident, implicated him instead in the death of "at least 60 children." In like manner, a special committee dispatched from Kigali, Rwanda (where the Franco-African summit was under way), concluded that the emperor "almost certainly" had been personally involved in some of the actual murders.[97]

The international revulsion that greeted Bokassa's latest atrocities sealed the emperor's fate. Following the incidents of January, exile elements, sensing that Bokassa's end was near, organized into liberation movements. These included "fronts" set up by General Sylvestre Bangui, who had resigned his ambassadorship to France and the U.K., and Ange Patasse, who was living in Paris at the time. Abel Goumba, Dacko's old protagonist and now a senior WHO official in Cotonou, Benin, had set up a moribund opposition movement in 1976 that was given a new lease of life at this time. The roughly 1,000-strong Association of Central African students in France issued a manifesto calling for a popular upheaval in Bangui and for the withdrawal of French support for the embattled emperor.

Despite intense domestic pressure to disengage from Bokassa, Paris equivocated until the Kigali committee report of August 19, which personally implicated the CAR dictator in the killings. The next day nearly all French financial aid was terminated. No longer merely a liability, Bokassa had become an unacceptable political embarrassment and his retention in office was a major blot on France's international reputation.

On September 20, Bokassa flew to Tripoli on a 48-hour state visit aimed at securing more Libyan fiscal aid and an enhanced military presence in Bangui. Libyan advance units were already in the CAR, and Libyan planes had already stockpiled war materiel in Bangui in August. (After the upheaval of September 20, French troops unceremoniously shipped out of the country thirty Libyan officers secretly residing in Bangui.)[98] Bokassa's intrigues were cut short, however, by Operation Barracuda, which airlifted into Bangui a contingent of French paratroopers as well as David Dacko, who had been in Paris at the time. Flanked by French troops, Dacko appealed over the radio for the Central African Army's acquiescence to the overthrow of Bokassa, and "formally" invited the French contingents to help police the capital during the transitional period.[99] Bokassa, having been refused asylum in France (following a dejected 60-minute wait at the Paris airport) flew to comfortable exile in Abidjan. There, after a period of uncharacteristic restraint, he began to disclose embarrassing details about his diamond "gifts" and other transactions with the president of France and his family. Revelations about his amassed fortune (allegedly worth $125 million)[100] and the discovery of mass graves outside Ngaragba prison, as well as the alleged discovery of four mutilated bodies in Bokassa's refrigerator in Bangui ("for the personal consumption of the former dictator," according to his personal chef)[101] aroused further furor at home and escalated demands that he be extradited to face criminal charges in Bangui.

The Legacy of Dictatorship

Despite the euphoria in Bangui over Bokassa's ouster, there was little jubilation over Dacko's return to power and considerable unease regarding the manner in which it had come about. Bokassa had been ousted by the force of foreign arms, and in his stead the metropole had imposed a leader who inspired no confidence. Although in Paris Dacko may have appeared the only acceptable alternate ruler, in Bangui he was viewed as a burnt-out leader with little credibility, tainted by the consultative role he had played in the last few years of the Bokassa regime.

Indeed, *all* the contenders who sprang up to claim the political throne of Central Africa were either too closely identified with the Bokassa dictatorship (e.g., Sylvestre Bangui, Henri Maidou, and Ange Patasse, the latter eleven times minister) or politically unacceptable to Paris. The only totally untarnished politician—Abel Goumba, who sought a comeback from self-exile with the WHO in Cotonou—was much too critical of France to be sponsored by Paris. Ange Patasse, who commanded considerable support among urban youth and from his northern Sara clientele (notwithstanding his role under Bokassa), was likewise unacceptable to Paris because of his pro-Libyan and quasi-radical inclinations.

The reconstruction of the much-brutalized socioeconomic polity was a task that would have taxed the efforts of the most astute successor regime. From the outset, Dacko appeared the wrong man for the task. His call for national reconciliation and mercy for the fallen dictator's henchmen was completely out of tune with popular sentiment in the capital and, indeed, simply did not ring true. At no time did his administration seriously press for Bokassa's extradition from the Ivory Coast to stand trial in Bangui. And although General Mayomokila and some of Bokassa's more notorious associates were ultimately placed on trial, some to be executed, the image Dacko projected was that of a leader reluctantly knuckling under popular pressure to perfunctorily prosecute his own relatives, former friends, and associates. Indeed, so insensitive was Dacko to popular sentiments in Bangui that he dropped from his cabinet some of his unpopular ex-Bokassa aides only after a special visit (and entreaties) by Martin Kirsch, the African Affairs adviser to the French president.

Dacko's stress on "political continuity" led him to include in his cabinet certain key figures of the antecedent regime. Yet continuity was not the correct mobilizational approach for a population straining for a total break with the past and, having progressively radicalized, even demanding an entirely different socioeconomic order. By setting up a wall-to-wall cabinet, Dacko may have temporarily defused the ambitions of a number of aspiring politicians, but he also further undermined his credibility among the masses. The fact that many familiar officials associated with the hated dictatorship still strutted on the political centerstage seemed to epitomize just how little of the evil had really been exorcised with Bokassa's ouster.

Some of the officials integrated into Dacko's government (such as Maidou, Bokassa's last premier and now Dacko's vice-president) may have been primarily guilty of failing to try to curb Bokassa's excesses. Others tapped by Dacko for high office came with much-sullied, even bloodied, hands. On March 22, 1980, Justice Minister François Gueret filed a report personally implicating some of Dacko's closest associates in both the massive embezzlement under Bokassa and the infamous 1979 massacre of schoolchildren. Gueret was summarily dismissed for his efforts; the associates implicated were dropped only later on, and then not as a result of the charges against them but because of increasing public pressure and civic unrest. As Gueret later publicly lamented, "on the judicial level the situation is blocked. . . . Bokassa's accomplices are not worried."[102]

Vacillating between firmness and weakness, much as he had done during his first presidency, Dacko proved incapable either of ameliorating the economic devastation of the country or of uniting behind his leadership the various political formations that sprang up with the liberalization of the political scene. The severe austerity regimen so needed to rein in the runaway budgetary deficits and the onerous national debt inherited from Bokassa clashed with the pent-up socioeconomic needs of the population. The national priority was to trim the largely unproductive, overwhelmingly (77 percent) Bangui-based civil service, which had mushroomed from 6,000 to 26,000 members in sixteen years and had consumed 88 percent of the national budget. The pruning of Bokassa's much-expanded army of 7,500 likewise demanded a firm hand, despite the explosive potential of this action. Nor were there any rosy promises to be made to school graduates in a country whose economy was decaying and whose employment opportunities in both the public and private sectors were virtually nonexistent. The ravaged economy was producing less coffee, diamonds, cotton, and tobacco than it had at independence, roads were in utter disrepair, commerce was at a total standstill, and state revenues were much contracted. As one French development official put it, "we have to rebuild the house from the inside, because the previous tenant left nothing but the walls."[103]

From the outset it was clear that Dacko's regime was in essence sustained by the "omnipresence of [2,000] French paratroopers and advisers"[104] in Bangui, without whom the regime would have collapsed like a house of cards. The wobbly economy continued to limp along thanks solely to infusions of French development aid and annual budget-balancing subsidies. Had it not been for the regular French budgetary subventions (of between 1 and 5 billion CFA francs), the monthly civil service payroll could not have been met. France remained the real power behind the political throne in Bangui, enmeshed in a quagmire not of its choosing, committed to a regime under attack from all directions, and progressively heavy-handed to boot. Taunted by labor and youth (who found their idol in Patasse) and constantly challenged by illegal strikes and budding conspiracies, Dacko's rule became authoritarian. Even as ex-Bokassa accomplices went free, politicians, union, and student leaders found themselves shipped to internal exile in distant provinces.

The presidential elections of March 1981 were supposed to resolve the post-Bokassa succession issue and legitimate the victor. But the results of the elections came under dispute, thus greatly exacerbating the social turmoil. Dacko narrowly avoided a second run-off poll and garnered 50.23 percent of the popular vote of 744,688. The five-cornered election included Patasse (who gained 38.11 percent of the vote), Pehoua (5.35 percent), Maidou (3.23 percent), and Goumba (1.42 percent). The results reflected Goumba's limited voter appeal following his fifteen-year absence from the country and Maidou's unpopularity due to his role under Bokassa. But the results also confirmed the power of the coalition forged by the demagogic Patasse, who linked his northern Sara support with the youth and labor in the capital (whom he had carried in the elections) to form an antiriverine alliance—and all this despite his lengthy former association with Bokassa.[105] Although the results appeared credible enough, they were rejected by the defeated candidates as fraudulent, and riots broke out in various centers as some of the contenders went underground to prepare for a popular upheaval. (Observers currently admit that electoral irregularities may indeed have resulted in doctored figures that favored Dacko.)

The escalating civil strife prompted Dacko to declare a state of emergency that strengthened the powers of the government. Later, the stipulated legislative elections (which, as was now clear, Dacko could neither have won nor rigged) were postponed indefinitely, and a wave of repression resulted in the imprisonment of several opposition leaders. Dacko's stalwarts were organized in an informal armed militia that was enjoined to liquidate the "serpent's head" of the opposition, especially in the troublesome capital. The country's sole trade union was neutralized when its right to strike was severely curtailed; and when it nevertheless called for a strike, it was forcibly disbanded. Strict censorship (reminiscent of the Bokassa era) was imposed on the press, and opposition leaders were formally denied access to the media. And like his immediate predecessor, Dacko appealed to Zaire's Mobutu for several companies of troops to serve as his Praetorian Guard, although he was rebuffed.

Ultimately, the embattled Dacko regime was ousted in much the same way it had come to power—by external design. The fall in Paris of President Valéry Giscard d'Estaing and the rise to power of the Socialist Mitterrand sealed Dacko's fate. Anxious to distance itself from Giscard's African policy, the new administration in France saw no merit in sustaining the unpopular and increasingly authoritarian regime in Bangui, which had merely substituted "compromised Ministers for compromised Ministers, corrupt men for corrupt men."[106] Since the disputed presidential elections, conditions had severely deteriorated. Several bombs had gone off in downtown Bangui, underground armed movements were springing up, student unrest was endemic, and farmers in the north (Patasse's ethnic area) were destroying cotton plants to decrease production and embarrass the regime. An aura of impending doom permeated the country, with no solution in sight.

For some time, the armed forces had been unhappy with their "political" task of enforcing the state of emergency, patrolling the capital in the aftermath of the Bangui bombings, and propping up the regime against domestic enemies. Informal contacts between Army Chief of Staff André Kolingba and official circles in Paris resulted in the consensus that Dacko would have to be ousted. Forewarned by the new French ambassador on August 31, 1981, that French troops would not intervene to defend him against a military coup, Dacko left Bangui for his farm. The next day, Major General André Kolingba assumed power in a peaceful coup d'état.

The Military Tries to Rule

After setting up a thirty-man Committee of National Recovery that included virtually the entire corps of senior officers (twenty-three of whom had also assumed ministerial duties), Kolingba declared a moratorium on political activity until the scars of the economy had been healed. In the interim, leading members of the various political formations were given sinecure positions; Abel Goumba, for example, was appointed rector of the University of Bangui.

The attempt to depoliticize the country was not successful, however. All those shut out of power during the Dacko interregnum regarded the hitherto irrelevent Central African army with condescension. And trimmed to 3,800 troops, the CAR Army remained one of the least trained and most underarmed military forces in the continent. Reflecting wider societal cleavages in its officer corps—composed of Mbaïka (the kinsmen of Bokassa and Dacko), Sara (Patasse supporters), and other riverine groups (the Yakoma, Kolingba's kin), the army was politically tugged in all directions. Sharply split into segments supporting one or the other of the civilian contenders, it was divided even about the merits of remaining in office beyond a brief transition period. These internal tensions within the army encouraged the formation of civil-military conspiratorial cliques, and the coalition that developed in support of Patasse's political ambitions triggered a bid for power in March 1982. The foiled putsch completely shattered the tenuous corporate integrity of the army's officer corps and, in turn, sealed the prospects (which were dim in any case) of a transfer of power to civilian authority.

The power gambit commenced with the return to Bangui of Ange Patasse from self-exile in Paris. Greeted at the airport by a crowd of 10,000 people, Patasse—"a man of few scruples and desperate for power"[107]—publicly declared that he had come to claim the political throne. As he put it, "the people are no longer afraid of guns. General Kolingba is a traitor to them. I alone represent constitutional legitimacy. I am now waiting for General Kolingba to pass power to me."[108] This challenge was followed by an attempted takeover by his military allies, headed by Generals Bozize and Mbaikoua, the ministers of information and of justice, respectively. The rather amateurish plot was immediately crushed by loyalist elements in the army. As ethnic demonstrations fanned out in support of Patasse's power-bid, troops loyal to Kolingba moved in to raze Patasse's residence (where as many as fifty armed militants may have died) after chasing him into political refuge at the French Embassy. A subsequent purge of the officer corps, cabinet, and senior civil service cleansed these groups of "Patassists." Apprehensions over the assumption that the power-bid was part of a "Left-wing Barracuda Operation" sponsored by Paris (given that the French Secret Service, the SDECE, was directly involved in the plot) were quelled only after President Mitterrand's African Affairs adviser visited Bangui to reassure the regime to the contrary.

Even after the elimination of the Patasse challenge, the highly atomized society inherited from the Bokassa dictatorship continued to prevent a coalescence of authority around Kolingba. Student unrest was a never-ending problem, with some of the riots allegedly sponsored by Patasse from abroad. Although Kolingba widened his cabinet to include civilians, such as François Gueret and Sylvestre Bangui (who, respectively, were dropped and arrested in 1984–1985), he continued facing challenges from all directions. In May 1982, the Libyan-trained followers of Iddi Lala's "liberation movement," who were responsible for the Bangui bombings of Dacko days, were put on trial for a plot to blow up the Bouar military camp. In August, Abel Goumba was arrested for setting up a "revolutionary" organization. And in August 1983, some seventy members of the Lala and Patasse clandestine movements met near the Chadian border to form a Central African Revolutionary Party (PRC) committed to ousting Kolingba and setting up a "progressive" civilian administration. Finally, in July 1986, a Patasse-Goumba alliance unified all of the anti-Kolingba elements in the country.

The frenzied atmosphere of Bangui, punctuated by periodic conspiracies reaching right into the military cabinet itself, underscored the vulnerability of Kolingba, who, it appeared, "could fall at any time."[109] By nature excessively prone toward delegating authority, Kolingba often withdrew to the sanctity of his heavily guarded and fortified private model farm at M'Boko, allegedly surrounded by the country's reserves of diamonds and cash. The protection of the regime was left at the hands of the French head of the Presidential Guard and the CAR Secret Service, Lieutenant Colonel Mansion. This "president of Kolingba" (as Mansion was referred to in Bangui), connected with ultra-right French and Gabonese economic interests as well as with mercenary groups,[110] was at times even given negotiating powers on behalf of the regime.

The economy remained in the doldrums. Cotton production, although it recovered to a level of 28,000 tons in 1983, was still far below the 60,000 tons recorded in the early 1970s. Servicing the national debt consumed a crippling 55 percent of budgetary revenues. Ongoing massive budgetary deficits still necessitated heavy foreign subventions. In 1983, the deficit was 10 billion CFAF, and total French public aid to Bangui had reached 15 billion CFAF. Nor were there signs that the deficits would be seriously reined in. The civil service had proven much too resilient to pruning: Still grossly overstaffed, corrupt, prone to embezzling, and characterized by crass absenteeism, it continued to consume some 90 percent of state revenues. In 1983, Kolingba even had to forgo valuable IMF standby credits because the conditions attached (requiring an immediate curb of the budgetary deficit) would have involved mass redundancies—an act of political suicide. At the same time, reports of the personal enrichment and economic entrenchment of key members of the Kolingba administration, including members of the president's family and his consorts, yet again attested to the difficulty of remaining a saint in Bangui. With few tangible economic successes to its credit, a united political opposition against it, and an increasingly odious record, the Kolingba administration began to pose a fundamental dilemma to Paris—with Goumba's name most often resurrected as a possible civilian alternative to the general.

On November 9, 1984, a guerrilla assault on a northern border town by pro-Patasse elements severely rattled Kolingba, possibly putting to rest the alternate scenarios discussed in an equally worried Paris. Earlier indications that the capital itself had been infiltrated by Libyan personnel, whose goal was to organize and arm youthful Patassists, invigorated the Bangui-Paris axis. (In 1986, a "Libyan connection" was also detected in a further series of bombs planted in Bangui.) The declaration on December 10 of a Patassist "Provisional Government for National Salvation in Exile" certainly underscored the fact that neither Ange Patasse nor the array of Libyan designs on the region was likely to disappear. The strengthened resolve of France to sustain Kolingba in office was coupled, however, with a demand that the regime civilianize itself and seek legitimation at the polls.

The August 1985 cabinet reshuffle thus saw both the integration of a number of civilians in top positions and the first concrete reference to a return to parliamentary rule; shortly thereafter, the foundations were laid for a building in Bangui destined to house the country's future deliberative assembly. By 1986, the process had gathered momentum. Kolingba announced the formation of the country's new single political party, the Central African Democratic Rally (RDC), which would include within it all political tendencies. Also formulated was a new constitution, allegedly unlike the one established by Dacko, "which had replaced tyranny with inefficiency, and terror with anarchy."[111] In the subsequent referendum aimed at the popular legitimation of the regime, 696,055 of the 763,451 who turned out to vote confirmed Kolingba's leadership. The liberalizations of 1986 were accompanied, however, by a number of restrictive edicts, including one, in May 1986, that unequivocally banned all student strikes in the country (the major thorn in Kolingba's side) at the pain of mandatory imprisonment.

It was in the midst of this slow political normalization, and during the minor amelioration of the economic scene, that the former dictator decided to play his much-threatened wild card. On October 23, 1986, he suddenly landed at Bangui airport. Whether he seriously expected to be greeted as a savior ("my people are anxiously waiting for my return. . . . I will soon be with them")[112] or was truly the pauper he claimed to be when his telephone, electricity, and water services were disconnected at his Chateau Hardricourt, or whether he was merely gambling that he would not be executed but, instead, would be allowed to live out his life in his homeland, is still a matter for conjecture. In any case, *West Africa* was most likely correct in stating that "reality had indeed left him long ago."[113]

However that may be, Bokassa's return "home" was a major political bonanza for Kolingba. The lengthy public trial may, at least psychologically, have sealed a dark chapter in the history of the Central African Republic. It certainly allowed the drawing of sharp contrasts between the "enlightened" administration of Kolingba and that of the aged (and by now alcoholic) ex-dictator. Bokassa's death sentence was "waived" following a secret meeting between him and Kolingba—an eventuality most commentators had fully expected. With the "Bokassa question" finally resolved, a major issue constantly plaguing Bangui was suddenly laid to rest.

Despite the short-lived euphoria accompanying the trial and sentencing of the former dictator, the consolidation of the Kolingba administration— which was under pressure to secure public legitimation—continued to encounter opposition. Legislative elections were held on July 31, 1987. Fully 62 percent of the voters abstained, with many of the 54 seats falling to local power-wielders in opposition to Kolingba but formally running on the RDC party slate. Although the cabinet has been civilianized and broadened to include former opponents tempted by positions of authority, Kolingba's rule still rests squarely and predominantly both on his control of the armed forces and on continued French fiscal, political, and military support.

More than 8,000 French troops and a squadron of Jaguar jets are now based in the country. In part the rear base for the Franco-Libyan standoff in Chad, this powerful force cannot but strongly intimidate the local opposition. In any case, many former political aspirants are in prison or under house arrest (e.g., Goumba); others (e.g., Patasse, now in Togo) have withdrawn to their professional lives or are plotting a comeback, usually from Libya or with Libyan support. In Bangui, the *éminence grise* of the country is still the French Colonel Jean-Claude Mansion, who "takes key decisions, is responsible for security and issues passports. No change in the country can take place without his approval. . . . Emperors and generals may come and go, but the French presence remains."[114]

Thus the Central African Republic remains beset by the very same socioeconomic and political cleavages that existed at the time of Bokassa's coup. The cleavages have been politicized, sharpened, and given an edge through the emergence of new class appeals for a fundamental rearray of political and economic power. Following its brutalization under Bokassa, the country is much more divided internally. And in the process of establishing the most fundamental features of public and political order, it finds itself virtually recolonized by French military force of arms.

Notes

1. Interview in Bangui, September 12, 1981.
2. The CAR was so-named after the two main rivers that either flow into the territory (Oubangui) or originate in it (Chari).
3. See the relevant entries in Samuel Decalo, *Historical Dictionary of Chad*, 2nd ed. (Metuchen, N.J.: Scarecrow Press, 1987).
4. Pierre Kalck, *La République Centrafricaine* (Paris: Berger-Levrault, 1971), p. 11.
5. Kalck, *Central African Republic: A Failure in Decolonization* (New York: Praeger Publishers, 1970), p. 11.
6. République Centrafricaine, *Journal Officiel* (September 1, 1966), p. 432.
7. See M. Georges, "La Vie rurale chez les Banda," *Cahiers d'Outre Mer*, vol. 26 (1963); and R.P. Daigre, "Les Banda de l'Oubangui-Chari," *Anthropos*, no. 16 (1931), and no. 27 (1932). See also Pierre Kalck, *Histoire de la République Centrafricaine* (Paris: Berger-Levrault, 1974), pp. 93–97.
8. See Captain Julien, "Mohammed es Senoussi et ses Etats," *Bulletin de la Société de Recherches Congolaises*, nos. 7–10 (Brazzaville, 1925–1929), pp. 104–177, 55–122, 49–96, and 45–88, respectively; and Dennis D. Cordell, *Dar el-Kouti and the Last Years of the Trans-Saharan Slave Trade* (Madison: University of Wisconsin Press, 1985).
9. John Hilberth, *The Gbaya* (Stockholm: Almquist and Wiksell, 1973); and Gabriel Gosselin, *Travail et Changement social en pays Gbaya* (Paris: Klincksieck, 1972), and "Histoire d'un clan Gbaya," *Geneva-Afrique*, vol. 12, no. 1 (Geneva, 1973), pp. 19–36.
10. E.E. Evans-Pritchard, *The Azande: History and Political Institutions* (Oxford: Clarendon Press, 1971); Arlette Thuriaux-Hennebert, *Les Zandé dans l'histoire du Bahr el Ghazal et de l'Equatoria* (Bruxelles: Institut de Sociologie de l'Université Libre, 1964); and Eric de Dampière, *Les Sultanats Zande de l'Oubangui* (Paris: Plon, 1967).
11. For details on the Sara, see B. Lanne, "Les Populations due Sud du Tchad," *Revue Française d'Etudes Politiques Africaines*, nos. 183–184 (July–August 1979), pp. 41–81; and J. Gayo Kogongar, "Introduction à la vie et à l'histoire precoloniales des populations Sara du Tchad" (Ph.D. thesis, University of Paris, 1971).
12. Actually the Oubangui River takes its name from this ethnic group. It is known by many different names depending upon the ethnicity controlling each segment. The French chose to name the river after the Bobangui. See Kalck, *"La République Centrafricaine,"* p. 5.

13. Kalck, *The Central African Republic*, p. 3.

14. The tension between Africans and Europeans in the CAR has been noted by many observers; see, for instance, Virginia Thompson and Richard Adloff, "Oubangui-Chari," in their *The Emerging States of French Equatorial Africa* (Stanford, Calif.: Stanford University Press, 1960), p. 385.

15. In an interview with a senior U.S. official at the U.S. Embassy, Bangui, June 1972.

16. See William B. Cohen, *Rulers of Empire* (Stanford, Calif.: Hoover Institution Press, 1971).

17. Brian Weinstein, "Felix Eboué and the Chiefs: Perceptions of Power in Early Oubangui-Chari," *Journal of African History* (1970), p. 111.

18. For a discussion of the concessionary system in Equatorial Africa, see Catherine Coquery-Vidrovitch's classic *Le Congo français au temps des grandes compagnies concessionaries* (Paris: Mouton, 1972); Kalck, *Histoire de la République Centrafricaine*, Chapter 8; Felicien Challaye, *Le Congo Français* (Paris: Elcan, 1909); and C. Tisserant, *Ce que j'ai connu de l'esclavage en Oubangui-Chari* (Paris: Plon, 1955). One good recent, if somewhat slanted, study of the history of the Central African Republic is Yarisse Zoctizoum's *Histoire de la Centrafrique*, 2 vols. (Paris: Harmattan, 1984).

19. Kalck, *The Central African Republic*, p. 49.

20. Kalck, *Histoire de la République Centrafricaine*, p. 181.

21. Weinstein, *Journal of African History*, p. 108.

22. See Thompson and Adloff, "Oubangui-Chari," pp. 392–393; and Marcel Homet, *Congo, Terre de Souffrances* (Paris: Montaigne, 1934).

23. Kalck, *Notes et Etudes Documentaires*, p. 11.

24. C. Mangin, *Souvenirs d'Afrique—Tournée d'Inspection au Congo, 1908* (Paris: Denoël, 1936).

25. Gide's exposé was even lodged as an official document before the International Labor Organization's investigation into forced labor in Africa. See André Gide, *Voyage au Congo* (Paris: Gallimard, 1927).

26. Interview with a senior official of the U.S. Embassy, Bangui, June 1972. Visitors were cautioned in case of trouble to avoid stopping in the countryside, where unpublicized incidents of spontaneous stoning or mobbing by antiwhite crowds had occurred.

27. Thompson and Adloff, "Obangui-Chari," p. 406.

28. This was the case despite its rank as fourth-lowest in population density in the continent. See Tables 1.5; 15.1, and 15.2 in Donald G. Morrison et al., *Black Africa: A Contemporary Handbook* (New York: Free Press, 1972).

29. The CAR possesses some of the finest game hunting in the continent in its eastern prefectures. In the 1970s, the wholesale slaughter of 80 percent of the CAR's elephant herds completely undermined the country's tourist prospects. See *Africa Research Bulletin*, Economic Series (October 1979).

30. Fully 95 percent of CAR's imports and exports utilize this river route; they are transshipped at Brazzaville (Congo) onto the railroad to the coast at Pointe Noire. Since the early 1970s, the river has been so shallow (or totally dry) that shipments halted for more than six months out of the year.

31. See Gosselin, *Travail et Changement*, pp. 239–241.
32. Kalck, *Central African Republic*, p. 72.
33. Ibid., p. 73.
34. Examples of prewar conflicts include the 1944 Baya disturbances, other localized riots, and the 1954 Berberati affair. For details on the latter event, see Thompson and Adloff, "Oubangui-Chari," pp. 392–393; and Kalck, *The Central African Republic*, pp. 89–90.
35. Boganda was elected on the MRP (Catholic Left) ticket and was encouraged into a political career by Grandin.
36. Born in Bobangui, Lobaye, in 1910, and educated at the Yaoundé (Cameroun) Seminary, Boganda was ordained a priest in 1935. While deputy to the National Assembly he married his French secretary and was defrocked, but this did not tarnish his charisma among the Oubanguians. According to one observer, Boganda was "the most prestigious and most capable of all the politicians of Equatorial Africa." See Georges Chaffard, *Les carnets secrets de la decolonisation* (Paris: Calman-Levy, 1967), p. 171. See also Jean-Pierre Rougeaux, "Le parti unique en R.C.A.: le MESAN" (Paris: Mémoire des Sciences Politiques, 1968), mimeo.
37. A few months before Boganda's death, a large crowd gathered at the Oubangui riverfront hoping to witness his crossing by walking over the water. See Victor LeVine, "The Central African Republic: Insular Problems of an Inland State," *Africa Report* (November 1968), p. 18.
38. See "L'Enquête sur le mort de M. Boganda," *L'Express* (Paris), May 7, 1959. See also Andrè Bussière, "La R.C.A. sans Boganda" (Paris, 1963), mimeo.
39. Born in Grimeri in 1926 and of Banziri origins, Goumba's father was interpreter to the French head of the Ouaka District.
40. Dacko, a Baya, was born in 1932 and was a teacher by profession. He was elected to the Territorial Assembly in 1957 and served as Boganda's minister of agriculture and later as minister of the interior. Kalck refers to him as "one of the most brilliant school teachers in French Equatorial Africa." See Kalck, *The Central African Republic*, p. 107. Faced with the concerted support for Dacko on the part of Boganda's widow, the colonial administration, and the expatriate community, Goumba was persuaded to cede the presidency for the sake of unity. According to John Ballard, "Dacko's rise to the presidency was primarily the work of a group of influential Europeans." See his "Four Equatorial States," in Gwendolen Carter (ed.), *National Unity and Regionalism in Eight African States* (Ithaca, N.Y.: Cornell University Press, 1966), p. 298.
41. Kalck, *Histoire de la République Centrafricaine*, pp. 121–122.
42. According to Kalck, "the clerks of yesterday, now Ministers of the Republic . . . [were] entirely indifferent to the low standard of living of the thousands in the villages" and solely concerned with their own comfort. See Kalck, *The Central African Republic*, p. 116.
43. Interview at the U.S. Embassy, Bangui, June 1972. For a similar assessment, see Guy de Lusignan, *French-Speaking Africa Since Independence* (New York: Praeger Publishers, 1969), p. 110.
44. François Constantin, "Centrafrique," *L'Année Politique Africaine 1964* (Paris: Pedone, 1965), p. 138.

45. See René Dumont, "Le difficile développement agricole de la République Centrafricaine," *Annales de l'Institut Agronomique*, vol. 4 (1966); Constantin, "Centrafrique," *L'Année Politique Africaine 1965* (Paris: Pedone, 1966), p. 141; and Gosselin, *Travail et Changement*, p. 52 and elsewhere. For a severe critique of the Dacko era, see also Jean D. Térivé, "Analyse d'un coup d'état," *France-Eurafrique* (March 1966), pp. 3–8; and *Terre Africaine*, nos. 77 and 78 (Brazzaville, May 15 and May 22, 1965). See also Jacque Serre, "Six ans de gouvernement Dacko," *Revue Française d'Etudes Politiques Africaines* (September 1975), pp. 73–104.

46. For background, see "Bokassa and the Two Chinas," *West Africa*, October 24, 1970. See also Victor LeVine, "The Coups in Upper Volta, Dahomey and the Central African Republic," in R. Rotberg and A. Mazrui (eds.), *Protest and Power in Black Africa* (London: Oxford University Press, 1970), and his article "The Coup in the Central African Republic," *Africa Today* (April–May 1968).

47. See Kalck, *The Central African Republic*, p. 152. See also Lee's comments about the ongoing civil-military competition for graft and the "best" mistresses in the capital, in J.M. Lee, *African Armies and Civil Order* (New York: Praeger Publishers, 1969), p. 100; and Térivé, "Analyse d'un coup d'état," p. 7.

48. In *Histoire de la République Centrafricaine*, Kalck also notes that Bokassa returned from Paris to Bangui in 1965 (despite orders from Dacko not to do so) to assume command of the armed forces (p. 329). At that time, the army numbered only 500 troops, the gendarmerie 450, the police 330, and the Republican Guard 700. Total allocations for all amounted to less than $1 million (250 million CFAF). See Constantin, *L'Année Politique Africaine 1964*, p. 150.

49. See Kalck, *The Central African Republic*; and LeVine, "The Coup in the Central African Republic." See also Michel Legris, "Esquisses Centrafricaines," *Le Monde*, January 4–5, 1966. Another version refers to the coup as retaliatory action for the 10:00 A.M. arrest of Bokassa on Dacko's orders. See Monique Sordet, "Jean-Bedel Bokassa," *Europe–France–Outremer* (December 1973), p. 9.

50. Although Dacko and Bokassa are cousins, Boganda was the latter's uncle.

51. Térivé, "Analyse d'un coup d'état."

52. C. Coulon and P.Y. Laporte, "Centrafrique," *L'Année Politique Africaine 1966* (Paris: Pedone, 1968), p. 182.

53. *Journal Officiel*, February 1, 1966, February 15, 1966.

54. Térivé, "Analyse d'un coup d'état."

55. These honors included the French Legion of Honor, the Medal of the Resistance and of Free France, and the Military Medal. See Sordet, "Jean-Bedel Bokassa," pp. 8–9.

56. Jean Revety, "L'Anomalie de Bangui," *Eurafrica* (January–March 1976), p. 80.

57. Kalck, *Central African Republic*, p. 165.

58. Ibid., p. 161.

59. See ibid. See also "République Centrafricaine: Un an de gouvernement Bokassa," *Europe–France–Outremer* (January 1967).

60. By the end of 1971, for example, there had been sixteen such shuffles; and the pace quickened in 1972.

61. Interview in Bangui, July 1972.
62. Ibid. Apart from Magalé, one could note Maurice Gouandjia, the former foreign minister. Twice purged for embezzlement and dragged out of government housing, after begging forgiveness, Gouandjia was posted as ambassador to Italy. "Lesser" officials, falling into disfavor, were rotated to the far north and more remote districts, before being repatriated to the capital, supposedly "purified."
63. Kalck, *The Central African Republic*, p. 177.
64. Ibid., p. 176.
65. "R.C.A.—Renforcement du regime policier," *Revue Française d'Etudes Politiques Africaines* (July 1969), p. 18.
66. *L'Année Politique Africaine 1970*, p. IV-18; Legum (ed.), *Africa Contemporary Record 1971-72*, p. B474.
67. "République Centrafricaine," *Année Africaine 1971*; Legum (ed.), *Africa Contemporary Record 1971-72*, p. B474.
68. Térivé, "Analyse de coup d'état," pp. 5-6.
69. Kalck, *Central African Republic*, p. 162.
70. "République Centrafricaine," *Année Africaine 1969* (Paris: Pedone, 1970), pp. 255-256; Fondation Nationale de Science Politique, *Chronologie Politique Africaine* (Paris, 1969), p. 85. See also *West Africa*, November 25, 1967.
71. Legum (ed.), *Africa Contemporary Record 1968-69*, p. 427.
72. *West Africa*, November 25, 1967; *Le Monde*, November 17, 1967.
73. "Tentative de coup d'état," *Afrique Contemporaine* (May-June 1969).
74. See Philippe Decraene, "Menace d'instabilité en République Centrafricaine," *Le Monde Diplomatique* (May 1969), p. 6. Because of this article, Decraene's writings were banned in Bangui. See "République Centrafricaine," *Année Africaine 1969*, p. 295. See also "The Two Professions," *West Africa*, April 19, 1969; "Central African Republic: Coup Foiled," *West Africa*, April 19, 1969; and "R.C.A.—durcissement français," *Revue Française d'Etudes Politiques Africaines* (December 1969).
75. "R.C.A.—Renforcement du regime policier," p. 18.
76. For a discussion of the vacillations in CAR foreign policy, see Robet Cornevin, "La Politique étrangére du gouvernement de Bangui," *Revue Française d'Etudes Politiques Africaines* (September 1975).
77. Legum (ed.), *Africa Contemporary Record 1970-71*, p. B269.
78. "Turmoil in Bangui," *Africa*, no. 6 (January 1972).
79. See Christian Casteran, "Le General Bokassa veut battre monnaie," *Revue Française d'Etudes Politiques Africaines* (November 1971). See also *West Africa*, August 15, 1970, and October 8, 1971.
80. Legum (ed.), *Africa Contemporary Record 1971-72*, p. B474; *Africa Research Bulletin*, Economic Series (April 1972).
81. See Legum (ed.), *Africa Contemporary Record 1972-73*, p. B512; Peter Enahoro, "Bokassa's Thieves," *Africa* (September 1972); *Africa Research Bulletin*, Political Series (August 1972); and *Le Monde*, August 2, 1972. A general amnesty had emptied the prisons in June, but catastrophic economic conditions made for alarming crime rates.
82. Interviews in Bangui, 1973. Originally strict prison sentences had been decreed for various offences: three years for "vagabonds," the cutting off of

one or both ears plus jail for theft, and amputation of the right arm and even death for recidivists. See *Africa Research Bulletin*, Political Series (August 1972); and *West Africa*, November 6, 1972.

83. See *West Africa*, December 4, 1972.

84. *West Africa*, September 1, 1972; Legum (ed.), *Africa Contemporary Record 1972-73*, p. 512.

85. Wishing to be reunited with a daughter sired while he served in Indochina, Bokassa dispatched a mission to Vietnam to search for her. The first "Martine" to arrive in Bangui was found to be an imposter, although Bokassa magnanimously adopted her. After the discovery of the true "Martine," Bokassa found husbands for both and joyfully presided over the double marriage. Both husbands were to suffer cruel fates, however; one was executed for a conspiracy against Bokassa. See the *New York Times*, November 27, 1972, January 17, 1973, and February 4, 1973; see also "Le Mariage de Deux Martines," *Bingo* (April 1973), p. 59.

86. Legum (ed.), *Africa Contemporary Record 1977-78*, p. B534, and *Africa Contemporary Record 1976-77*, p. B477.

87. See Kalck, *Central African Republic*, p. 167. And for the composition of the armed forces, see *The Military Balance 1980-81* (London: Institute for Strategic Studies, 1981).

88. *West Africa*, May 7, 1973; "The Perils of Bokassa," *Africa Confidential*, June 22, 1973.

89. *Marchés Tropicaux*, January 16, 1976.

90. Legum (ed.), *Africa Contemporary Record 1975-76*, p. B454; Bernard Loubat, *L'Ogre de Berengo* (Paris: Editions Alain Lefeuvre, 1981).

91. Bokassa had eight wives and thirty-odd mistresses; his thirtieth legitimate child was born in 1978. In 1974 he married a Lebanese girl, and in 1975 a Romanian dancer.

92. *West Africa*, January 25, 1975.

93. Legum (ed.), *Africa Contemporary Record 1976-77*, p. B473.

94. Both Tombalbaye of Chad and Mobutu of Zaire had seriously considered this option.

95. As one French envoy stated, "Personally I find it perfectly abnormal to criticize what is about to take place in Bangui while finding the Queen of England's Jubilee ceremony all right. It smacks of racism." Cited in Legum (ed.), *Africa Contemporary Record 1977-78*, p. B531. Legum also provides a quasi-psychological rationalization of Bokassa's motives in declaring himself emperor. For a representative cross-section of the literature of this subject, see "Papa Bok," *Africa* (November 1977); John Howe, "Captains and Kings," *Africa* (February 1978); John Crabb, "The Coronation of Emperor Bokassa," *Africa Today* (July-September 1978); and Jeremy Hunter, "The Coronation of an Emperor," *Africa* (January 1978).

96. See *Le Monde*, January 24, 1979; and *West Africa*, January 29, 1979. See also S. Nyama, "Dark Clouds over the Court of Berengo," *Africa* (June 1979); and *Africa Research Bulletin*, Political Series (February 1979).

97. *West Africa*, May 21 and 28, 1979, and June 11, 1979. See also *Le Monde*, June 17, 1980; and *Africa Research Bulletin*, Political Series (June and September 1979).

98. *Daily Telegraph,* September 29, 1979.

99. See *Africa Research Bulletin,* Political Series (October 1979); and Irving Howe, "Kitchen Comedy," *Africa* (November 1979).

100. Bokassa's amassed fortune included a chateau in Loire, a fifty-room mansion in Paris, houses in Cannes and Toulouse, and a villa in Berne. When French soldiers broke into the Imperial Palace (to sequester sensitive documents on France-CAR relations), they also discovered several chests of diamonds (one with 14,000 rough stones, one with 2,000 cut gems), diamond-encrusted clocks, a 62-carat ring, and Bokassa's marshal's baton valued at nearly $2 million. There were also more than 200 cameras and accessories. Some of the valuables (including diamonds) mysteriously disappeared after the invasion.

101. *Daily Telegraph,* September 26, 1979.

102. See *West Africa,* July 14, 1980. See also the April 7, 1980, issue; and Legum (ed.), *Africa Contemporary Record 1980–81,* p. B404.

103. *Africa Research Bulletin,* Economic Series (March 1980).

104. "Central African Republic: Dacko Dangles," *Africa Confidential,* February 27, 1980.

105. See "La réelection au premier tour de President Dacko," *Afrique Contemporaine* (May–June 1981), p. 24. See also *Africa Contemporary Record,* Political Series (April 1981).

106. Cited in Legum (ed.), *Africa Contemporary Record 1981–82.*

107. *Le Monde,* March 20, 1982.

108. *West Africa,* March 22, 1982.

109. "C.A.R.: Les operations," *Africa Confidential,* November 30, 1983.

110. "C.A.R.: Before the Storm," *Africa Confidential,* August 1, 1984.

111. See "Kolingba's Promises," *West Africa,* June 30, 1986. And for a critical look at Kolingba's regime, see Roger Delpey, *Affaires Centrafricaines* (Paris: Jacques Grancher, 1985).

112. Cited in "Bokassa Bounces Back," *West Africa,* May 27, 1985.

113. See "Bokassa's Comeback," *West Africa,* December 8, 1986. See also "Bokassa's Return," *West Africa,* November 3, 1986; T.M. Azongo, "The Trial Resumes," *West Africa,* December 22, 1986; and Didier Bigo, "Le Retour de Bokassa," *Politique Africaine* (December 1987).

114. *Africa Confidential,* August 27, 1987.

5 The Authoritarian Syndrome in Africa

The Roots of Tyranny

The previous three chapters outlined some of the pertinent socioeconomic features of Uganda, Equatorial Guinea, and the Central African Republic, and the political backgrounds against which personal dictatorship emerged in these three countries. Included in these chapters was an analysis of the factors that helped shape the personalities and orientations of the tyrants in question, the salient characteristics of the course of the dictatorial era, and the traumatic and destabilizing legacy it left behind to plague successor regimes.

Throughout these case studies, the analytic focus was directed to the *specific* socioeconomic and political conditions that helped catapult each tyrant into office and to the *specific* idiosyncrasies that manifested themselves in each case through the dictatorial modality of governance established by each tyrant. Although in every instance brutal personal dictatorship arose as a result of societal characteristics unique to the country concerned, and although the unique personality of each tyrant molded the features of dictatorship in each country, *systemically* both sets of factors have several important points of similarity that now bear underscoring.

We turn first to the societal context. In Uganda, the systemic conditions that helped catapult Amin to power were the growing economic malaise following Obote's "Move to the Left" initiative, the political deflation of central legitimacy and, especially, of Obote's personal authority, and ongoing political strife. Amidst this turmoil unfolded the personal estrangement between the chief executive (Obote) and the chief of staff (Amin), and the personal threat to the latter's status and hegemony over the armed forces constituted the actual triggering cause of the coup.

In the Central African Republic, the factors underlying Bokassa's seizure of power were, likewise, the complete erosion of authority on the part of the political leadership (David Dacko) and progressive economic decay. The imminence of a bid for power on the part of a clique headed by the chief of police (which might have derailed the professional career of Bokassa) was the ultimate spark in an increasingly volatile situation. Bokassa's own personal role-aggrandizing inclinations also played a role in the New Year's Eve coup.

The circumstances in Equatorial Guinea were similar. There was a plot (a parliamentary plot, in this instance) to oust Nguema from his tenuous leadership in the National Assembly, set against the background of an extremely splinterized array of political power and a society completely divided on many dimensions. Moreover, the country's originally somewhat healthier economy (several of its indicators at independence were on a par with those of the Ivory Coast) has to be seen in the context of its overwhelming domination by haughty expatriate (and absentee landlord) interests and a colonial heritage of socially stagnant and politically oppressive Spanish rule.

A comparative overview of the conditions that ushered in personal dictatorship in Uganda, Equatorial Guinea, and the Central African Republic would thus point up the fact that, in all three cases, there was a coalescence of three common vectors. First, the *structural background conditions* to the pending political upheavals in all three countries were identical: an acute deflation of central authority coupled with, or consequent to, a combination of intense social division and strife, economic malaise, and political polarization. Second, the *behavioral contexts* of the coup leaders were similar: Purely personal motivations were at the core of the coups that led to dictatorship. In each case there was a clear, unequivocal, direct, and personal threat to the prestige, status, power hegemony, and even personal security of the individual who was ultimately to ward off these assaults on his position by seizing power. Bokassa's personal motives for his takeover in Bangui—in response to the threat to his continued leadership of the armed forces in the event of Izamo's coup—were further sharpened, as noted, by his existing personal (as opposed to political) ambitions for an enhanced power role for purposes of self-gratification.

Finally, and most important to the purposes of our comparative analysis, what could be termed the *idiosyncratic* variable was remarkably similar in all three countries. In this case the common "random" variable was the fact that the three individuals who seized power in Kampala, Malabo, and Bangui had seriously malintegrated and force-oriented personalities. This commonality in some of the basic personality traits of Amin, Nguema, and Bokassa axiomatically ensured that their regimes would manifest highly aberrant and tyrannical characteristics as compared to the more "pedestrian" traits and preoccupations of other African regimes, including the authoritarian/dictatorial ones similarly ushered in by personalist motivations in contexts of societal strife and deflation of central authority. Indeed, this idiosyncratic input is what sharply sets off the three dictatorships of Amin, Nguema, and Bokassa (which, strictly speaking, should be seen as *personal tyrannies*, as already suggested) from other authoritarian/dictatorial regimes in Africa. The specific nature of the personal tyrannies that emerged in Kampala, Malabo, and Bangui had thus much more to do with the aberrant personalities of those who seized power than with the socioeconomic deficiencies facing the antecedent administrations in these three countries.

The meshing of these three factors—personalist power-grabs by maladjusted and malevolent leaders in a societal context of intense division and a legitimacy void—goes a long way toward explaining the roots of aberrant personal dictatorship in Africa. The visible deflation of central authority and political legitimacy in Kampala, Malabo, and Bangui—a consequence of the erosion (or nonexistence) of societal consensus regarding the most fundamental dimensions of the political system—whetted the ambitions of many political aspirants who were plotting behind the scenes in all three countries. But in the specific cases of Amin, Nguema, and Bokassa, their drives for supremacy were triggered less by a desire to provide better leadership to the ship of state, to correct societal grievances, or to set alternate policies—less by the existing political vacuum itself—than by the threat to their personal status. Favorable socioeconomic and political conditions were clearly supportive of a power-grab, but they were not the root cause of the coups that took place.

In a similar vein, it was specifically the deviant, malintegrated, and force-oriented personalities of Amin, Nguema, and Bokassa that set the stage for the bizarre flights of fancy and frightful brutalities that were to transpire in Kampala, Malabo, and (to a lesser extent) in Bangui, and not any societal context or drive, nor any subsequent threat to the paramountcy of the three dictators once power was securely in their hands. Even in Uganda, where both internal and external threats to Amin's power hegemony (i.e., the ethnic composition of the army and its constant unruliness, and Obote's loyalist forces poised across the border in Tanzania) were clearly relevant factors objectively calling for coercive measures, the incredible reign of terror that he unleashed on the country was simply unnecessary—indeed, counterproductive—and primarily a manifestation of his own deranged personality. Numerous personal autocracies, both civil and military, have surfaced in Africa, through coups or otherwise, establishing both benign as well as socially oppressive regimes. But even the most authoritarian—even those that are little more than plundering "personal governments" (to use a term increasingly applied to describe a number of venal personal dictatorships) are devoid of the wildly idiosyncratic behavior and widespread random brutality that manifested themselves in Uganda, Equatorial Guinea, and the Central African Republic.

The different personalities of the three tyrants—their predispositions, biases, value systems, and self-conceptions—were in each case powerfully and indelibly reflected in the policies they set into motion in their societies. As noted, Africa has seen an array of erstwhile *caudillos*—headstrong, charismatic, or authoritarian civil and military leaders, who for better or worse have forcefully stamped their unique imprints on their countries' political heritages. (Cogent examples abound, including Thomas Sankara in Burkina Faso, Julius Nyerere in Tanzania, Jomo Kenyatta in Kenya, Maummar Qadaffi in Libya, Mobutu Sese Seko in Zaire, Kamuzu Banda in Malawi, Sekou Toure in Guinea, and Kwame Nkrumah in Ghana.) But none truly approximated the impact that Amin, Nguema, and Bokassa had in their respective countries and, indeed, on the outside world. The systemic brutalization of their populations, the utter pulverization of the societal fabric of Uganda and Equatorial Guinea, and the fundamental socioeconomic dislocations in the Central African Republic simply have no match elsewhere on the continent. Outside Africa, probably an entire generation of laypersons became familiar with Uganda only after Amin thumbed his nose at the West and committed his widely reported domestic atrocities. And if there is any awareness at all of the existence of the Central African Republic, it is due mostly to Bokassa's bizarre antics and celebrated Napoleonic coronation. (Equatorial Guinea and Nguema's reign of terror, however, still remain virtually unknown abroad.) Apart from these three potentates, many of the harsher edges and more idiosyncratic features of the colorful personalities that Africa has produced have been blanched or blunted by healthy doses of realistic pragmatism and moderated by the constraints of a measure of collegial power-sharing, which even authoritarian regimes often possess.

Not so with Amin, Nguema, and Bokassa, whose personal idiosyncracies (which, as we have seen, varied markedly) were rather precisely mirrored in the processes they set into motion in their respective countries. One need not engage in armchair psychology (although psychological analysis, sadly absent, is certainly tempting and, if embarked upon, would be extremely rewarding given the availability of rich details on the social backgrounds, formative experiences, core values, attitudes, and behaviors of the three dictators) to detect the direct linkage between the personality of each tyrant and his actions in office. Bokassa's flights of imagination, fanciful behavior, and visions of personal grandeur did not stem from societal inputs but, rather, were a reflection of his personal needs and whims. Nguema's morose withdrawal into an inner world of witchcraft and a bygone parochial era can be directly traced to his own personality anachronisms and maladjustments. Indeed, the more "normal" (i.e., venal) dictatorship that supplanted his own in Malabo, headed by a cross-section of his former henchmen, cogently underscores the *personal* roots of the madness of Nguema's reign. And the virtual rudderless and policy-sterile eight-year rule of Amin in Uganda was likewise a direct manifestation of that tyrant's own arid and disorderly personal universe and limited horizons.

It is here that one encounters the second set of commonalities in the case studies. Although the specific idiosyncrasies of each dictator differed markedly from country to country, numerous generic similarities abound. These relate to the *systemic* nature of the personal dictatorships that were established in Kampala, Malabo, and Bangui, for many of the dimensions of the reigns of Amin, Nguema, and Bokassa are closer to the features implicit in the classical (though little-used) concept of personal tyranny than to those associated with the more current idea of personal dictatorship, no matter how authoritarian. It is therefore in their establishment of personal tyrannies in their respective fiefdoms—and not by virtue of their *specific* policy idiosyncrasies—that the three dictators share similarities.

What was strikingly similar and systemically common in all three regimes was the personal, aberrant, and tyrannical dimensions of dictatorship, and it is these traits that set them apart from other instances of authoritarian rule on the continent. These features, common to all three tyrants, include (1) the awesome totality of power (social, economic, political, military, religious, even divine) that each tyrant arrogated to himself; (2) the excessively brutal and predominantly force-oriented manner in which the three potentates utilized these powers to gratify their every personal whim and to secure their continued and unchallenged personal paramountcy in society (In this connection, even Bokassa, on the whole the most socialized of the trio, fits squarely into the tyrannical mold given his utterly unnecessary murder of the infant of his son-in-law as well as his rampages against pupils who would not wear his effigy-imprinted uniforms); and (3) the absence of even a semblance of moral, collegial, or pragmatic restraints on the highly arbitrary and brutal utilization of these powers. (One could also add, as an aside, the absence of any serious interference in these reigns of terror from the world community of nations.)[1]

Additional similarities shared by all three dictatorships were (4) the total absence of any sectional, regional, ethnic, corporate, religious, secterian, or class legitimacy; and (5) the fact that the personal autocracies of Amin, Nguema, and Bokassa were supported primarily, and at times solely, by cowed cohorts and sycophantic power-seekers (in the Central

African Republic), family relatives and kinsmen (in Equatorial Guinea), and virtual outright mercenaries (in Uganda). They also reflected (6) a total lack of concern with the plight of society at large, ignoring (in the case of Bokassa, only intermittently) virtually anything unsupportive of their egos or unrelated to their personal whims, interests, and preoccupations.

Finally, (7) the manner in which the social order was forcefully restructured to better conform with each tyrant's personal self-image or perverted vision of the world (as in Equatorial Guinea and Uganda) or harnassed to provide the backstage for the dictator's flights of fantasy (as in the Central African Republic) was common to all three potentates. Thus, despite the only obvious differences between the personal idiosyncrasies of Amin, Nguema, and Bokassa, their regimes are bound together by the personal, aberrant, and tyrannical features of the regimes they set up.

The Future of Dictatorship in Africa

Based on the insights gleaned from these three case studies, one can now attempt to assess the tentative conclusions that can be drawn about the possible emergence of further aberrant regimes in Africa. Are the case studies to be regarded as fundamentally *sui generis*—that is, as the product of the intermeshing of unique sets of circumstances unlikely to be replicated in the future and, hence, of only marginal academic interest except to the specialist? Or are the generic conditions favorable to the rise of personal tyrannies actually common on the continent?

More specifically, how likely is it that these conditions might synchronize again elsewhere on the continent, spewing out other maladjusted leaders who will further devastate African societies? After all, as the case studies have demonstrated, aberrant personal dictatorships emerged in countries that could hardly be more geographically separated—in countries distinctly different from one another on virtually every dimension, including colonial background. Does this suggest the existence in Africa of a fertile topsoil within which personal dictatorship can take root irrespective of the historical, cultural, political, or colonial context of the country concerned?

Such analysis is necessarily speculative, of course. The field of authoritarian rule in Africa has been little plowed, and the phenomena of dictatorship and tyranny on the continent have barely been explored. As Amos Perlmutter has noted, even contemporary definitions of tyranny, dictatorship, autocracy, and authoritarianism are not distinct and tend to blur.[2] And only recently has there been a strong trend among Africanists to reconceptualize political leadership in Africa in terms of the personalist dimension—an approach that meshes well with that of this study.

Furthermore, the three instances of personal dictatorship under analysis are hardly an adequate data-set from which firm generalizations can be drawn. Personal dictatorship, as here defined, is a unique form of autocracy at the tyrannical extreme along the spectrum of authoritarianism, characterized by the personal, aberrant, and tyrannical nature of the despotic power exercised. The analysis of this phenomenon, moreover, inevitably involves some assessment of personality traits, the weighing of often-covert motivations for coups or aspirations for power, and the detection of linkages among formative experiences, values, attitudes, and political behavior. All such endeavors are, by definition, academically hazardous and replete with potential pitfalls. Beyond the superficial and anecdotal, very little empirical research has been conducted along these lines; Africanists often tend, instead, to be fixated on socioeconomic and structural explanations for political behavior. And as J. Gus Liebenow has suggested in a somewhat different context, much of the data needed for this kind of analytical focus may, indeed, be difficult to obtain, except ex post facto—that is, until *after* the emergence of a malevolent personal dictator; hence any predictive or probabilistic insights these data might otherwise have generated are obviated.[3]

With these qualifications in mind, we can now attempt to assess the probability that such aberrant personal tyrannies will be replicated elsewhere on the continent. Three issues lie at the core of this analysis: (1) the personal dimension of political power in Africa, (2) the personal motivations that permeate many power-grabs on the continent, and (3) the relative prevalence of maladjusted personalities in positions of authority.

Personal Rule in Africa

Political power is highly personalized in Africa, and personal rule is virtually the norm. This holds true for most political systems on the continent, whether civilian or military, elitist (as most are, in any case) or overtly populist, or conservative or radical. It is true of those countries whose systems are "legitimated" by one or more political parties, and true of those without any political parties whatsoever. It is equally true of those countries that overtly espouse liberal and democratic values, as well as of those permeated by a clearly authoritarian ethos. Personal rule is likewise the common denominator in polities projecting a semblance of collegial power-sharing as well as in those clearly ruled by a sole maximum leader or dictator. Indeed, so prevalent is the phenomenon of personal rule and the personalist basis of power on the continent that one might even be tempted to conclude that its erosion—in African societies characterized by a multiplicity of cleavages and by the absence of a strong political core—will inevitably lead to instability. Certainly, in the three case studies in this work, the erosion of the personal power bases of Milton Obote, Macias Nguema, and David Dacko (and not just the erosion of the "legitimacy" of their regimes) was one of the factors that set the stage for the coups that ushered in dictatorship.

The concept of personal rulership, and of the personal aspect of power in Africa, has in recent years been developed, refined, and applied with great utility by a number of prolific scholars.[4] At the core of this reconceptualization of political power is one fundamental axiom: Irrespective of the peculiarities of the political leader in question, and regardless of the modalities of governance in Africa (i.e., the political structures, political parties, elections, constitutions, centralizing ideologies, etc.), political power in each polity is tightly centralized in the hands of a political leader who stands at the center of a (primarily) modern clientelist network of personal alliances that links to him secondary civil and military leaders.

At times accompanied by a personality cult aimed at drumming up wider popular support, or projecting its existence for purposes of conveying systemic legitimacy, the personal ruler is the center of his political universe. All senior social, economic, political, military, educational, and at times even religious appointments stem from him, and all policies of any import bear his personal sanction or imprint. In more open political systems, the immediate circle of associates surrounding the personal ruler may, in exchange for total fealty, actively participate in the process of decisionmaking. Tapping patronage by virtue of their privileged position, dispensing it downwards thus solidifying their own status, these associates form a political system that calls to mind the concept of division of power—though always within strict limits set by the personal ruler. Elsewhere the personal ruler's allies are clearly little more than administrative aides with little scope for independent action, even within their tightly circumscribed domains. (President Kamuzu Banda, for instance, is fond of referring to his cabinet ministers as "my boys" and personally assesses every application for a business license in Malawi.) The specific style of governance adopted by the personal ruler—whether active or passive, open or authoritarian—reflects his personality, thus allowing for a variety of possible typologies of personal rule,[5] even though the centrality of the personal basis of power is common to all.

Personal rule can thus be seen as a fundamentally elitist style of governance that trades off patronage and societal rewards to other political aspirants or socially influential figures in exchange for personal support and political quiescence. It binds to the persona of the ruler alternate loci of political power (and hence of potential threat), buying off, imprisoning, and if necessary physically eliminating recalcitrant individuals who challenge the system with populist, ethnic, or class appeals. Such a system of governance rests, as one scholar has put it, on "mercenary support" for the personal ruler, who acquires "instrumental allegiance from influential individuals and groups through patronage."[6]

Personal rule is above all a modality of governance aimed at ensuring the *retention* of power in conditions of extreme social flux—conditions that are characteristic of modernizing societies. It aims at "locking in" power in the hands of a political hierarchy whose core membership is frozen in time, assuming a lifelong (if not dynastic) tenure of office. It is one outcome of—and even a solution to—the problems of governing and securing political compliance in complex multi-ethnic societies marked by multiple cleavages (ethnic, regional, religious, class). These problems are compounded by the fact that African ruling hierarchies tend to be narrowly based as well as internally divided, and head relatively ineffective ("soft") instruments of popular mobilization, national integration, social control, and coercion.

Personal rule need not be authoritarian, although, by definition, it is autocratic and inimical to the development of a completely open and competitive political system. Despite populist rhetoric to the contrary, personal rulership in Africa is fundamentally not accountable for the exercise of power to the wider society at large, and it tends to remain beyond the purview of the structural mechanisms for governance and accountability that may exist in the polity. It opens the door for significant social waste, graft, and corruption (the necessary prices of securing the allegiance of the ruler's cohorts) and thus inevitably serves the personal and sectional interests of the ruling group first and the wider society last. When such a system of personal rule is headed by a totally illegitimate or venal leader, by an individual with headstrong paternalistic inclinations, or by one suffused by millenial or visionary goals, it may evolve into an autocracy (as in Samuel Doe's Liberia or Mobutu Sese Seko's Zaire), a benevolent personal dictatorship (as in Kamuzu Banda's Malawi), or a highly idiosyncratic authoritarian regime (as in Qadaffi's Libya).

Although personal rule can be relatively stable (as evidenced by the extraordinarily long terms in office of those African leaders not yet toppled by coups), it carries within itself fundamental anomalies. In a system devoid of alternate sources of power and independent and viable structures capable of mediating conflict, where power is highly personalized and where access to its apex is severely limited, intra-elite friction tends to be personalized. Indeed, one is struck by the number of political tugs-of-war in Africa that essentially stem from personality cleavages and personal vendettas.

Personal rule cannot bind *all* power-aspirants to the center—certainly not those who fundamentally reject the system itself on programmatic or ideological grounds. Since personal rule is anchored in patronage and the spoils of office (both of which are limited, even in the wealthiest African states such as Libya and Gabon), it encompasses only a segment of all power-aspirants, shunting aside others. The intra-elite seasaw between the "ins" and the "outs" is sharpened by the fact that few opportunities exist for upward social mobility outside the lucrative public domain; indeed, in many countries the sole key to economic success is a civil service appointment that allows access to public funds and services—but this venue is locked in the hands of the ruling elite.

One should also note that many African societies are rapidly developing. The needs and demands of a growing intelligentsia, the glaring inconsistencies of widening class cleavages and income disparities, the burdens of servicing onerous national debts with the dwindling resources of often shrinking or flagging economies, the rural-urban drift of an often nihilistic age-group of unemployed youth, and the increasingly coercive measures adopted by insecure leaders facing waning systemic legitimacy—all of these factors sap the founts of personal power in systems that are inherently ossified, where prospects of political choice, change, and peaceful transition from one set of rulers to another is precluded except through coup d'état.

The Personalist Coup

In countries without viable, autonomous, or meaningful political structures capable of mediating conflict, assessing priorities, and objectively legitimating power by endowing it with authority (as is the case in most African states), and where political power is highly concentrated and power relationships are personalized, political conflict is likely to be highly personalized as well. In zero-sum (winner-take-all) contexts, where personal competitions cannot be adjudicated impartially (electorally or otherwise) and where independent loci of power are regarded as threatening and are consequently suppressed, plotting, subversion, and power bids manifest themselves with great regularity and coups tend to be the only method of effecting change. Indeed, where societal choice and prospects of political change are permanently frozen by personal rule (whether authoritarian or relatively benevolent), coups may be seen as the functional equivalent of elections, replacing one set of political actors for another. Existing civil-military alliances and power pyramids (two of the personal ruler's tools of governance) break down at various levels as a result of civil-military personality clashes and fundamental programmatic differences. And although some of the resultant coups may aim at cleansing society of the ills of the antecedent administration and transferring political power to alternate leaders, many tend to be triggered by little more than narrow corporate and personalist motivations.

At any point during the past two decades, half of Africa and (given Nigeria's record of instability) more than 60 percent of the continent's population have been governed by military hierarchies. Coups and military rule have been one of the most frequent and persistent features of the continent. In an increasing number of countries, permanent military rule has become the norm, anchored in either ideological or programmatic justifications; in some, rule by civilian politicians is but a fleeting, distant memory. Military coups have afflicted a wide variety of countries. Both the relatively better-governed regimes and those that are crassly mismanaged and corrupt have suffered takeovers by their armed forces; both those with relatively healthy economies and those suffering considerable economic stress have seen the military intrude into the political arena. As Aristide Zolberg concluded nearly two decades ago, it "is impossible to specify as a class countries where coups have occurred from others which have so far been spared."[7]

Although a voluminous literature has mushroomed as Africanists have attempted to come to grips with the generic causes of coups on the continent, considerable controversy remains in the discipline. The absence of political legitimacy, failures of institutionalization and leadership, economic stress, corruption, ethnicity, and a host of other factors have been pinpointed and, more recently, quantitatively isolated in increasingly sophisticated research as the root causes of the coup phenomenon on the continent.[8] But one major side-effect of the preoccupation with the more easily analyzable and quantifiable structural and systemic deficiencies of African states is the empirical neglect of the behavioral dynamics of the coup context. The consequence has been a gross underemphasis of the personalist motivations underlying a large number of Africa's military upheavals. Although the systemic factors that cause instability in Africa certainly play a role in triggering military upheavals, empirical research often reveals a multitude of other factors. Fluid societies with lifeless political structures headed by personalist leaders tend to encourage dynamic power interplays, gambits, and seizures by ambitious personalities, civilian as well as military. Noble overt rationalizations for extraconstitutional takeovers, even when they objectively reflect reality, may well be the camouflage for covert personal takeovers.

In short, systemic stresses and imbalances often form the backdrop against which covert motivations play the predominant or even sole role in power-grabs. In many instances, military officers are no doubt reacting (reluctantly, at times) to a political and legitimacy void; in other cases, however, they are utilizing unsettled societal conditions as the legitimating cloak for the attainment of purely sectional and personal aspirations. It is often taken for granted that civilian aspirants seek political power for a multiplicity of reasons (some noble, others not so noble) in their quest for political power, but that military officers are immune to the temptations of ambition, greed, personal self-aggrandizement, and intervene in the political arena merely as a result of objective societal factors.

The case studies in this work vividly illustrate the variety of parochial motives potentially underlying personalist military coups. The specific rationalizations offered by the three tyrants that came to power need not detain us, inasmuch as these rationalizations clearly bore no relationship to the true and covert reasons for their power seizures. Notwithstanding the White Paper issued by Amin in justification of his takeover, and the objective validity of nearly every charge he levied against Obote, the coup in Uganda was really triggered by Amin's fear of eclipse in the army and of possible imprisonment. The history of Africa is, indeed, replete with similar instances of purely personalist motivations for coups, camouflaged by layers of noble justifications.[9]

But it is important to stress that personalist motivations are not necessarily the predominant triggering factor in Africa's spate of coups since independence. (Most of the coups in Nigeria, for example, appear to have been remarkably free of such personalist motivations.) No scholar has yet tabulated the relative frequency of personalist ingredients in the cauldron of motivations underlying military coups in Africa, although references to such motivations abound in the professional literature. Such endeavors would require detailed empirical analysis of highly sensitive issues relating to intramilitary behavioral dynamics, with all the methodological pitfalls inherent in research that is both behavioral and subjective. However, the high incidence of personalist coups in Africa can be ignored only at the risk of allowing fundamental errors to creep into the emerging theories of African political behavior.

More important, an awareness of the true motivations behind coups in Africa may be critical to the study of dictatorship and tyranny on the continent. Where the drive to the presidential office stems from purely personal and parochial considerations, the policies of the resultant regime will likely reflect the personal interests and preoccupations of the military junta first and those of society last, if at all. Of course, military rule can also be benevolent and enlightened, for a host of other factors may come into play once power is consolidated. But the temptations inherent in high office unaccountable to other societal actors enhance the chances that military leaders with such motivational pedigrees will perpetuate themselves in power. When the regime is politically sterile, venal, and utterly devoid of popular backing, a harsh military dictatorship may well ensue. And if headed by the "right" aberrant leader, a personal tyranny might emerge. In Kampala, Bangui, and Santa Isabel, tyranny sprang up precisely through the convergence of such conditions—namely, a deflation of the power base of personal rule coupled with a personalist coup led by an aberrant personality. Similar convergences of societal conditions and aberrant profiles, it may be argued, are likely to produce identical outcomes elsewhere on the continent.

The Aberrant Personality in Africa

The major dimension that sets apart the tyrannies under analysis from other instances of personal dictatorship on the continent concerns the aberrant personality of the autocrats in question. In the final analysis, it is aberrant leadership, and not legitimacy voids and personalist motivations for takeovers, that characterizes personal tyrannies, at least on the African continent.

As earlier noted, in the absence of this idiosyncratic factor, different forms of autocracy might have developed in Kampala, Bangui, and Malabo. Were it not for the maladjusted, anachronistic, and socially destructive personality of Nguema at the fulcrum of power in Equatorial Guinea, the country might well have developed into "merely" another rudderless personal dictatorship like that of Samuel Doe in Liberia. In like manner, it was the fact that Idi Amin headed the armed forces—and not merely the emergence of the military at the fulcrum of power—that led to the post-1971 reign of terror in Uganda. In the presence of a less deranged personality than that of Amin, a Mobutu-style vandalizing military autocracy might have been the outcome. And there is little doubt that no military regime in Bangui except Bokassa's could have produced the policy aberrations that occurred in 1966–1979. The erosion of the personal power base of the antecedent political leadership in the three countries created power vacuums that could have sucked in a variety of alternate leaders and regimes, including nonauthoritarian ones. And if authoritarian, they could have been venal, mercenary, personalist, and even brutally protective of their power hegemonies when necessary, but devoid of policies utterly counter productive to the personal interests of the potentate himself and of the systematized random terror that characterized the interregnums of Amin, Nguema, and Bokassa.

It is virtually impossible to assess even superficially the likely prevalence of such personality configurations in Africa. African studies provide an absolute minimum of guidance inasmuch as empirical research is literally nonexistent. The study of personality, political psychology, even political leadership—vibrant subfields in mainstream political science—has barely extended to the Third World and hardly touched the dark continent. A survey of the contemporary political leadership of Africa is of little assistance for, apart from the trio under current analysis, no instances of either tyranny or aberrant leadership, as here defined, have emerged. Aberrant personalities are in the minority in any society, although, as contemporary psychological research suggests, they are not randomly distributed. Moreover, only a small number of such individuals are likely either to seek political power or to attain it.

As noted, Africa has produced an abundance of headstrong and idiosyncratic civil and military leaders, but none in the mold of Amin, Nguema, and Bokassa. The tight personal rule of the mercurial and visionary Qadaffi in Libya, for example, essentially aims at redistributing global power and restructuring the socioeconomic universe. Though fueled by an assortment of personality idiosyncrasies that authoritative sources have identified, Qadaffi is not in the tyrannical mold, no matter how repugnant he may be to Americans, or how authoritarian and personalist his regime may be. In addition (and this is an observation often ignored in assessments of Qadaffi), some of the fundamentalist features and expansionary inclinations of the Libyan Jamahariya have both popular support within the country and roots in its recent history, as none of the three personal dictators under study could claim. The brutal war in Eritrea, the bloody purges in Addis Ababa, and the social violence and class warfare intermittently unleashed in Ethiopia by Mengistu Haile Mariam have solid programmatic roots and ideological anchors, as well as socioeconomic origins; moreover, they are not *prima facie* manifestations of aberrant tyranny, no matter how harsh the regimes in question. And the iron-handed paternalism and strong personal idiosyncrasies of Kamuzu Banda in Malawi, Jerry Rawlings in Ghana, and Omar Bongo in Gabon likewise pale into insignificance when compared to the essence of tyranny, even though these regimes show different gradations of dictatorial rule.

At least part of the answer lies in a more critical examination of the original conditions under which the three potentates under analysis surfaced to prominence in their respective civil and military hierarchies. Individuals such as Amin, Nguema, and Bokassa—given their severe personal, social, professional, and political limitations (Bokassa included, due to his excess vanity, ebulience, alcoholism, in a career fundamentally requiring balance of judgment and moderation)—would not normally be expected to rise to positions of importance, let alone to the pinnacles of their civil or military careers, on their own merits. The chances are overwhelming that political and military figures with such personality traits or deficiencies (illiterate, brutal, and disorganized officers, inchoate drug-addicted politicians, etc.) will remain frozen in secondary positions at the lower extremities of the civil administration and armed forces.

The three personal dictators were both products of decolonization and answers to the urgent need for indigenization of previously expatriate political and military hierarchies. Hence their personal advancements were unique, and the chances of similar replications are highly unlikely. They were "first-generation" leaders, who, despite well-known personal deficiencies and potentials for aberrant behavior, slipped through the much looser net, so to speak, that was relaxed at the eve of independence to accommodate the exigencies of imminent independence. They moved up the civil and military rungs to the pinnacles of their professional careers due to circumstances that objectively had little to do with their own actual qualifications or merits. The fact that other "first-generation" leaders also emerging in positions of power in Africa at the heyday of independence did *not* become tyrants reflects minority status of the aberrant personality in any society.

Nguema penetrated Equatorial Guinea's elitist senior administrative hierarchy solely as a result of Spanish colonial favoritism for its rare loyal Fang (he could not have passed the qualifying examinations on his own, having failed them several times already). Nominated *alcalde* (mayor) by the Spanish authorities (in a town where he was disliked, and where an election would have seen his defeat—as later occurred in the open 1968 presidential elections), he automatically became a member of the very small National Assembly as well as cabinet minister. With his career subsequently furthered by expatriate mercantile interests seeking a role in the post-colonial era, he was able to develop the power base that was his springboard to dictatorship. Given his abrasive, antisocial, and incoherent style, and the presence of other articulate and intellectual power-aspirants in Santa Isabel, it is highly doubtful whether Nguema, on his own, could have triggered the bandwagon coalescence of political support in the National Assembly.

Amin, by contrast, was a product of overly rapid Africanization. Evidence of merit or of suitability for higher office was, in his case, specifically sacrificed on the altar of nationalist expediency by both the British colonial administration and the nascent African leadership in Kampala. Suitably placed for a quantum jump to officerhood as an *effendi* and clearly a popular platoon leader (he seemed potentially able to provide leadership to a larger military machine), Amin was rapidly advanced beyond his native abilities. If objective criteria had been applied to his candidacy, or if he had been subjected to the array of technical and literacy proficiency tests and the other senior-officer staff-training courses routinely required of subsequent generations of officer cadets, there is little doubt that Amin would have remained an NCO for life. Although the current Ugandan officer corps does not invite direct comparison (it was drawn from Museveni's liberation elements and is only now being trained, locally, by a British military mission), the rigorous screening and training programs in African armies elsewhere leave little chance for individuals such as Amin to penetrate the officer fraternity, let alone to acquire the base for a seizure of power.

Bokassa was also automatically placed in command of the nascent Central African forces on the eve of colonialism in Equatorial Africa, in the absence of alternate or more suitable Oubangui-Chari officers in the demobilized French Colonial Armies. Although his educational and military credentials were certainly superior to those of Amin in Uganda, if there had been a choice (or less urgency in the indigenization of the military command), he might well have been passed over because of his personality idiosyncrasies, which were well known in French military circles prior to independence.

However unique the circumstances that permitted the rise to power of Amin, Nguema, and Bokassa, there can be no assurance that other aberrant personalities are not lurking near the summit of civilian or military power in some other African state, biding their time. Military officers catapulted into power through personalist coups (and not through the rough give-and-take process of forging personal alliance pyramids and political networks) might, in the absence of widespread systemic support, move into the tyrannical mold in an effort to retain ultimate power. Civilian rulers, too, can establish tyrannical regimes, especially if they possess a tight control over the coercive instruments of power in their society. However, the latter outcome is unlikely except in very small polities (such as Equatorial Guinea), given the multiplicity of ethnic groups and the sectional and personal tensions that suffuse most armed forces. Finally, it is possible that *unsuccessful* power-grabs from the lower ranks of African armies have already been triggered, or will yet be initiated by individuals with highly idiosyncratic power-drives. The personality configurations and motivations of unsuccessful coup-leaders attract even less academic attention in the discipline, and empirical ex post facto analysis is obviously difficult, if not impossible. (Among other things, some of these individuals have been executed.) Supportive data are therefore even sparser in this area—but the attempted coup of 1976 in Niger, for example, appears to have been sponsored by an officer with a highly aberrant personality, and certain other military upheavals might likewise bear closer scrutiny.

In essence, therefore, it is difficult—if not inherently impossible—to obtain even suggestive evidence about either the relative prevalance of aberrant personalities in high civil and military positions in Africa or the prospects of further instances of tyrannical rule. The only conclusions one can draw with reasonable certitude are these: (1) In the three cases of such regimes on the continent (and there are only these three), extraordinary circumstances unlikely to repeat themselves (except in completely different contexts) were at work. But, conversely, (2) within the inherently authoritarian framework of personal rule and personal dictatorship that is the norm in much of Africa, and especially in the context of the multiplicity of personalist power-grabs that tend to erupt in such systems, the *potential* that such a tyrannical leader will emerge is heightened.

In assessing the systemic after-effects of personal dictatorship following the collapse of tyranny in Uganda, Equatorial Guinea, and the Central African Republic, one is struck by the continuing social and economic dislocations. In Equatorial Guinea, of course, Nguema's ouster was more in the nature of a changing of the guard—the replacement by a vandalizing personal dictatorship of the demented tyranny of yesteryear. Much of the regressive brutality and senseless devastation of society have ended, but oppressive personal rule remains. In Kampala and Bangui, beleaguered successor regimes are to this day battling a multitude of destabilizing and fissiparous tensions set loose by the physical brutalization of society and the devastation of their national economies during the dictatorial era. Civil war continues to afflict Uganda along its north-south (Bantu-Nilotic) axis, with part of the country in a state of anarchy, prey to armed marauders of all kinds from all directions. And in the Central African Republic, only a virtual recolonization by France has stabilized the bankrupt economy and cauldron of tensions of this utterly splinterized society.

In each case, personal dictatorship fundamentally and unequivocally shattered the social, economic, and political status quo. Though under severe stress immediately prior to the rise of dictatorship, the mutually antagonistic segments of the three countries remained largely bound by the social glue imposed by colonial rule. If the bonds of nationhood were embryonic at the time of the emergence of dictatorship, they are possibly weaker today; even the concept of statehood is currently under challenge in Uganda, Equatorial Guinea, and the Central African Republic. A confusing array of powerful ethnic separatist movements, national liberation fronts, and (in Bangui and Kampala) private armies consisting of anarchic armed groups, have sprung up in the countries under study, taxing the energies of successor regimes.

Faced with such disintegrative societal challenges, and saddled with virtually bankrupt economies inherited from the antecedent tyrannies, the weak, beleaguered successor administrations in Kampala, Bangui, and Malabo have increasingly begun to react with authoritarian policies and social repression. In the absence of the most fundamental aspects of systemic support, reliance on brute force has supplanted efforts to develop societal legitimacy and personal authority.

This shift from authority to force as the governing modality not only results in further political decay but also fuels new tensions, frustrations, and divisive tendencies. A vicious circle is established, severely constraining socioeconomic reconstruction and the development of at least a tacit political status quo. Telling is the experience of Uganda, which after the euphoria of liberation (even in Idi Amin's home district), slid into civil war, repression, even genocide under the post-Amin administration of Milton Obote; and, more recently, following the briefest of honeymoons under Yoweri Museveni, is perilously poised at the brink of a similar situation.

The experiences of Uganda and the Central African Republic suggest that political institutionalization and socioeconomic rehabilitation in the post-liberation era are likely to be riddled with pitfalls and discontinuities—hardly the anticipated unilinear progression from devastation to reconstruction. As the process is prolonged due to the continued political imbroglio and the wastage of effort and resources on retaining political power at the center, mushrooming social frustrations further hinder reconstruction by triggering intermittent and politically debilitating power-grabs. Any such derailment of political and socioeconomic normalization (now so cogently visible in Uganda and the Central African Republic) may acquire a *leitmotif* of its own, permanently stultifying attempts at cleansing society of the ravages of dictatorship. The socially destructive legacy of personal tyranny in Africa may thus yet rival the actual ravages of the dictatorial era itself.

Notes

1. The crowning insult may indeed have been France's active collaboration in, and financing of, Bokassa's coronation; in so doing, it defended the creation of an imperial dynasty in Bangui by comparing it to the existence of monarchy in Great Britain. (See Chapter 3 of this volume.)

2. Amos Perlmutter, *Modern Authoritarianism* (New Haven, Conn.: Yale University Press, 1981), p. 170.

3. J. Gus Liebenow, "The Military Factor in African Politics: A Twenty-Five Year Perspective," in G.M. Carter and P. O'Meara (eds.), *African Independence:*

The First Twenty-Five Years (Bloomington: Indiana University Press, 1985), p. 127.

  4. See, in particular, the work of Robert H. Jackson and Carl G. Rosberg, especially their seminal *Personal Rule in Black Africa: Prince, Autocrat, Prophet, Tyrant* (Berkeley: University of California, 1982). See also J. Cartwright, *Political Leadership in Africa* (New York: St. Martin's Press, 1984); and Guenther Roth, who originally applied this concept to the study of the contemporary Third World in his "Personal Rulership, Patrimonialism, and Empire-Building," *World Politics* (January 1968).

  5. See, for instance, the Prince/Autocrat/Prophet/Tyrant typology in Jackson and Rosberg, *Personal Rule in Black Africa.*

  6. Richard Sandbrook, *The Politics of Africa's Stagnation* (Cambridge: Cambridge University Press, 1985), p. 83.

  7. Aristide Zolberg, "Military Intervention in the New 'States' of Africa," in Henry Bienen (ed.), *The Military Intervenes* (New York: Russell Sage Foundation, 1968), p. 71.

  8. The literature on coups is too voluminous to cite, even selectively. For some of the more germane research and overviews, see Samuel Decalo, *Coups and Army Rule in Africa: Studies in Military Style* (New Haven, Conn.: Yale University Press, 1976); Steffan Wiking, *Military Coups in Sub-Saharan Africa* (Uppsala: Scandinavian Institute of African Studies, 1983); and Robert W. Jackman, "The Predictability of Coups d'Etat: A Model with African Data," *American Political Science Review* (September 1978).

  9. For a more thorough exploration of this theme, and many more examples, see Decalo, *Coups and Army Rule*, as well as "Military Rule in Africa: Etiology and Morphology," in Simon Baynham (ed.), *Military Power and Politics in Black Africa* (London: Croom Helm, 1986), and *Military Rule in Africa: Motivations and Constraints* (New Haven, Conn.: Yale University Press, forthcoming).

Selected Bibliography

Aasland, Tertit, "On the Move to the Left in Uganda 1969–71" (Uppsala: Scandinavian Institute of African Studies, Research Paper No. 26, 1974).
Adoko, Akena, *Uganda Crisis* (Kampala: African Publishers Ltd., 1970).
Africa Research Bulletin (1965–1987).
Ake, Claude, "Political Integration and Political Stability," *World Politics*, vol. 19, no. 4 (1967).
Akinyeni, Bolaji, "Nigeria and Fernando Poo 1958–1966," *African Affairs*, no. 276 (July 1970), pp. 236–249.
Alexandre, Pièrre, "Proto-histoire du groupe beti-bulu-fang," *Cahiers d'Etudes Africaines*, vol. 5, no. 20 (1966).
Alexandre, Pièrre, and Jacques Binet, *Le Groupe dit Pahouin (Fang–Bulu–Beti)* (Paris: Institut International Africain, Presses Universitaires de France, 1958).
Année Politique Africaine (Paris: Pedone, 1963–1979).
Apter, David, *The Political Kingdom in Uganda* (Princeton, N.J.: Princeton University Press, 1961).
Aranzadi, I.X. de, *En el bosque fang* (Barcelona, 1963).
———, "Rio Muni ayer y hoy," *Guinea Española*, vol. 62, no. 1598 (Santa Isabel, 1965).
Avirgan, Tony, and Martha Honey, *War in Uganda: The Legacy of Idi Amin* (London: Zed Press, 1982).
Ayemi, Antonio, *Los Bubis en Fernando Poo* (Madrid: Direccion General de Marruecos y Colonias, 1942).
Azongo, Tikum Mbah, "Assertions and Denials," *West Africa*, August 4, 1986.
———, "Breaking New Ground," *West Africa*, February 3, 1986.
———, "The Trial Resumes," *West Africa*, December 22, 1986.
Baguena Corella, L., "Sobre los grupos humanos de la Provincia Española de la Guinea," *Africa* (February 1957), pp. 16–26.
Balandier, Georges, "Social Change Among the Fang of Gabon," in George Balandier, *Sociology of Black Africa* (New York: Praeger Publishers, 1955).
Ballard, John, "Four Equatorial States," in Gwendolen Carter (ed.), *National Unity and Regionalism in Eight African States* (Ithaca, N.Y.: Cornell University Press, 1966).

Barber, J.P., "The Karamajoa District of Uganda," *Journal of African History*, vol. 3, no. 1 (1962).
Beattie, J.H.M., *Bunyoro: An African Kingdom* (New York: Holt, Rinehart and Winston, 1960).
_____, *The Nyoro State* (Oxford: Oxford University Press, 1971).
_____, *Understanding an African Kingdom: Bunyoro* (New York: Holt, Rinehart and Winston, 1965).
Beltran, L., "L'Afrique d'expression espagnole: la région autonome de la Guinea equatoriale," *Etudes Camerounaises*, vol. 10, no. 5 (Kinshasa, September–October 1967).
Berman, Sanford, *Spanish Guinea: An Annotated Bibliography* (Washington, D.C.: Multen Library of the Catholic University of America, 1971).
_____, "Spanish Guinea: Enclave Empire," *Phylon*, vol. 18 (October 1957).
Bienen, Henry, "Public Order and the Military in Africa," in Henry Bienen, *The Military Intervenes* (New York: Russell Sage Foundation, 1968).
Bigo, Didier, "Le Retour de Bokassa," *Politique Africaine* (December 1987).
Blomstrom, Bruce A., "Capital Flight in East Africa," in Tom J. Farar (ed.), *Financing African Development* (Cambridge, Mass.: MIT Press, 1965).
"Bokassa and the Two Chinas," *West Africa*, October 24, 1970.
"Bokassa Bounces Back," *West Africa*, May 27, 1985.
"Bokassa's Comeback," *West Africa*, December 8, 1986.
"Bokassa's Return," *West Africa*, November 3, 1986.
Bowles, B.D., "Nationalism in Uganda 1950–62" (Ph.D. thesis, Mekerere University, 1971).
Brett, E.A., *Colonialism and Underdevelopment in East Africa* (New York: NOK Publishers, 1973).
Brown, R.T., "Fernando Poo and the Anti-Sierra Leonean Campaign 1826–34," *International Journal of African Historical Studies*, vol. 6, no. 2 (1973), pp. 249–264.
Buganda, Department of Interior, "Buganda's Independence" (Kampala: Buganda Department of Information, 1960).
_____, "Buganda's Position" (Kampala: Buganda Department of Information, 1960).
Bundy, Emory, "Uganda's New Constitution," *East African Journal* (June 1966).
Burke, Fred G., *Local Government and Politics in Uganda* (Syracuse, N.Y.: Syracuse University Press, 1964).
Bussières, André, "La R.C.A. sans Boganda" (Paris, 1963), mimeo.
"C.A.R.: Before the Storm," *Africa Confidential*, August 1, 1984.
"C.A.R.: Les operations," *Africa Confidential*, November 30, 1983.
Cartright, J., *Political Leadership in Africa* (New York: St. Martin's Press, 1984).
Casteran, Christian, "Le General Bokassa veut battre monnaie," *Revue Française d'Etudes Politiques Africaines* (November 1971).
Castillo-Fiel, Conte de, *Notas para un estudio antropologica y etnologico del Bubi de Fernando Poo* (Madrid: Instituto de Estudios Africanos, 1949).
"Central African Republic: Coup Foiled," *West Africa*, April 19, 1969.

"Central African Republic: Dacko Dangles," *Africa Confidential*, February 27, 1980.
Chaffard, Georges, *Les carnets secrets de la decolonisation* (Paris: Calman-Levy, 1967).
Challaye, Felicien, *Le Congo Français* (Paris: Elcan, 1909).
Chick, John D., "Uganda: Quest for Control," *The World Today* (June 1984).
Cohen, D.W., "The Political Transformation of Northern Busoga 1600–1900," *Cahiers d'Etudes Africaines*, vol. 22, no. 2-3 (1982), pp. 465–488.
Cohen, William B., *Rulers of Empire* (Stanford, Calif.: Hoover Institution Press, 1971).
Constantin, François, "Centrafrique," *L'Année Politique Africaine 1964* (Paris: Pedone, 1965).
_____, "Centrafrique," *L'Année Politique Africaine 1965* (Paris: Pedone, 1966).
Coquery-Vidrovitch, Catherine, *Le Congo français au temps des grandes compagnies concessionaires* (Paris: Mouton, 1972).
Cordell, Dennis, *Dar el-Kouti and the Last Years of the Trans-Saharan Slave Trade* (Madison: University of Wisconsin Press, 1985).
Cornevin, Robert, "La Politique étrangére du gouvernement de Bangui," *Revue Française d'Etudes Politiques Africaines* (September 1975).
Cossio, R. de Cossio y de, "Problemas que afectan la estractura economica de la Guinea continental española," *Africa*, vol. 21 (July 1964).
Coulon, C., and P.Y. Laporte, "Centrafrique," *L'Année Politique Africaine 1966* (Paris: Pedone, 1968).
Crabb, John, "The Coronation of Emperor Bokassa," *Africa Today* (July–September 1978).
Cronje, S., "Equatorial Guinea—The Forgotten Dictatorship" (London: Anti-Slavery Society, 1976).
Daigre, R.P., "Les Banda de l'Oubangui-Chari," *Anthropos*, no. 16 (1931) and no. 27 (1932).
Dampière, Eric de, *Les Sultanats Zande de l'Oubangui* (Paris: Plon, 1967).
Davis, David H., *The Economic Development of Uganda* (Baltimore: Johns Hopkins Press, 1962).
Decalo, Samuel, *Coups and Army Rule in Africa: Studies in Military Style* (New Haven, Conn.: Yale University Press, 1976).
_____, *Historical Dictionary of Chad*, 2nd ed. (Metuchen, N.J.: Scarecrow Press, 1987).
_____, "Libya's Qaddafi: Bedouin Product of the Space Age," *Present Tense* (New York, January 1974).
_____, "Military Rule in Africa: Etiology and Morphology," in Simon Baynham (ed.), *Military Power and Politics in Black Africa* (London: Croom Helm, 1986).
_____, *Military Rule in Africa: Motivations and Constraints* (New Haven, Conn.: Yale University Press, forthcoming).
Decraene, Philippe, "Le Putsch de Guinée Equatoriale," *Revue Française d'Etudes Politiques Africaines* (September–October 1979).
_____, "Menace d'instabilité en République Centrafricaine," *Le Monde Diplomatique* (May 1969).

Delpey, Roger, *Affaires Centrafricaines* (Paris: Jacques Grancher, 1985).
Dominguez, Ramon Garcia, *Guinea: Macias, la ley del silencio* (Barcelona: Plaza & James, 1976).
Dumont, René, "Le difficile développement agricole de la République Centrafricaine," *Annales de l'Institut Agronomique*, vol. 4 (1966).
Dunbar, A.R., *A History of Bunyoro-Kitara* (Nairobi: Oxford University Press, 1969).
Dyson-Hudson, Neville, *Karamajong Politics* (Oxford: Oxford University Press, 1960).
Elkan, Walter, *The Economic Development of Uganda* (London: Oxford University Press, 1961).
Enahoro, Peter, "Bokassa's Thieves," *Africa* (September 1972).
———, "Tyranny in Equatorial Guinea," *Africa* (August 1976).
Engholm, G.F., "The Westminster Model in Uganda," *International Journal* (Autumn 1963).
Engholm, G.F., and Ali Mazrui, "Violent Constitutionalism in Uganda," *Government and Opposition* (July 1967).
"Enquête sur le mort de M. Boganda," *L'Express* (Paris), May 7, 1959.
"Equatorial Guinea: A Coup Dissected," *Africa Confidential*, October 17, 1979.
"Equatorial Guinea: Nguema's Chamber of Horrors," *New African* (February 1976).
"Equatorial Guinea: Silence Is Dangerous," *Africa* (February 1979).
España en el Africa Ecuatorial (Madrid: Instituto de Estudios Africanos, 1964).
Evans-Pritchard, E.E., *The Azande: History and Political Institutions* (Oxford: Clarendon Press, 1971).
Fallers, Lloyd A., "Ideology and Culture in Ugandan Nationalism," *American Anthropologist*, vol. 63, no. 4 (1961).
———, *Inequality: Social Stratification Reconsidered* (Chicago: University of Chicago Press, 1972).
———, *The King's Men: Leadership and Status in Buganda on the Eve of Independence* (London: Oxford University Press, 1964).
Fernandez, Rafael, *Guinea: Materia Reservada* (Madrid: Sedmay Ediciones, 1976).
First, Ruth, "Uganda: The Latest Coup d'Etat in Africa," *The World Today* (March 1971).
Fondation Nationale de Science Politique, *Chronologie Politique Africaine* (Paris, 1969).
Garcia, H.R. Alvarez, *Leyendos et mitos de Guinea* (Madrid: Instituto de Estudios Africanos, 1951).
Garcia, T. Martinez, *Fernando Poo* (Santa Isabel: Instituto "Claret" de Africanistas, 1968).
Gard, Robert C., "Equatorial Guinea: Machinations in Founding a National Bank," *Munger Africana Library Notes*, no. 27 (October 1974).
Georges, M., "La Vie rurale chez les Banda," *Cahiers d'Outre Mer*, vol. 26 (1963).
Gershenberg, Irving, "Slouching Towards Socialism: Obote's Uganda," *African Studies Review* (April 1972).

Gertzel, Cherry, "How the Kabaka Yekka Came to Be," *Africa Report*, vol. 9, no. 9 (1964).

———, *Party and Locality in Northern Uganda 1945-62* (London: Athlone Press, 1974).

———, "The Lost Counties," *Africa Report*, vol. 7, no. 5 (1962).

———, "Uganda After Amin: The Continuing Search for Leadership and Control," *African Affairs* (September 1980).

Ghai, P. Dharam, "The Bugandan Trade Boycott," in Robert Rotberg and Ali Mazrui (eds.), *Protest and Power in Black Africa* (New York: Oxford University Press, 1970).

Ghai, P. Dharam, and Yash Ghai (eds.), *Portrait of a Minority: Asians in East Africa* (Nairobi: Oxford University Press, 1970).

Gide, André, *Voyage au Congo* (Paris: Gallimard, 1927).

Gingyera-Pinyewa, A.G.G., "On the Proposed Move to the Left in Uganda," *East African Journal* (February 1970).

Glentworth, G., and I. Hancock, "Obote and Amin: Change and Continuity in Modern African Politics," *African Affairs* (July 1973).

Gomez, A. Panyella, "El individuo y la Sociedad Fang," *Archivos del Instituto de Estudios Africanos*, no. 46 (Madrid, September 1958).

———, *Esquema et etnologia de los Fang-Ntumu de la Guinea Española* (Madrid: Instituto de Estudios Africanos, 1959).

Gomez, E. Arrojes, "Los territorios españoles del Golfo de Guinea," in *España en Africa* (Madrid: Instituto de Estudios Africanos, 1950), pp. 19-32.

Gosselin, Gabriel, "Histoire d'un clan Gbaya," *Geneva-Afrique*, vol. 12, no. 1 (Geneva, 1973), pp. 19-36.

———, *Travail et Changement social en pays Gbaya* (Paris: Klincksieck, 1972).

Green, Reginald H., "Magendo in the Political Economy of Uganda" (Brighton: University of Sussex, Institute of Development Studies, 1981).

Greenstein, Fred I., "Personality and Political Socialization: The Theories of Authoritarian and Democratic Character," *Annals of the American Academy of Political and Social Science*, no. 361 (1965), pp. 81-95.

———, *Personality and Politics: Problems of evidence, Inference, and Conceptualization* (New York: W.W. Norton, 1975).

Greenstein, Fred I., and Michael Lerner, *A Source Book for the Study of Personality and Politics* (Chicago: Markham, 1971).

"La Guinée Espagnole," *Revue Française d'Etudes Politiques Africaines*, vol. 13, no. 4 (September 1963).

Gukiina, Peter, *Uganda: A Case Study in African Political Development* (Notre Dame, Ind.: University of Notre Dame Press, 1972).

Hancock, I.R., "Patriotism and Neo-Traditionalism in Uganda: The Kabaka Yekka," *Journal of African History*, vol. 11, no. 3 (1970).

Hansen, H.B., *Mission, Church and State in a Colonial Setting: Uganda 1890-1925* (London: Heinemann, 1984).

Hayward, Fred, "Political Participation and Its Role in Development: Some Observations from the African Context," *Journal of Developing Areas*, vol. 7 (1973).

204 Selected Bibliography

Heraud, G., "Aperçu sur l'organisation des territoires espagnols d'outre mer," *Revue Juridique et Politique*, no. 8 (July–September 1954).
Hilberth, John, *The Gbaya* (Stockholm: Almquist and Wiksell, 1973).
Homet, Marcel, *Congo, Terre de Souffrances* (Paris: Montaigne, 1934).
Hopkins, Terence, "Politics in Uganda: The Buganda Question," in Jeffrey Butler and A.A. Castagno (eds.), *Boston University Papers on Africa* (New York: Praeger Publishers, 1967).
"The Horror of Equatorial Guinea," *West Africa*, October 16, 1978.
Howe, John, "Captains and Kings," *Africa* (February 1978).
———, "Kitchen Comedy," *Africa* (November 1979).
"Human Rights in Uganda" (London: Amnesty International, June 1978).
Hunter, Jeremy, "The Coronation of an Emperor," *Africa* (January 1978).
Ibingira, Grace S.K., *The Forging of an African Nation* (New York: Viking Press, 1973).
Iglesias de la Riva, A., *Politica Indigena en Guinea* (Madrid: Instituto de Estudios Africanos, 1947).
Ingham, Kenneth, *The Kingdom of Toro in Uganda* (London: Methuen, 1975).
———, *The Making of Modern Uganda* (London: Allen and Unwin, 1958).
Institute for Strategic Studies, *The Military Balance 1980–81* (London: ISS, 1981).
International Bank for Reconstruction and Development, "The Economy of the Republic of Equatorial Guinea," *International Development Association Report*, no. AW-37a (November 27, 1972).
International Monetary Fund, "Equatorial Guinea," *Surveys of African Economies*, vol. 5 (Washington, D.C.: IMF, 1973), pp. 314–353.
Israel, Ministry of Foreign Affairs, "Israel and Uganda" (Jerusalem, 1972).
Jackman, Robert W., "The Predictability of Coups d'Etat: A Model with African Data," *American Political Science Review* (September 1978).
Jackson, Robert H., and Carl G. Rosberg, *Personal Rule in Black Africa: Prince, Autocrat, Prophet, Tyrant* (Berkeley: University of California Press, 1982).
Jorgensen, J.J., *Uganda: A Modern History* (London: Croom Helm, 1981).
Julien, Captain, "Mohammed es Senoussi et ses Etats," *Bulletin de la Société de Recherches Congolaises*, nos. 7–10 (Brazzaville, 1925–1929).
Kalck, Pierre, *Central African Republic: A Failure in Decolonization* (New York: Praeger Publishers, 1970).
———, *Histoire de la République Centrafricaine* (Paris: Berger-Levrault, 1974).
———, *La République Centrafricaine* (Paris: Berger-Levrault, 1971).
Kasfir, Nelson, "Cultural Sub-Nationalism in Uganda," in Victor A. Olorunsola (ed.), *The Politics of Cultural Sub-Nationalism in Africa* (New York: Anchor Books, 1972).
———, "Explaining Ethnic Political Participation," *World Politics* (April 1979).
Kiwanuka, M.S.M., *Amin and the Tragedy of Uganda* (Munich: Weltforum Verlag, 1979).
———, "Nationality and Nationalism in Africa: The Uganda Case," *Canadian Journal of African Studies*, vol. 4, no. 2 (Spring 1970).
Klinteberg, Robert af, *Equatorial Guinea, Macias Country* (Geneva: International University Exchange Fund, 1978).

———, "L'Enfer de la Guinée Equatoriale," *Revue Française d'Etudes Politiques Africaines* (July–August 1979).
Kobel, A.E., "La République de Guinée Equatoriale: Ses resources potentialles" (Ph.D. thesis, University of Neuchatel, 1976).
Kogongar, J. Gayo, "Introduction à la vie et à l'histoire precoloniales des populations Sara du Tchad" (Ph.D. thesis, University of Paris, 1971).
"Kolingba's Promises," *West Africa*, June 30, 1986.
Kyemba, Henry, *State of Blood* (London: Corgi, 1977).
"La Guineé equatoriale et les travailleurs nigerians," *Marchés Tropicaux*, January 2, 1976.
Lanne, B., "Les Populations du Sud du Tchad," *Revue Française d'Etudes Politiques Africaines*, nos. 183–184 (July–August 1979), pp. 41–81.
"La reélection au premier tour de President Dacko," *Afrique Contemporaine* (May–June 1981).
Lawrence, J.C.D., *The Iteso: Fifty Years of Change in a Nilo-Hamitic Tribe of Uganda* (London and Oxford: Oxford University Press, 1957).
Lee, J.M., *African Armies and Civil Order* (New York: Praeger Publishers, 1969).
Legris, Michel, "Esquisses Centrafricaines," *Le Monde*, January 4–5, 1966.
Legum, Colin, "Behind the Clown's Mask," *Transition* (Accra, October 1975–March 1976).
Legum, Colin (ed.), *Africa Contemporary Record* (London: Rex Collings, 1966–1987).
"Le Mariage de Deux Martines," *Bingo* (April 1973).
"Les Institutions Monetaries de la République de Guinèe Equatoriale," no. 186 (Paris: Banque Centrale des Etats de l'Afrique de l'Ouest, July 1971).
LeVine, Victor, "The Central African Republic: Insular Problems of an Inland State," *Africa Report* (November 1968).
———, "The Coup in the Central African Republic," *Africa Today* (April–May 1968).
———, "The Coups in Upper Volta, Dahomey and the Central African Republic," in R. Rotberg and A. Mazrui (eds.), *Protest and Power in Black Africa* (London: Oxford University Press, 1970).
Leys, Colin, *Politicians and Policy: An Essay on Politics in Acholi 1962–65* (Nairobi: East Africa Publishing House, 1967).
Liebenow, J. Gus, "The Military Factor in African Politics: A Twenty-Five Year Perspective," in G.M. Carter and P. O'Meara (eds.), *African Independence: The First Twenty-Five Years* (Bloomington: Indiana University Press, 1985).
"Life on Devil's Island," *Africa* (June 1974).
Liniger-Goumaz, Max, *Guinea Ecuatorial: Bibliografia General*, 2 vols. (Berne: Commission Nationale Suisse pour l'Unesco, 1976).
———, "Guinea Ecuatorial—Population, Bibliographie," *Journal de la Société des Africanistes*, vol. 42, no. 1 (1971), pp. 195–206.
———, *Historical Dictionary of Equatorial Guinea* (Metuchen, N.J.: Scarecrow Press, 1980).
———, *La Guinée Equatoriale: Pays Méconnu* (Paris: Editions Harmattan, 1980).

———, "La République Guinée Equatoriale—une independence à refaire," *Afrique Contemporaine* (September–October 1979), pp. 8–21.
Listowel, Judith, *Amin* (London: Irish University Press, 1974).
Loubat, Bernard, *L'Ogre de Berengo* (Paris: Editions Alain Lefeuvre, 1981).
Low, Donald A., *Buganda in Modern History* (Berkeley: University of California Press, 1971).
———, *Political Parties in Uganda 1946–1962* (London: Athlone Press, 1962).
———, *The Mind of Buganda: Documents of the Modern History of an African Kingdom* (Berkeley: University of California Press, 1971).
Low, Donald A., and R. Cranford Pratt, *Buganda and British Over-Rule 1900–1955* (London: Oxford University Press, 1960).
Lusignan, Guy de, *French-Speaking Africa Since Independence* (New York: Praeger Publishers, 1969).
Majuju, A.B., "The Gold Allegations in Uganda," *African Affairs* (October 1987), pp. 479–504.
Mamdani, Mahmood, "Class Struggles in Uganda," *Review of African Political Economy*, no. 4 (1975).
———, *Politics and Class Formation in Uganda* (London: Heinemann, 1976).
Mandelbaum, May Edel, "African Tribalism: Some Reflections on Uganda," *Political Science Quarterly*, vol. 80, no. 3 (1965).
Mangin, C., *Souvenirs d'Afrique—Tournée d'Inspection au Congo, 1908* (Paris: Denoël, 1936).
Mangongo-Nzambi, A., "La Delimitation des frontières du Gabon 1885–1911," *Cahiers d'Etudes Africaines*, vol. 9, no. 33 (1969).
Martin, David, *General Amin* (London: Faber & Faber, 1974).
Matate, Gordon, "Exit Africa's Triad of Tyrants," *Africa* (London, November 1979), pp. 12–18.
Mazrui, Ali, "Leadership in Africa: Obote of Uganda," *International Journal* (Summer 1970).
———, "Phallic Symbols in Politics and War: An African Perspective," *Journal of African Studies*, vol. 1, no. 1 (1974).
———, "Racial Self-Reliance and Cultural Dependence: Nyerere and Amin in Comparative Perspective," *Journal of International Affairs*, vol. 27, no. 1 (1973).
———, "Resurrection of the Warrior Tradition in African Political Culture," *Journal of Modern African Studies* (March 1975).
———, *Soldiers and Kinsmen in Uganda: The Making of a Military Ethnocracy* (Beverly Hills, Calif.: Sage, 1975).
Middleton, John, *The Lugbara of Uganda* (New York: Holt, Rinehart and Winston, 1965).
Middleton, John, and D. Tait (eds.), *Tribes Without Rulers* (London: Routledge and Kegan Paul, 1958).
"Modern Caligula," *Der Spiegel*, December 27, 1976, pp. 67–68.
Molino, A. Martin del, "Origen del pueblo Bubi de Fernando Poo," *Guinea Española*, vol. 60, no. 1569 (Santa Isabel, 1963).
Molubuela, E. Gori, *Etnologia de los Bubis* (Madrid: Instituto de Estudios Africanos, 1955).

Momoh, Eddie, "Equatorial Guinea: Mr. Botha's Long Hand," *West Africa*, November 30, 1987.
Moraleda, A. Itozano, "El patronato de Indigenas de Guinea: institucion ejamplar," *Archivos del Instituto de Estudios Africanos*, vol. 40 (March 1957).
Morris, H.F., *A History of Ankole* (Kampala: East African Literature Bureau, 1962).
Morris, H.F., and James S. Read, *Uganda: The Development of Its Laws and Constitution* (London: Stevens, 1966).
Morris, H.M., *The Indians in Uganda: Caste and Sect in a Plural Society* (London: Weidenfeld and Nicolson, 1968).
Morrison, Donald G., et al., *Black Africa: A Comparative Handbook* (New York: Free Press, 1972).
Mutesa II, *Desecration of My Kingdom* (London: Constable, 1967).
Mveng, M., "Notes sur l'emigration des Camerounais a Fernando Poo entre les deux gueres mondiales," *Abbia*, no. 23 (Yaoundé, September–December 1969).
Nigeria, Legislative Council, "Parliamentary Delegation to Fernando Poo and Rio Muni" (Lagos, 1957).
Nigeria, Legislative Council, "Report on Employment of Nigerian Labourers in Fernando Poo" (Lagos, Sessional Paper No. 38, 1929).
Nyama, S., "Dark Clouds over the Court of Berengo," *Africa* (June 1979).
Obote, Milton, *Myths and Realities* (Kampala: African Publishers Ltd., 1970).
———, "The Common Man's Charter, with Appendices" (Entebbe: Government Printer, 1970).
O'Brien, Justin, "General Amin and the Ugandan Asians," *Round Table* (January 1973).
Oded, Arye, *Islam in Uganda* (New York: John Wiley and Sons, 1974).
Odetola, T.O., *Military Regimes and Development* (London: George Allen & Unwin, 1982).
Osoba, S.O., "The Phenomenon of Labour Migrations in the Area of British Colonial Rule," *Journal of the Historical Society of Nigeria*, vol. 4, no. 4 (1969).
Pain, Dennis, "The Nubians: Their Perceived Stratification System and Its Relation to the Asian Issue," in Michael Twaddle (ed.), *Expulsion of a Minority: Essays on Ugandan Asians* (London: Athlone Press, 1975).
"Papa Bok," *Africa* (November 1977).
Parson, Jack, "Africanizing Trade in Uganda: The Final Solution," *Africa Today*, vol. 29, no. 1 (1973).
Patel, H., "General Amin and the Indian Exodus from Uganda," *Issue* (Winter 1972).
Pélissier, René, "Equatorial Guinea: Autopsy of a Miracle," *Africa Report* (May–June 1980).
———, "Fernando Poo ou la politique de l'insularité," *Revue Française d'Etudes Politiques Africaines*, no. 36 (December 1968).
———, "Fernando Poo: Un archipel hispano-guinéen," *Revue Française d'Etudes Politiques Africaines*, no. 33 (September 1968).
———, "Guinée Equatoriale: au seuil de l'independence," *Revue Française d'Etudes Politique Africaines* (October 1968).

_____, "Guinée Equatoriale: embuches sur la voie de l'independence," *Revue Française d'Etudes Politiques Africaines* (October 1967).
_____, "Guinée Equatoriale: la crise," *Revue Française d'Etudes Politiques Africaines* (April 1969).
_____, "Guinée Equatoriale: Les Debuts de l'Independence," *Afrique Contemporaine* (November–December 1968).
_____, "Guinée Equatoriale: mourir pour Corisco," *Revue Française d'Etudes Politiques Africaines* (October 1972).
_____, "Le Mouvement nationaliste en Afrique espagnole," *Revue Française d'Etudes Politiques Africaines* (July 1966).
_____, "Les suicides de Papa Macias," *Revue Française d'Etudes Politiques Africaines* (March 1975).
_____, "Political Movements in Spanish Guinea," *Africa Report* (May 1964).
_____, "Spain's Discrete Decolonization," *Foreign Affairs* (April 1965).
_____, "Spanish Guinea: An Introduction," *Race*, vol. 6, no. 2 (1964).
_____, "Uncertainties in Spanish Guinea," *Africa Report* (March 1968).
Peris Tores, S.V., "La isla de Annobon," *Archivos del Instituto d'Estudios Africanos*, no. 57 (January 1961).
Perlmutter, Amos, *Modern Authoritarianism* (New Haven, Conn.: Yale University Press, 1981).
Picho, Ali, "The 1967 Republican Constitution of Uganda," *Transition* (Kampala, December 1967–January 1968).
Pinillos de Cruells, M., "Guinea Española: la secta del Mbueti," *Africa*, vol. 86 (February 1949).
Posner, Michael H., *The Lawyers' Committee for International Human Rights* (New York: International Commission of Jurists, June 1978).
Pratt, R.C., "Nationalism in Uganda," *Political Studies*, vol. 9, no. 2 (June 1961).
"R.C.A.—durcissement français," *Revue Française d'Etudes Politiques Africaines* (December 1969).
"R.C.A.—Renforcement du regime policier," *Revue Française d'Etudes Politiques Africaines* (July 1969).
Renwick, Allan, "Makerere and Uganda's Elite," *Africa Today* (December 1963).
République Centrafricaine, *Journal Officiel* (Bangui, 1960–1987).
"République Centrafricaine: Un an de gouvernement Bokassa," *Europe–France–Outremer* (January 1967).
Revety, Jean, "L'Anomalie de Bangui," *Eurafrica* (January–March 1976).
Rishworth, S.K., "Spanish-Speaking Africa: A Guide to Official Publications" (Washington, D.C.: Library of Congress, 1972).
Roberts, A.D., "The Sub-Imperialism of Buganda," *Journal of African History*, vol. 3, no. 3 (1962).
Roberts, Andrew R., "The Lost Counties of Bunyoro," *Uganda Journal*, vol. 26, no. 2 (1962).
Roscoe, John, *The Baganda* (London: Frank Cass, 1965).
Roth, Guenther, "Personal Rulership, Patrimonialism, and Empire-Building," *World Politics* (January 1968).

Rothchild, Donald, and Michael Rogin, "Uganda," in G. Carter (ed.), *National Unity and Regionalism in Eight African States* (Ithaca, N.Y.: Cornell University Press, 1966).
Rougeaux, Jena-Pierre, "Le parti unique en R.C.A.: le MESAN" (Paris: Mémoire des Sciences Politiques, 1968), mimeo.
Ryan, Selwyn, "Economic Nationalism and Socialism in Uganda," *Journal of Commonwealth Political Studies*, vol. 10, no. 2 (July 1973).
Sandbrook, Richard, *The Politics of Africa's Stagnation* (Cambridge: Cambridge University Press, 1985).
Sandinot, E., "Guinea Ecuatorial española," *Cuadernos del Ruedo Ibérico*, nos. 13–14 (Madrid, July–September 1967).
Sathyamurthy, T.V., *The Political Development of Uganda 1900–1986* (London: Gower, 1986).
_____ , "The Social Bases of the Uganda People's Party," *African Affairs* (October 1975).
Saul, John S., "The Unsteady State: Uganda, Obote and General Amin," *Review of African Political Economy*, no. 5 (January–April 1976).
Serre, Jacques, "Six ans de gouvernement Dacko," *Revue Française d'Etudes Politiques Africaines* (September 1975), pp. 73–104.
Shaw, Timothy, "Uganda Under Amin: The Costs of Confronting Dependence," *Africa Today* (Spring 1973).
Sniderman, Paul M., *Personality and Democratic Politics* (Berkeley: University of California Press, 1974).
Sordet, Monique, "Jean-Bedel Bokassa," *Europe–France–Outremer* (December 1973).
Southall, Aidan W., *Alur Society* (Nairobi: Oxford University Press, 1970).
_____ , "The Concept of Elites and Their Formation in Uganda," in P.C. Lloyd (ed.), *The New Elites in Tropical Africa* (New York: Oxford University Press, 1966).
Steinhart, Edward I., *Conflict and Collaboration: The Kingdoms of Western Uganda, 1890–1907* (Princeton, N.J.: Princeton University Press, 1977).
Strate, Jeffrey J., "Post-Military Coup Strategy in Uganda: Amin's Early Attempts to Consolidate Political Support" (Athens, Ohio: Papers in International Studies, Africa Series No. 18, 1973).
Sundiata, I.K., "A Note on an Abortive Slave Trade: Fernando Poo 1778–81," *Bulletin d'IFAN*, vol. 34, no. 4 (Dakar, October 1973), pp. 793–804.
_____ , "Prelude to Scandal: Liberia and Fernando Poo, 1880–1930," *Journal of African History*, vol. 15, no. 1 (1974), pp. 97–112.
_____ , "The Fernandinos: Labor and Community in Santa Isabel 1827–31" (Ph.D. thesis, Northwestern University, 1972).
_____ , "The Importance of Fernando Poo: Humanitarians and Africans" (Paper presented at the African Studies Association meeting, Boston, 1976).
Tandon, Yash, "The Asians in Africa in 1972," in Colin Legum (ed.), *Africa Contemporary Record 1972–73* (New York: Africana Publishing Co., 1973).
"Tentative de coup d'état," *Afrique Contemporaine* (May–June 1969).
Térivé, Jean D., "Analyse d'un coup d'état," *France–Eurafrique* (March 1966), pp. 3–8.

Terre Africaine, nos. 77 and 78 (Brazzaville, May 15 and 22, 1965).
"The Cocoa-Slaves of Fernando Poo," *The Guardian*, November 21, 1976.
"The Man the Churches Call the Caligula of Africa," *Times Review* (London), December 29, 1974, p. 6.
"The Perils of Bokassa," *Africa Confidential*, June 22, 1973.
The Rehabilitation of the Economy of Uganda (London: Commonwealth Secretariat, 1979).
"The Report of the Commission of Inquiry in the Case of the Two Missing Americans in Uganda," *Transition*, no. 42 (1972).
"The Two Professions," *West Africa*, April 19, 1969.
Thompson, Virginia, and Richard Adloff, "Oubangui-Chari," in Virginia Thompson and Richard Adloff, *The Emerging States of French Equatorial Africa* (Stanford, Calif.: Stanford University Press, 1960).
Thuriaux-Hennebert, Arlette, *Les Zandé dans l'histoire du Bahr el Ghazal et de l'Equatoria* (Bruxelles: Institut de Sociologie de l'Université Libre, 1964).
Tisserant, C., *Ce que j'ai connu de l'esclavage en Oubangui-Chari* (Paris: Plon, 1955).
Twaddle, Michael, "The Amin Coup," *Journal of Commonwealth Studies* (July 1971).
Twaddle, Michael (ed.), *Expulsion of a Minority: Essays on Ugandan Asians* (London: Athlone Press, 1975).
"Uganda: Nubians and Southern Sudanese," *Africa Confidential*, May 3, 1974.
"Uganda Under Military Rule," *Africa Today*, vol. 20, no. 2 (Spring 1973).
"Uganda v. Commissioner of Prisons *ex parte* Matovu," *East African Law Reports* (1966), pp. 514–546.
United States, *Area Handbook for Uganda* (Washington, D.C.: Government Printing Office, 1969).
Unzueta y Yuste, A. de, "Etnografia de la Guinea Española, los Bengas," *Estudios Geograficos*, vol. 6, no. 19 (May 1945).
———, *Guinea Continental Española* (Madrid: Instituto de Estudios Africanos, 1944).
Velarde, Juan Fuentes, "El Plan de Desarrollo economico y social de Fernando Poo y Rio Muni," *Archivos del Instituto d'Estudios Africanos*, vol. 28, no. 71 (January 1966).
———, "Problemas de empleo en la Guinea ecuatorial," *Revista de Trabajo*, vol. 6, no. 2 (1964).
Vilaldach, Antonio de Veciana, *La Secta del Bwiti en la Guinea Española* (Madrid: Instituto de Estudios Africanos, 1958).
Wanji, Barri A., "The Nubi Community: An Islamic Social Structure in East Africa" (Sociology Working Paper No. 115, Makerere University, n.d.).
Weinstein, Brian, "Felix Eboue and the Chiefs: Perceptions of Power in Early Oubangui-Chari," *Journal of African History* (1970).
———, *Gabon: Nation-Building on the Ogoue* (Cambridge, Mass.: MIT Press, 1966).
Welbourn, F.B., *Religion and Politics in Uganda, 1952–62* (Nairobi: East Africa Publishing House, 1967).

Wiking, Steffan, *Military Coups in Sub-Saharan Africa* (Uppsala: Scandinavian Institute of African Studies, 1983).
Willetts, Peter, "The Politics of Uganda as a One Party State," *African Affairs*, vol. 74 (July 1975).
Wolfenstein, E. Victor, *The Revolutionary Personality* (Princeton, N.J.: Princeton University Press, 1967).
Woodward, Peter, "Ambiguous Amin," *African Affairs* (April 1978).
Yaniz, J.P., "La Guinea Ecuatorial española: de la occupation a la independencia," *Historia y Vida*, no. 84 (Madrid, 1975).
Young, Crawford M., "The Obote Revolution," *Africa Report*, vol. 11, no. 6 (1966).
Zoctizoum, Yarisse, *Histoire de la Centrafrique*, 2 vols. (Paris: Harmattan, 1984).
Zolberg, Aristide, *Creating Political Order: The Party-States of West Africa* (Chicago: Rand-McNally, 1966).
————, "Military Intervention in the New 'States' of Africa," in Henry Bienen (ed.), *The Military Intervenes* (New York: Russell Sage Foundation, 1968).
————, "The Structure of Political Conflict in Africa," *American Political Science Review* (June 1968).

Index

Aberrant leadership, 191–195
Abidjan, 164
Acholi, 13, 81, 82, 87, 89, 93, 94, 98, 100, 101, 102, 117–118
Adama-Tamboux, Michel, 144
Adamawa emirates, 36
Addis Ababa, 192
Adoko, Akena, 94, 123(n39)
Adrisi, Mustafa (General), 111
AEF. *See* French Equatorial Africa
Africa, 43
   administrative weakness, 2, 3, 26
   authoritarianism, 1, 2, 184–185
   coups, 1, 11, 188–191
   dictatorships, 3
   elections, 1, 2
   personal rule, 185–188
   rapid Africanization, 9, 10
   social inertia, 26
Africa Confidential, 67
Africa Contemporary Record, 70
Africa Research Bulletin, 50
Air Centrafrique affair, 21, 150, 154–155
Ali, Moses (Brigadier General), 26, 112, 117
Ali, Waris (Lt. Colonel), 97
Alur, 102
Amin, Idi, 4, 9, 19, 21, 53, 94, 95–113, 146, 149
   accused of cowardice, 94, 123(n44)
   army composition, 13, 93, 94, 97–98
   and Asian community, 7, 15, 97, 99, 106, 109–111, 180
   and Britain, 10, 106–107, 109
   brutality, 13, 24, 96, 99
   and Buganda, 99, 100, 104
   cabinet meetings, 13–14, 98, 104, 105
   cannibalism, 15
   childhood and family background, 5, 6, 7, 24, 95
   and China, 107
   coup d'état, 11, 12, 92, 94, 99, 104, 179, 181, 190
   decisionmaking style, 18–19, 98–99, 105, 106
   and divine guidance, 15–16, 97, 106, 109
   ethnic recruitment and promotions, 11, 13, 97–98, 99
   and France, 107–108
   gold and ivory affair, 7, 89
   in international affairs, 15, 106–108, 126(n91)
   invasion of Tanzania, 112, 113
   Libyan aid, 16, 107, 108, 111, 112, 113, 116
   liquidations, 13, 16, 58, 96, 99–102
   medical maladies, 24, 95, 124(n47)
   military career, 7, 8, 9–10, 13, 93, 94, 95–97, 124(n51), 193–194
   mismanagement of funds, 7, 11, 94, 98
   murder of Archbishop Luwum, 16, 103, 108
   and Nubians, 97, 105, 112, 124(n56)
   and Okoya's murder, 11, 13, 94, 98
   ouster, 111–113
   peer groups, 18, 19, 97, 106, 124(n56)
   personal characteristics, 13, 24, 93, 95–97, 103–104, 106, 180
   plots against, 15, 103–104
   policies, 14, 17, 18, 96, 98–99, 104–106, 109–111
   proposes monument to Hitler, 107, 125(n81)
   psychology of, 24, 97, 183
   religious favoritism, 16, 105
   sexual proclivities, 96
   and United States, 100, 108, 117
   See also Uganda, armed forces
Ankole. *See* Banyankole
Annobon, 33, 63, 71(n4)
Anya Nya, 94, 97
Arabs, 16, 107, 110, 112
Arube, Charles (Brigadier General), 98, 102
Astles, Bob, 110
Ateba, Clemente, 43

Authoritarian rule, 1, 2, 3, 28(n8)
  difficulties in comparison of, 3–4
  prevalence and reasons for, 2, 22
  repercussions of, 2–3
  See also Dictatorship; Tyranny

Babinga, 132
Baguirmi, 131
Bahr el Ghazal, 132
Bakouma, 139
Balandier, Georges, 36
Balboa, Armando, 48
Bambara, 131
Bambari, 132
Banda, Kamuzu, 3, 182, 186, 187, 192
Banda, 131
Bandio, Jean Arthur, 145
Bangui, Sylvestre (General), 163, 164, 169
Bangui, 25, 134, 136, 140, 142, 150, 160, 162. *See also* Central African Republic
Banyankole, 80, 102, 108, 116, 118, 126(n96)
Banza, Alexandre (Colonel), 8, 15, 145, 146, 148, 150, 151, 152, 158
Banziri, 132, 174(n39)
Basoga. *See* Busoga
Bata, 17, 44, 47, 49, 54, 58, 62, 63, 68
Batore, 80. *See also* Toro
Baya. *See* Gbaya
Beka (Major), 97
Berengo, 161
Bhang, 23, 54
Biéri cult, 37, 53
Binaisa, Godfrey
  dismisses Oyite-Ojok, 115
  presidency, 114–115, 117
Bobangui, 132, 146, 149, 172(n12), 174(n36)
Bobossa, 139
Boboua, 139
Boganda, Barthélemy, 136, 141–142, 143, 145, 174(nn 35, 36, 37)
Bogoin, 139
Bokassa, Catherine, 8, 162
Bokassa, Jean-Bedel, 4, 14, 20, 25, 53, 146–164, 175(n55)
  Air Centrafrique affair, 21, 150, 154–155
  and Alexandre Banza, 8, 15, 145, 146, 148, 150, 151, 152
  armed forces, 15, 145, 146, 157–158
  assault on prison inmates, 8, 14, 15, 148, 150, 155, 176(n82)
  brutality, 8, 14, 15, 145, 146, 150, 163
  cabinet appointments, 20–21, 145–147, 148, 153, 157, 161, 175(n60)
  cannibalism, 15, 164
  childhood and family background, 5–6, 7, 136, 145, 146
  coronation, 14, 16, 20, 25, 129, 147, 160–161, 177(n95), 196(n1)
  and corruption, 14, 145, 148, 152–153, 157, 158–159, 176(n62)
  coup d'état, 11, 14, 20, 144–146, 150, 179–180
  and diamonds, 20, 139, 164, 178(n100)
  different from other tyrants, 20, 21, 25, 149, 194
  divine inspiration, 16
  economic mismanagement, 20, 21, 137, 140, 154, 159
  flights of fancy, 20, 22, 25, 148, 149, 154, 160–161
  and France, 10, 25, 129, 146, 147, 150, 151, 152, 153–154, 156–157, 161, 163–164
  ideological/international vacillations, 20, 21, 149–150, 153
  and Libya, 16, 150, 163
  liquidations under, 14, 15, 25
  and Magalé, 145, 148, 157, 158
  and Mandaba, 152, 157, 158
  military career, 6, 7, 9, 10, 145, 147–148, 175(n48), 194
  Operation Barracuda, 129, 157, 158, 162–163
  personal characteristics, 10, 11, 14, 20, 21, 147, 150–151, 180
  playacting, 16, 21, 26
  policies, 17, 20–21, 146, 149–150, 151–155, 160
  Presidential/Imperial Guard, 157–158, 162–163
  psychological insights into, 25, 171, 177(n95), 182
  and religion, 16, 20, 21, 150
  return (aborted) to Bangui (1983), 25, 26
  return to Bangui (1986), 25, 149, 151, 170–171
  sources of support, 156–158
  sexual proclivities, 8, 25, 177(n91)
  student riots, 8, 14, 15, 129, 150, 156–157, 158, 162–164, 165
  and sycophants, 20, 148–149
  "Two Martines" affair, 151, 155, 177(n85)
  vanity, 8, 14–15, 21, 149
  See also Central African Republic
Bongo, Omar, 2, 3, 192. *See also* Gabon
Bororo, 132
Bouar, 132, 139, 157, 158, 162
Bourguiba, Habib, 2
Bozize (General), 168

Index

Brazil, 34, 40
Brazzaville, 134, 141, 147, 149
Bria, 131
Bridge of Blood, 100
Britain, 38
  on Fernando Póo, 34, 37
  and Uganda, 106–107, 109, 126(n85)
  and Uganda's Army, 9–10, 13
Bubi, 6, 34, 35, 47, 48, 58, 61, 62, 68, 69
  fear of Fang domination, 45, 46
  in politics, 42, 43, 45
Buganda, 78, 79, 80, 83, 88, 108, 116
  attempted secession, 87, 89, 90, 93, 121(n24)
  kabaka of, 80, 83, 86, 87, 88, 90, 100, 121(n23)
  Katikiro, 83, 88, 122(n26)
  Lukiiko, 86, 87, 88, 122(n29)
  protectorate status, 80, 86
  religious cleavages, 83, 86, 116
  See also Uganda
Bunyoro, 80, 87, 88, 89
Buraka, 132
Burkina Faso, 3, 182
Busoga, 80, 81, 87, 122(n29)
Bwiti, 37, 53

Caligula, 49, 54
Cameroun, 33, 35, 36, 37, 42, 43, 44, 45, 57, 59, 62, 73(n32), 131
Campo River, 36
Cannibalism, 15, 164
CAR. *See* Central African Republic
Catherine (Empress), 8
Censorship
  in CAR, 151, 167
  in France, 25, 155
  in Spain, 23, 53
Central African Democratic Rally (RDC), 170, 171
Central African Republic (CAR), 4, 22, 129, 130(map)
  armed forces, 10–11, 12, 145, 165, 168, 175(n48)
  Berberati affair, 135, 174(n34)
  Boganda, Barthélemy, 136, 141–142, 143, 174(n40)
  Central African Democratic Rally, 170
  and China, 144, 146, 153
  colonial rule, 5, 132–138, 140–142
  concessionary system, 133, 134, 135
  corruption, 142, 143–144
  cotton, 136, 137–138, 140, 143, 150, 170
  coup of 1966, 8, 11–12, 14, 144–145, 179–180
  Dacko, David, 142–145, 163–167, 179

  demography, 131–133, 136–137
  economy, 137–140, 143, 170
  ethnic representation in cabinets, 147
  and France, 140, 150, 156–157, 165, 166, 167, 171
  Gbaya, 134, 135, 142, 146, 174(n34)
  Goumba, Abel, 141–142, 163, 164, 168, 169, 170, 171, 174(nn 39, 40)
  Kolingba in power, 167–172
  Mandjia, 134, 135, 142
  Mbaïka, 5, 146, 152, 157, 162, 163, 168
  MEDAC, 142
  MESAN, 141, 142, 144, 146, 160
  Oubanguians. *See* Central African Republic, riverine groups
  Oubangui river, 132, 134, 137, 159, 173(n30)
  Patasse, Ange, 145, 161, 163, 164, 166, 167, 168, 169, 170, 171
  presidential elections (1981), 166
  primacy of Lt. Col. Mansion, 169
  reconstruction, 27, 164–165
  referendum (1986), 170
  riverine groups, 5, 6, 132, 168
  Sara, 131, 132, 164, 166, 168
  slave raids, 131, 132, 133
  unrest since Bokassa's demise, 167–171
  See also Bangui; Bokassa, Jean-Bedel
CFA franc, 29(n30), 69
Chad, 43, 131, 132, 134, 136, 151, 171, 177(n94)
China, 40, 57, 59, 60, 68, 107, 144, 146, 150, 153
CMS. *See* Supreme Military Council
CNLGE. *See* Cruzada Nacional de la Liberacion de la Guinea Ecuatorial
Common Man's Charter, 91
Concessionary system, 133, 134, 135
Congo, 43, 89, 134
Congo/Kinshasa. *See* Zaire
Congo-Ocean Railroad, 134
Conservative party (Uganda), 116
Corisco, 33
Coups d'état
  behavioral context, 180–183
  in CAR, 11–12, 180–181
  idiosyncratic variable, 180
  motivations for, 11, 12, 179, 181–182, 188–191
  structural background conditions, 180
  in Uganda, 11, 12, 179
Creoles, 34, 35, 36
Cruzada Nacional de la Liberacion de la Guinea Ecuatorial (CNLGE), 43
Cuba, 34, 40, 57, 60, 65, 66
Customs Union for Central Africa (UDEAC), 21, 69, 151

Index

Dacko, David, 15, 20, 142–145, 150
  challenged by Goumba, 142
  corruption under, 143
  deflation of power, 143
  France's choice, 156
  overthrown, 145, 167
  personal background, 174(n40)
  retains Bokassa henchmen, 164–165
  second presidency, 163, 164–167
  weak leadership, 142–143, 165
  See also Central African Republic
Dar-es-Salaam, 108. *See also* Tanzania
Darfur, 131
Dar Kouti, 131, 132
Dar Rounga, 131
Decraene, Phillipe, 151
Defence Council (Uganda), 101, 105, 111
Democratic party (Uganda), 83, 87
  in 1980 elections, 116
Dictatorship, 4, 26, 69, 77
  absence of coherent policy, 17
  academic interest in, 21–22
  comparative analysis, 179–197
  conditions conducive to, 184–191
  cultural marginality of, 15, 22
  legacy of, 4, 25–26, 27, 196
  levels of terror, 4, 22, 57, 61
  modality of rule, 4, 12, 17, 70, 77
  and personal rule, 185–187
  post-liberation events, 26, 115–119
  victims of, 26, 29(n31)
  See also Authoritarian rule; Tyranny
Dideo, Bosio, 58
Doe, Samuel, 187, 191. *See also* Liberia
Domitien, Elizabeth, 160
Douala. *See* Cameroun
Drugs, 6, 23, 54
Dumont, René, 144

East African Community, 84, 100
Eastern bloc, 17, 40, 53, 59, 63
East Germany, 40, 59
Effendi, 9, 96
Efik, 36
Egoué estuary, 33, 60
Ekwele, 68
Ela, Salvador (Captain), 65, 68
Elar ayong, 36
Elobey Islands, 33
El Pais, 67
El Tigre, 52
El Unico Miraclo, 16, 17
Emancipado status, 7, 10, 73(n26)
Emperor. *See* Bokassa, Jean-Bedel
Entebbe, 19, 80, 100
Entebbe Operation, 107, 125(n82)
Epota, José Perea, 43

Equatorial Guinea, 4, 5, 6, 7, 8, 22, 25, 26, 31(map), 31–76
  Annobon, 33, 63
  arrests and liquidations in, 12–13, 31, 47, 48, 49, 57–59
  Autonomous Republic, 43, 44, 58
  cocoa plantations and exports, 19, 34, 35, 36, 37, 39, 40, 49, 56–57, 66, 69
  coffee, 36, 37, 39–40
  collapse of administration, 16, 17, 18, 49, 55, 57, 60
  colonial rule, 35, 37, 38, 42, 51
  and Communist bloc, 40
  constitution, 44, 45, 46, 49, 61, 68
  Corisco, 33
  Creoles, 34, 35
  Dachau of Africa, 49, 58
  depopulation, 57, 59
  dictatorship in, 12, 33, 49, 60
  economy of, 38–40, 41, 57
  elections, 38, 44, 46, 47
  Elobey Islands, 33
  expatriates in, 7, 10, 47, 48–49
  fincas, 34, 42, 55
  forced labor, 18, 31, 33, 49, 57, 60, 66
  and France, 59, 66, 69
  Garcia-Trevijano, 10, 46, 50–51, 55, 56
  National Assembly, 10, 12, 48, 68
  Nigerian contract labor, 36, 37, 38, 49, 55, 56, 66
  offshore oil, 33, 60
  Ondu Edu government, 44, 46, 50
  political evolution, 42–43, 44, 46, 49, 60, 180
  post-Nguema dictatorship, 26, 31–32, 33, 66–70
  referenda (1963, 1968, 1982), 44–45, 68
  regional disparities, 33–34, 42
  religion, 16, 66
  roots of dictatorship, 61–62
  security services, 61–62, 63, 65
  and Spain, 12, 47, 48, 66
  Spanish exodus, 47–49
  territory and population, 33, 71(n6), 72(n15)
  timber, 39, 41, 69
  See also Fernando Póo; Nguema, Francisco Macias; Obiang, Teodoro Nguema Mbasogo
Eritrea, 192
Esengui, 5, 49, 62, 68
Evinayong, 44

Fang, 5, 6, 10, 35, 36, 44, 45, 46, 49, 58, 68
  cleavages among, 36, 44, 45
  and coffee cultivation, 36, 37

Index   217

fetishes and magic, 15, 52
  in politics, 42
  revivalist movements, 36–37
  in Río Muni, 34, 35, 36, 37
  in security services, 62
Fatouma, 139
Fernandinos, 6, 36, 42, 45, 61
Fernando Póo, 6, 10, 29(n33), 31, 33, 34, 37, 48, 63, 71(n4)
  Bubi of, 6, 34, 35, 42, 43, 45, 46, 47, 48, 58, 61, 62, 68, 69
  cocoa plantations, 35, 37, 38, 40, 49, 56–57, 66, 69
  collapse of the economy, 38, 40, 49, 56
  Creoles, 35, 36
  Europeans in, 34, 38, 41, 47–49, 68
  Fernandinos, 36
  gauleiter of, 29(n33), 33, 64
  Nigerian contract labor, 36, 37–38, 49, 56, 66
  pro-Spanish, 35, 42
  separatist movements, 42, 45
  See also Equatorial Guinea; Nguema, Francisco Macias
Fernao do Po, 34
Fincas, 34, 42, 55
Forsythe, John, 61
Fort Sibut, 131
France, 15, 156, 161, 168
  colonial rule of CAR, 5, 132, 133–138, 140–142
  colonial rule of Gabon, 36
  and Equatorial Guinea, 59, 66
French Equatorial Africa (AEF), 134, 141
Fulani, 132

Gabon, 3, 6, 33, 36, 42, 43, 44, 45, 47, 49, 57, 59, 60, 67, 169, 188, 192
Ganda, 80, 87, 90. See also Buganda
Garcia Dominguez, 54
Garcia-Trevijano, Antonio, 10, 46, 50–51, 55, 56
Gbaya, 134, 135, 146, 152
General Service Units (Uganda), 92, 94, 104, 123(n39)
Ghana, 40, 97, 182, 192
Gibraltar, 38
Gide, André, 135, 173(n25)
Giscard d'Estaing, Valery, 156, 161
Gold and ivory affair (Uganda), 7, 89
Gouandjia, Maurice, 176(n62)
Goumba, Abel, 141, 142, 163, 164, 168, 169, 170, 171, 174(nn 39, 40)
Gowon, Yufu (Major General), 112
Green, Reginald, 115
Guardia Civil, 48, 61
Guardian, The, 101

Gueret, François, 165, 169
Guinea, 3, 182
Guwedeko, Smuts (Brigadier General), 94, 98

Hallucinogenics, 23, 54
Hills, Dennis, 107
Hispano-Guineans, 26, 29(n31), 38, 57, 67, 69, 70
Hitler, 49, 95, 107, 124(n81)
Holy Spirit Battalion, 119
Houphouët-Boigny, Félix, 2. See also Ivory Coast
Hypomania, 24, 95, 124(n47)

Ibingira, Grace, 89, 122(n32)
Idea Popular de la Guinea Ecuatorial (IPGE), 43, 45
Imperial modality of rule, 4, 28(n8)
Indochina wars, 6, 8, 25, 147
International Commission of Jurists, 102
International Monetary Fund, 42, 67
IPGE. See Idea Popular de la Guinea Ecuatorial
Ismail (Captain), 97
Israel, 107, 125(n82), 126(n83)
Italians, 126(n83)
Iteso, 90, 102. See also Teso
Ivory Coast, 31, 164, 180
Izamo, Jean, 14, 145, 180

Jamaica, 34
Jerusalem. See Israel
Jinja, 6, 95
Juma (Major), 100

Kabaka, 28(n10), 80, 88, 100, 121(n23), 122(n29). See also Buganda
Kabaka Yekka (KY), 87, 88, 104, 122(n31)
  alliance with UPC, 88
  factionalism, 88
  See also Kabaka
Kagera Salient, 113
Kakwa, 5, 18, 24, 81, 93, 95, 97, 98, 100, 101, 102, 112
Kampala, 25, 80, 81, 88, 117
  falls to Museveni, 118
  liberated from Amin, 15, 113
  See also Uganda
Karamojong, 81, 96, 100, 118
Karume Falls Bridge, 100
Katikiro, 83, 88, 122(n26). See also Buganda
Kenya, 13, 19, 80, 81, 84, 92, 95, 98, 100, 101, 105, 107, 108, 182
Kenyatta, Jomo, 90, 182. See also Kenya

Kerekou, Mathieu, 2
Kezza, Antoine, 145
Kigali. *See* Rwanda
Kikuyu, 124(n51)
King Carlos, 66
Kirsch, Martin, 165
Kiwanuka, Benedicto, 83, 87, 122(n26)
Klinteberg, Robert af, 49, 52, 54, 57, 59
Koboko County, 95
Kolingba, André (Major General)
  military rule in CAR, 167–172
Kolotto, 152
Kondoism, 92
Kouango, 134
KY. *See* Kabaka Yekka
Kyabazinga. *See* Busoga

Lake Victoria, 78, 79, 80, 95
Lala, Iddi, 169
Langi, 13, 81, 82, 87, 89, 94, 98, 100, 101, 102, 117–118
League of Nations, 31
Legum, Colin, 106
Liberia, 37, 187, 191
Libreville, 43, 60
Libya, 108, 171, 182, 187, 188, 192
  aid to Amin, 16, 107, 108, 111, 112, 113
  and CAR, 16, 163, 164, 169, 170
Liebenow, J. Gus, 185
Lingopou, Martin (General), 158
Lobaye, 142
"Lost Counties," 80, 87, 88, 89
Luganda, 7, 105
Lugazi, 95
Lugbara, 6, 81, 95, 97, 100, 101, 102, 112
Lukaya, 113
Lukiiko, 87, 88, 122(n29). *See also* Buganda
Lukwena, Alice, 119
Lule, Yusuf, 114, 115, 117
Lumago, Isaac (Major General), 111
Luo, 108
Lusaka. *See* Zambia
Luwero Triangle atrocities, 117–118
Luwum, Janani (Archbishop), 16, 103, 108

Madi, 81, 94, 100, 101, 102
Madrid, 10, 31, 34, 38, 42, 45, 57, 67, 68. *See also* Spain
Mafioso, 17, 18, 29(n33), 54, 64
Magalé, André Dieudonné (Brigadier General), 145, 148, 157, 158, 176(n62)
Maho, Luis, 43
Maidou, Henri, 161–162, 164, 166
Makerere University, 82, 99

Malabo, 8, 10, 16, 25, 51, 54, 57, 62, 66. *See also* Equatorial Guinea; Fernando Póo
Malawi, 3, 182, 186, 187, 192
Malbrant, René, 140
Malendoma, Timothée (Lieutenant), 145
Maleombho, Pierre, 142, 145
Malera, Hussein (Brigadier General), 98
Malire Mechanized Regiment, 93, 100, 102
Maliyamunya, Isaac (Brigadier General), 111
Mandaba, Jean Claude (General), 152, 157, 158
Mandjia, 134, 135, 142
Mangin (General), 135
Mansion, Jean-Claude (Colonel), 169
Mao, 107
Mariam, Mengistu Haile, 192
Martin, David, 96
Materia reservada, 23, 53
Mau Mau rebellion, 13, 96
Mauritius, 2
Mawanga, Paolo, 114, 118
Mayanja, Abu, 104
Maye, Mo, 62
Maye Ela, Florencio, 62, 68
Mayomokila, Josephat (General), 157–158, 164
Mba, Leon, 43
Mbaïka, 5, 132, 146, 152, 157, 162, 163, 168
Mbaikoua (General), 168
Mbarara, 97, 100, 102, 126(n96)
M'Bongo, Auguste (Major), 158
MEDAC. *See* Mouvement pour l'Evolution Démocratique de l'Afrique Central
MESAN. *See* Mouvement d'Evolution Sociale en Afrique
Mitterrand, François, 167, 168
Mmengo Hill, 90. *See also* Buganda
MNLGE. *See* Movimento Nacional de la Liberacion de la Guinea Ecuatorial
Mobutu Sese Seko, 162, 167, 177(n94), 182, 187. *See also* Zaire
Mogadishu, 103
Mohammed es-Senoussi, 131
Moka, King, 35
Mombasa, 80
MONALIGE. *See* Movimento Nacional de la Liberacion de la Guinea Ecuatorial
Mongomo, 12, 17, 18, 49, 50, 52, 54, 62, 63
Monrovia, 37
Moro, 100
Morocco, 17, 52, 65, 68, 70
Morris, H.M., 85

Moshi Conference, 114, 115
Moummié, Felix, 73(n32)
Mouvement pour l'Evolution Démocratique de l'Afrique Central (MEDAC), 142
Mouvement d'Evolution Sociale en Afrique (MESAN), 141, 142, 144, 146, 160
Movimento de Union Nacional de la Guinea Ecuatorial (MUNGE), 43, 44, 46, 47
Movimento Nacional de la Liberacion de la Guinea Ecuatorial (MONALIGE), 43, 44, 46, 47
Movimento pro-Independencia de la Guinea Ecuatorial (MPIGE), 43
Moyo, 100
M'Patou, 139
MPIGE. *See* Movimento pro-Independencia de la Guinea Ecuatorial
MUNGE. *See* Movimento de Union Nacional de la Guinea Ecuatorial
Musa (Lt. Colonel), 97
Museveni, Yoweri, 27, 115, 116, 117, 118, 126(n96), 194
   National Resistance Army, 119
   and Obote, 117–118, 126(n96)
   resistance to, 119
   Union of Patriotic Masses, 116
Mutesa. *See* Kabaka
Mvet praise singers, 53
Mwami, 107. *See also* Rwanda

Naguemon, Kombot, 154
Nairobi, 101, 103, 106, 108, 117. *See also* Kenya
Napoleonic coronation, 20, 25, 160–161
National Rescue Front, 117
National Resistance Army, 119
NCC. *See* Uganda, National Consultative Council
Ndélé, 131, 139
Ndjamena, 149. *See also* Chad
Ndong Miyone, Atanasio, 12, 43, 46, 47, 54, 73(n32), 74(n44)
Nekyon, Adoko A., 89, 91
New York Times, 49
Ngadé, 139
Ngounio, Etienne, 142
Nguema, Francisco Macias, 4, 21, 31, 49–76, 146, 149
   and Annobon, 33, 63
   arrests and liquidations under, 12–13, 31, 48, 54, 57–59, 64–65
   brutality, 8, 49
   cannibalism, 15
   childhood and family background, 5, 6, 7, 49, 50, 52, 73(n26)
   closure of ministries, 17, 57, 61
   and crisis of 1969, 12, 47–49
   and drugs, 6, 23, 53, 64
   "El Unico Miraclo," 16, 53, 54
   family mafioso, 62, 64
   and Garcia-Trevijano, 10, 46, 50–51, 55, 56
   lauds Hitler, 49, 124(n81)
   medical problems, 8, 23, 53–55
   and Obiang, 29(n33), 64, 65
   overthrow of, 16–17, 31, 33, 52, 64–65
   personal characteristics, 6, 7, 8, 23, 49–52, 55, 180
   policies and policymaking, 7, 17–18, 54–55, 60, 64
   power base, 10, 43, 46, 47–48, 50–53, 54, 61–62
   psychological insights into, 23–24, 51–52, 55, 183
   question of sanity, 23, 53
   and religion, 16, 53
   rise to power, 12, 46, 47, 48, 49–52, 192
   sexual proclivities, 8–9, 52
   and Spain, 10, 12, 46, 47, 48, 49
   supernatural powers, 15, 16–17, 52, 61, 65
   withdrawal to Mongomo, 17, 54, 63–64
   See also Equatorial Guinea; Fernando Póo
Nguema Esona, Bonifacio, 62
Nguema Essono, Nchama, 68
Nguesso, Sassou, 2
Niger, 194
Nigeria, 38, 40, 56, 58, 59, 60, 66, 139, 189, 190
Nigerian contract labor, 36, 37–38, 49, 56, 66
   repatriation, 36, 38, 55
Niger River, 34
Nile River, 78, 98, 100, 134
Nilotics, 79, 81, 93
Nixon, Richard, 108
Nkrumah, Kwama, 182
North Korea, 59, 65
Nseng, Ela, 62
Nsué, Micha, 62
Ntumu Fang, 36
Ntutumu, Eugene, 62
Ntutumu, Masié, 62
Nubians, 13, 18, 81, 93, 95, 102
   in Amin's Army, 97, 98, 99, 101, 102, 105, 112
Nyasanyong, 50, 63

Nyerere, Julius, 90, 108, 113, 114, 126(n91), 182. *See also* Tanzania
Nzakara, 135

OAU. *See* Organization of African Unity
Obiang, Teodoro Nguema Mbasogo (Colonel), 29(n33), 33, 68
  breaks with Eastern Europe, 60
  compared to Nguema, 66–67, 69–70
  corruption under, 67–68
  dictatorship, 64, 66–70
  overthrows Nguema, 64–65
  relationship to Nguema, 33, 62
Obote, Milton Apollo, 83, 87, 113
  abolition of traditional monarchies, 90
  Acholi/Langi power base, 13, 81, 87, 116, 117–118
  and Amin, 9–10, 11, 92, 94, 179
  attempted assassination of, 8, 11, 92, 94, 123(n44)
  challenged from within UPC, 88–89, 91
  comeback (1980), 114, 116
  Common Man's Charter, 91
  Luwero Triangle atrocities, 117–118
  Move to the Left, 84, 91–92, 104, 179
  and Oyite-Ojok, 94, 118
  personal traits, 90
  referendum on the "Lost Counties," 80, 89
  refuge in Tanzania, 108
  second overthrow, 118
  showdown with *kabaka*, 28(n10), 89–90
  suspends constitution, 89–90
  See also Uganda
Obrou, Fidel, 15
Ocheng, David, 89, 122(n31)
Ogoué River, 34
Okak Fang, 36
Okello, Basilio (General), 118
Okello, Tito (General), 108
Okoya, Pierino Yere (Brigadier General), 13, 94, 96, 98, 123(n44)
Onama, Felix, 89, 91, 94
Onana, Mba, 62, 68
Ondogo, Michael (Colonel), 102
Ondu Edu, Bonifacio, 12, 44, 46, 47, 54, 57
Operation Barracuda, 163
Opolot, Shaban (Brigadier-General), 28(n10), 90, 93
Organization of African Unity (OAU), 13
Oris, Juma (Lt. Colonel), 112
Osa, Clara, 62
Ouadai, 131
Oubanguians. *See* Central African Republic
Oubangui-Chari, 6, 129, 133–136, 172(n2). *See also* Central African Republic
Oubangui River, 132, 134, 137, 159, 172(n12), 173(n30)
Owono Asongono, Evuna, 62
Oyem, 49
Oyite-Ojok, David (Colonel), 94, 108, 114, 115, 118, 126(n96)
Oyono, Feliciano, 62
Oyono Ayingono, Daniel, 62

Pahouin, 36
Pakistanis, 110
Palestinians, 108, 113
Pamué, 36
Paris-Match, 147
Patasse, Ange, 163, 164, 166, 167, 168, 169, 171
  attempted putsch, 168, 170
  under Bokassa, 145, 161
Patronato de indigenas, 37, 38, 51
Pehoua, 166
Pélissier, René, 42, 53
Perlmutter, Amos, 3, 184
Personal rule, 4, 185–188
Personal tyranny. *See* Tyranny
Playeros, 45
Political psychology, 21–25, 28(nn 16, 24), 182–183, 192–195
Pompidou (President), 154
Port Iradier, 42
Portugal, 34
Pretoria. *See* South Africa
Prince, The (Machiavelli), 22
Prince George, 161
Psychology. *See* Political psychology
Public Safety Units (Uganda), 99–100, 112
PUNT party, 60, 62

Qadaffi, Muammar, 107, 150, 182, 187, 192. *See also* Libya

Rabah, 131, 132
Rawlings, Jerry, 2, 192
RDC. *See* Central African Democratic Rally
Riabbo, 35
Río Benito, 36, 45, 48, 49
Río Campo, 36
Río Muni, 6, 33–34, 42, 45, 47, 48, 51, 62, 66, 68, 69
  Bieri cult, 37
  Bwiti cult, 37
  coffee, 37
  corvee labor, 37
  crisis of 1969, 47–49
  Elar ayong, 36

Europeans in, 34, 41, 48, 66
Fang in, 6, 10, 36, 37, 44, 45
features of, 33, 34
referendum results (1963), 45
revivalist movements, 36–37
timber, 34, 41, 48, 59, 66, 69
See also Equatorial Guinea; Fernando Póo
Riverine groups. *See under* Central African Republic
Riyadh, 113
Romania, 8, 139, 153, 177(n91)
Rwanda, 101, 107, 108, 163

San Carlos Bay, 34, 60
Sango, 132, 162
Sankara, Thomas, 2, 3, 182
Santa Isabel, 8, 10, 33, 34, 46, 47, 50, 53, 71(n4), 77. *See also* Equatorial Guinea; Fernando Póo; Malabo
Santiago de Baney, 43
Sao Tomé, 40
Sara, 131, 132, 164, 166, 168
Saudi Arabia, 5, 108, 112, 113
Saza, 83
Secretariado Conjunto, 46
Sierra Leone, 34, 139
Sikara, Tarao (Pastor), 43, 46, 48
Singapore, 94, 95
Slave labor, 31, 37, 60, 66
Soumaliot rebellion, 89
South Africa, 2, 15, 70, 107
Spain, 7, 23, 31, 34, 53, 58
  colonialism, 10, 33, 34, 36, 37, 38, 48, 51, 71(n3)
  materia reservada, 23, 53, 59
  medical treatment to Nguema, 23
  ouster from Equatorial Guinea, 47–49, 68
  reconstruction aid, 67, 68
  and the "Three Flags" incident, 12, 47–48
  See also Equatorial Guinea
Special Forces (Uganda), 92, 123(n39)
Ssemogerere, Paul, 116, 118
State Research Bureau, 99–100
Stroh/Seidle murders, 97, 100–101, 108
Sudan, 5, 81, 82, 94, 95, 108, 112, 113, 131, 132, 139, 162
Sudanese, 13, 18, 93, 97, 98, 101
Sunday Times Magazine, 95
Supreme Command Council (Uganda), 18
Supreme Military Council (CMS), 68

Taban, Hassan (Colonel), 111
Tanga, 107

Tanzania, 84, 92, 100, 101, 102, 105, 107, 108, 182
  desire to disengage from Uganda, 116
  invaded by Uganda, 112–113
  liberation of Uganda, 8, 15, 16, 107, 113
Terror, 22, 52, 57, 61. *See also* Tyranny
Teso, 81, 82. *See also* Iteso
Tombalbayé, François, 177(n94)
Toro, 87
Touré, Sékou, 3, 182
Towelli, Ali, 99–100, 112
Treaty of Tordesillas (1494), 34
Tripoli. *See* Libya
Turkana, 81
Tyranny, 2, 4, 180
  characteristics of, 183–184
  consequences of, 4
  cultural marginality of, 15
  modality of rule, 4, 180–181
  roots of, 181
  See also Authoritarian rule; Dictatorship

UDEAC. *See* Customs Union for Central Africa
Uganda, 5, 7, 22, 25, 26, 78(map), 79(map)
  Anglo-Buganda alliance, 80
  armed forces, 8, 9–10, 11, 13, 19, 82, 89, 90; ethnic composition under Amin, 13, 93, 94, 97–98, 101; Defence Council, 101, 105, 111, 112; as a destabilizing force, 92, 101; ethnic recruitment drives, 93, 94, 101; falling apart of Acholi and Langi, 117–118; increase in size, 92–93, 100–101; invasion of Tanzania, 112–113; Langi/Acholi component, 93, 94, 98; Luwero Triangle atrocities, 117; Malire Mechanized Regiment, 93, 97; massacres, 13, 99, 100–101; mutiny of 1964, 92; operational commands, 93, 94, 96; politicization, 93; promotions under Amin, 97–98; Public Safety Units, 99–100; purges of Acholi/Langi, 13, 99–100; State Research Bureau, 99–100; Supreme Command Council, 181
  Asian community, 15, 19, 84–85, 101, 103, 109–111, 116
  Binaisa presidency, 114–115, 117
  Bunyoro, 80, 87, 89
  cleavages in, 26, 82, 86, 87, 113–114, 116
  coffee, 19, 80, 84, 111
  collapse of coalition with KY, 89–90
  copper, 84, 111

cotton, 80, 84, 111, 116
coup d'état of 1971, 11, 12, 92, 93, 94, 99, 104, 179
crime levels, 92, 115, 116–117
Democratic party, 83, 87, 88, 116
dislocations, 101, 103, 109, 115
economic collapse, 19, 49, 98, 110–111, 116
economy, 19, 84–85, 91–92, 98, 109–111
elections, 86, 87, 88, 116
federal system, 87, 90
Independence Constitution, 88, 89
invasion of 1972, 102, 108
kabaka, 28(n10), 80, 88, 90, 100, 121(n23)
Kabaka Yekka, 87, 88, 89, 90, 91, 116
liberation, 1, 8, 26, 102, 107, 113
"Lost Counties" dispute, 80, 89
Lule presidency, 114–115
Move to the Left, 84, 91–92, 104, 109
Muslim community of, 16, 91–92
National Consultative Council (NCC), 114, 115
nostalgia for Amin era, 117
Obote's comeback, 115
Okoya's murder, 13
political parties in, 85–92
population, 78–80
post-Liberation problems, 27, 114–119
refugees, 99, 101, 102
Stroh/Seidle murders, 97, 108
tea-estates, 19, 84, 85, 116
UPC, 83, 87, 88, 89, 91, 116
See also Amin, Idi; Buganda; Obote, Milton Apollo
Uganda National Congress (UNC), 87
Uganda National Liberation Army (UNLA), 118
Uganda National Liberation Front (UNLF), 114, 115
Uganda People's Congress (UPC), 83, 86, 87, 88, 89
electoral victory in 1980, 116

factionalism, 88, 91
Socialist goals, 89, 91
sources of support, 87
UNC. *See* Uganda National Congress
UNDP. *See* United Nations Development Program
Union of Central African States, 151
Union of Patriotic Masses, 116
United Nations, 36, 45, 48, 55, 59, 62, 66, 67, 68, 70, 122(n32), 155
United Nations Development Program, 59
United States, 59, 100, 108, 117, 151
UNLA. *See* Uganda National Liberation Army
UNLF. *See* Uganda National Liberation Front
UPC. *See* Uganda People's Congress
USSR, 40, 59–60, 66, 124(n81)

Vatican, 53
Vietnam, 151

Wakhweya, Andrew, 105
Waldheim, Kurt, 155
Warlords, 17, 19
Washington. *See* United States
Watergate, 108
West Africa, 2, 171
West Nile District, 5, 93, 94, 95, 98, 102, 111
Willetts, Peter, 92
Woleu Ntem, 36, 49

Yakoma, 168
Yaoundé, 43
Youlou, Fulbert, 141

Zaire, 2, 7, 48, 81, 89, 112, 113, 151, 162, 167, 177(n94), 187
Zairiens, 13, 98, 101
Zambia, 118
Zande, 131
Zolberg, Aristide, 1, 27, 189